T0306158

Strategic Marketing

This book is a unique collection of comprehensive cases that explore concepts and issues surrounding strategic marketing. Chapters explain what strategic marketing is, and then discuss strategic segmentation, competitive positioning, and strategies for growth, corporate branding, internal brand management, and corporate reputation management. With case studies from a broad range of global contexts and industries, including Burger King, FedEx, and Twitter, readers will gain a working knowledge of developing and applying market-driven strategy. Through case analysis, students will learn to:

- examine the role of corporate, business, and marketing strategy in strategic marketing;
- recognize the implications of markets on competitive space with an emphasis on competitive positioning and growth;
- interpret the various elements of marketing strategy and apply them to a particular real-world situation;
- apply sound decision-making strategies and analytical frameworks to specific strategic marketing problems and issues;
- apply ethical frameworks to strategic marketing situations.

Strategic Marketing: Concepts and Cases is ideal for advanced undergraduate and postgraduate students, as well as those studying for an MBA or executive courses in strategic marketing or marketing management.

Russell Abratt is a Professor of Marketing in the Huizenga College of Business at Nova Southeastern University. His research has been published in the *Journal of Advertising Research*, *California Management Review*, *Industrial Marketing Management*, *Journal of Business Ethics*, and *European Journal of Marketing*, among others.

Michael Bendixen is a Professor of Marketing in the Huizenga College of Business at Nova Southeastern University. His research has been published in the *Journal of International Business Studies*, *Journal of Business Ethics*, *Industrial Marketing Management*, *Journal of Business Research*, and *European Journal of Marketing*, among others.

Strategic Marketing

Concepts and Cases

Russell Abratt and Michael Bendixen

Routledge
Taylor & Francis Group

LONDON AND NEW YORK

First published 2019
by Routledge
2 Park Square, Milton Park, Abingdon, Oxon OX14 4RN

and by Routledge
711 Third Avenue, New York, NY 10017

Routledge is an imprint of the Taylor & Francis Group, an informa business

British Library Cataloguing-in-Publication Data
A catalogue record for this book is available from the British Library

Library of Congress Cataloging-in-Publication Data
A catalog record has been requested for this book

ISBN: 978-1-138-59363-3 (hbk)
ISBN: 978-1-138-59364-0 (pbk)
ISBN: 978-0-429-48932-7 (ebk)

Typeset in Gill Sans
by Out of House Publishing

This book is dedicated to my grandchildren; Jacob, Hannah, and Luke.
(Russell Abratt)
Dedicated to those who smile at those special moments of great learning.
(Michael Bendixen)

Contents

About the authors

Russell Abratt

Russell Abratt is a Professor of Marketing at the H. Wayne Huizenga College of Business and Entrepreneurship, Nova Southeastern University, Fort Lauderdale, Florida. He is also Professor Emeritus at the Wits Business School, University of the Witwatersrand, Johannesburg, South Africa. He completed his B.Com at the University of the Witwatersrand and his MBA and Ph.D. at the University of Pretoria, South Africa. Professor Abratt has also taught at the Ohio State University, University of Florida, Warwick University, Rotterdam School of Management, University of Rome, and Victoria University of Wellington as a visiting scholar. Before entering the academic world he held executive management positions in retailing and wholesaling. He is the co-author of a number of books on marketing and sales management. His research has been published in the *California Management Review, Business Horizons, European Journal of Marketing, Journal of Advertising Research, Journal of Business Ethics, Industrial Marketing Management, Journal of Marketing Management, Journal of Marketing Theory and Practice, Journal of Brand Management*, and *Journal of Product and Brand Management*, among others. He has also had wide consulting experience in marketing planning and strategy.

Michael Bendixen

Michael Bendixen is a Professor of Marketing at the H. Wayne Huizenga College of Business and Entrepreneurship, Nova Southeastern University, Fort Lauderdale, Florida. He completed his degree in Chemical Engineering at the University of the Witwatersrand, Johannesburg, South Africa, his Master of Business Leadership at the University of South Africa, Pretoria, and his Ph.D. at Wits Business School, University of the Witwatersrand. He has taught academic programs in South Africa, Mauritius, Italy, the Bahamas, Bermuda, Jamaica, and the U.S. as well as executive education programs in South Africa, Botswana, Ghana, Kenya, and Nigeria. Professor Bendixen has executive management experience as well as extensive consulting experience particularly in management of service industries. He has been published in *Business Horizons, European Journal of Marketing, Industrial Marketing Management, International Journal of Bank Marketing, Journal of Business Ethics, Journal of Business Research, Journal of International Business Studies, Journal of Marketing Management, Journal of Product and Brand Management*, and *Journal of Services Marketing*, among others.

Preface

This book is a collection of cases that explore strategic marketing concepts. We look at marketing from a strategic point of view and the decisions that top management, including the Chief Marketing Officer, has to make with regard to marketing. Chapters explain what strategic marketing is, and then discuss strategic segmentation, competitive positioning, and strategies for growth, corporate branding, internal brand management, and corporate reputation management. Each chapter has examples and at least two case studies. Readers will gain a working knowledge of strategic marketing management by learning how to develop and apply market-driven strategy. The book concentrates on the application of various marketing topics through the use of case studies in different contexts and industries. Students will be able to make strategic choices and propose solutions to real-world marketing problems.

The book is intended for the capstone course in marketing on a MBA course or executive courses in marketing. It presumes that students have completed a core marketing course and/or have marketing experience.

The objectives of this book are through case analysis to:

1. Examine the role of corporate, business, and marketing strategy in strategic marketing.
2. Recognize the implications of markets and competitive space with an emphasis on competitive positioning and growth.
3. Interpret the various elements of marketing strategy and apply them to a particular real-world situation.
4. Apply sound decision-making strategies and analytical frameworks to specific marketing problems and issues.
5. Apply ethical frameworks to strategic marketing situations.

Instructors will get access to an instructor's notes on the cases along with PowerPoint slides.

All the cases in this book are intended for classroom use only. They are not intended to demonstrate effective or ineffective handling of a business situation. The cases were originally written by members of a MBA class and then edited by the authors. We wish to acknowledge the following people who authored cases:

XFINITY from Comcast: the quest for better customer service case: Stephanie Arboleda, Luxio Bosquez, Hannel Pina, and Angelica Sanchez.
Spirit Airlines: Devondrius Brown, Varun Desai, Katrina Garcia, Soraya Noel, and Mona Petre.

Burger King identity crisis: who are they now?: Fatima Ahmed, Liliana Bastidas, Stian Berg, Caridad Cabrera, and Jordan Ufer.

Florida Blue: the blues of the Affordable Care Act: Althia Carty, Manuel Malo, Krystal Minor, Steve Mogerman, and Jessica Steiner.

McDonald's all-day breakfasts: Dayana Barrientos Duffoo, Khurram Bukhari, Claudia Espinoza Hernandez, Eric Levy, and Angela Nunez.

FedEx: how to beat the competition: Abdulaziz Alobaikan, Lesley Green, Kristie Gusow, Janelle Gutierrez, Alysse Llerena, and Gleness Moore.

Twitter: Mariangelix Cordero, Eryn Crane, Kelly Ferreira de Souza, Diana Gonzalez, and Martine Pierre.

CrossFit SOFLA: growing pains: Michelle Lara, Keyondra LeCounte, Evelyn Nina, Maria Julia Salmio, and Josh Thompson.

Cadillac: the battle to recapture the luxury car market: Mabel Lora, Teresa Francine Rodriguez, Berkin Tetik, and Ivy Velasquez.

Uber Technologies Inc.: managing the repercussions of #DeleteUber: Rajaa Amir, Jennifer Corujo, Paulina Lardizabal, Alicia Rowe, and Jordan Thorpe.

World Fuel Services: leading internal marketing: Limongy Jean, Asher McQueen, Carolina Sanchez, Miriam Sirotzky, and Kimberly Woods.

Weatherby Healthcare: increasing turnover and declining engagement: Amy Coelho, Debbie Fearon, Lauwana Glymph, Joshua L. McGlothlin, and Danielle Schey.

Lennar Corporation: Brittany Bucknor, Flavio Devoto, Razia Gonzalez, and Kaylee Rodriguez.

Chipotle: the cost of fresh fast food: Marcia Perez-Del Valle, Ivy Aparicio, Ashley Auger, Matthew DeBruin, and Kemelly Figueroa.

No book is complete without recognizing the many people that contributed to its success. First, we would like to thank our students for all their efforts in developing the cases. Without them, this book would not exist. Second, we would like to thank the administration of the Huizenga College of Business and Entrepreneurship at Nova Southeastern University for giving us the time to conduct research amongst our teaching and service duties. Third, we would like to thank our publishers, Taylor & Francis Group, and especially Alex Atkinson, Jess Harrison, and Sophia Levine, as well as our copy-editor Penny Harper, for their professional guidance in preparing this manuscript.

Chapter 1

Strategic marketing

The Chief Marketing Officer (CMO) is usually part of the senior executive team responsible for the formulation of the vision, mission, and corporate strategy of an organization. Once this has been approved by the board, it is the responsibility of the CMO and her team to devise and implement the marketing strategy to realize the mission. This all seems very straightforward until it comes down to actually articulating what a marketing strategy comprises, and thus having a clear understanding of strategic marketing. Varadarajan (2010, p. 130) defines the concept as follows:

> Marketing strategy refers to an organization's integrated pattern of decisions that specify its crucial choices concerning marketing activities to perform and the manner of performance of these activities, and the allocation of marketing resources among markets, market segments and marketing activities toward the creation, communication and/or delivery of a product that offers value to customers in exchanges with the organization and thereby enables the organization to achieve specific objectives.

While these lofty words convey a precise academic meaning, what do they mean in practical terms? What decisions does the marketing team, under the leadership of the CMO, actually have to make? In essence, marketing strategy answers the following questions for the organization:

- How to compete?
- Where to compete?

In answering these two questions, the marketing team will make decisions about its competitive positioning, strategic segmentation, corporate and internal branding, as well as how it builds and maintains a good reputation. It must also ensure that it has a "license to operate," by behaving ethically, and implementing sustainability policies so that it does not harm the environment, and behaves as a good corporate citizen.

Strategic marketing decisions tend to be long term in nature, and involve high risk. They tend to be irreversible, certainly in the short term, as they usually involve resource commitments such as the purchase of real estate, capital plant and equipment, and technology. The main aim of investments of this kind is to give the organization a sustainable differential advantage. These investments are typically substantial, and therefore involve trade-offs. These strategic decisions are strategic and usually require input from and coordination with other senior executives, including the Chief Financial Officer and the Chief Operating Officer (Varadarajan, 2010).

Sustainable competitive advantage

A concept that is important in strategic marketing is the resource-based view of the firm (RBV) (Barney, 1991). It starts off with the assumption that the outcome of the top management effort within the organization is a sustainable competitive advantage (SCA). RBV emphasizes strategic choice. The CMO, along with other senior executives, must identify, develop, and deploy key resources with the intention of obtaining targeted returns on the investments. The provision of greater value to customers and other stakeholders is a way of gaining competitive advantage and is likely to result in stakeholder satisfaction, good return on investment, and greater market share.

The RBV of the firm recognizes that not all resources are of equal importance and some may not possess the potential to be a source of competitive advantage. According to Barney (1991), advantage-creating resources must meet four conditions, namely, value, rareness, inimitability, and nonsubstitutability. Customer value is an important element of competitive advantage, and market-orientation is an essential business philosophy. Value is also important for other stakeholders, and employees as a key resource have a major role to play in proving value to these stakeholders. An element of the RBV is the inability of competitors to duplicate resources. Even though some resources can be duplicated, they can be legally protected through trademarks, patents, and copyright. Brands fall into this category and are an important strategic resource of many organizations.

An organization's resources comprise of three subgroups; tangible assets, for example good locations; intangible assets, for example well-known brands and reputation; and capabilities, for example skills of employees. Of course, the management of all three subgroups by top management is a key resource by itself which can lead to a sustainable competitive advantage.

Gaining strategic competitive advantage

The CMO and the marketing team should follow a process of analysis in order to develop strategies with the aim of gaining an SCA. This involves an analysis of the strategic situation, making a determination of the current situational advantages, making decisions on the strategic marketing objectives, identifying and evaluating strategic alternatives, and making decisions with regard to what strategy to select and implement.

Analysis of the strategic situation

An examination of the environmental forces, the industry dynamics, the competitive situation, the structure of the market, and the organization itself will be the first logical step in the strategic analysis. Environmental forces, which are largely uncontrollable by the organization, include economic, social, political, techno-logical, and natural forces. The organization must analyze how these forces influence it currently, and how this is likely to change in the future. The organization must look for future opportunities or threats from these environmental forces. An industry and competitor analysis should be performed because the organization's resources, relative to its competitors', create important market advantages and strategic weaknesses. The structure of the market creates various strategic situations. Saturated markets or mature markets intensify competition. Organizations need to make decisions on competitively positioning themselves and also need to choose segments of the market that they will serve, and more importantly understand the market segments that they will not serve relative to some of their competitors. As part of the analysis of the strategic situation, management must take a good look at the organization. They must understand what resources the organization has, its capabilities, and its performance. This will determine its strengths and weaknesses.

The current situational advantages

The competitive position of the organization, whether it has a competitive advantage or not, the existence of various segments of the market with different needs and wants, and whether the industry is mature or new, all determine the situational advantage. The different strategic-situation types include market development, market domination, market selectivity, differential advantage, and no advantage (Cravens, 1986). The first organization to enter a new market usually plays a leading role in developing that market. The market-domination situation is the market leader in an established market. Market selectivity is a situation when the market has many segments as a result of customer differentiation. There are many small organizations serving niche markets in this situation. The differential advantage situation happens when an organization possesses one or more sustainable advantages. The last situation is no advantage where suppliers offer similar products because customers are not differentiated.

Strategic marketing objectives

The CMO and team must set performance expectations for the organization. The strategic objectives must concern the organization's market position, market share, and performance.

Identifying and evaluating strategic alternatives

Management must consider the strategic alternatives available to them. This will include decisions on market segmentation and positioning, and the use of the marketing mix elements of product, pricing, distribution, and communication strategies. They must also consider strategic alternatives that involve corporate social responsibility programs, corporate branding and reputation, and internal and external corporate branding issues.

Strategy to select and implementation

Any decision on the strategy chosen should take into account all the alternatives discussed by management but also consider whether the chosen alternative will give the organization a sustainable competitive advantage. Obviously resource requirements need to be considered including the organization's tangible assets, intangible assets, and capabilities of the employees.

The market-driven organization

In order to achieve objectives, an organization must be market driven. To be market driven, it must have a customer focus and at the same time have an awareness of the needs and expectations of other stakeholders such as suppliers, the community, employees, and government. In order to do so, it must be able to obtain intelligence about its competitors, understand the law, engage with the community and other stakeholders, and understand what customers value. The organization will have to work under the philosophy of being marketing orientated which is made operational under the marketing concept. This means that the firm will have to organize its resources toward satisfying customers' needs and developing market offerings that create value for customers and other stakeholders. The organization will make profit from doing this better than its competitors.

In order do this efficiently and effectively, an organization must look within as well. It must have a clear understanding of its resources and capabilities, and have intra-departmental coordination so that everyone in the organization understands what the firm is trying to achieve and understand what part they have to play to see to it that objectives are achieved and performance is on target.

The CMO is the organization's executive who is responsible for the strategic marketing of the firm and represents marketing at board level. The CMO's job includes participating in the organization's strategy formulation and the development of corporate-level marketing strategies and integrating them with the firm's other functional strategies. Normally the marketing department staff report to the CMO.

The strategic marketing process includes the following steps:

1. Identify market opportunities
2. Define market segments
3. Evaluate competition
4. Assess the organization's strengths and weaknesses.

Developing strategies include:

- Market targeting
- Competitive positioning
- Corporate brand management and internal branding
- Managing the organization's reputation.

Many of these will be discussed in the following chapters.

Conclusion

This chapter highlights the fact that strategic marketing is marketing viewed from the corporate perspective by top management and the resource commitments are long term. It also highlights the fact that organizations need to seek a sustainable competitive advantage, and ways of doing this are highlighted. This chapter also discusses the market-driven organization and emphasizes the need to have a customer focus. Last, the strategic marketing process is highlighted.

References

Barney, J. (1991). Firm resources and sustained competitive advantage. *Journal of Management*, 17 (March), 99–120.

Cravens, D. (1986). Strategic forces affecting marketing strategy. *Business Horizons*, Sept–Oct, 77–86.

Varadarajan, R. (2010). Strategic marketing and marketing strategy: domain, definition, fundamental issues and foundational premises. *Journal of the Academy of Marketing Science*, 38(2), 119–140.

XFINITY from Comcast: the quest for better customer service

Carrie, a loyal customer and a graduate student, sat at her dining table staring at her laptop contemplating her next phone call to Comcast. After weeks without service and little response from the cable provider, her frustration with the company's customer service department is over the top. Due to sidewalk repairs in her neighborhood, the physical cable providing service to her home was accidentally cut by construction workers when her sidewalk was rebuilt about a week ago. Carrie called Comcast one day after her service went down and explained the reason for the service outage in detail. The customer service representative was sympathetic and apologized to Carrie for the inconvenience. She assured Carrie that a technician would be there the next day to resolve the issue. This promptness was a huge relief and made Carrie very happy.

The next day, no one showed up to Carrie's house, no one called her to cancel or reschedule the appointment, and Carrie is confused and upset. Now it was the weekend, and that means Carrie would have to wait at least two more days until Monday. Finally, Monday came, and Carrie called Comcast once again only to learn that it could not send someone to her house until Thursday. Carrie's frustration is growing while her patience is running low. What happened next would drive anyone to insanity. A Comcast technician finally showed up on Thursday.

After Carrie explained the situation to him he checked on the outside cable connection and confirmed her story. The technician went on to explain that this type of situation requires him to request a special technician and that the soonest he can get someone out there would be in 16 days. The technician did offer a glimmer of hope by saying that if anything were to become available before then, she would be notified. It has been eight days without any service except the weak signal of the XFINITY Wi-Fi hotspot available, and Carrie is feeling hopeless and unvalued as a customer.

Over the next couple of days, she called once a day asking, begging, and pleading for someone on the other end of the phone to show some compassion and dig deeper to offer her a better solution. Now on her umpteenth call to Comcast within the month, she once again vented her frustrations to this customer service representative and begged for clarification of how Comcast internal workflows and escalations are handled. Carrie was particularly interested in learning the escalation procedure for a situation in which a customer's service was suddenly and unexpectedly interrupted. On this particular call, the customer service representative offered apologies and reassured her that the issue would be escalated to the proper department immediately. Another week would pass before Carrie made the next call. Still, no progress had been made, and life goes on. Work needed to get done, papers had to be written, so Carrie temporarily moved out of her place to stay with her boyfriend since she needed the Internet to work from home and get her school work done.

Through it all, Carrie could not help but wonder how Comcast could mess this up so badly. What is the internal process in the company for an issue of this kind and what should it be? Why is this so complex to resolve? And why isn't there a direct number to call to report these specific issues, such as the utility company, FPL, has when a power line goes down? These were all questions that tormented Carrie for weeks, and if only she could get to the right ears and vent her frustrations, perhaps someone with more power and autonomy could ensure that the issue would be taken care of and provide a date and time. "Wishful thinking," she thought. Every representative she spoke to sounded as if he/she was just reading a script.

Comcast's customer service is infamous for horrible communication and poor ease of resolution to interrupted service. The company has seen significant advancement in improvements to the product, which has increased demand and revenue, but it has a way to go to achieve world-class customer service. How can this be? How can a company so well versed in customers' needs not know how to fix this ongoing issue?

Industry

It has been nearly a decade since the creation of cable television that took America by storm. Having started in only three states – Arkansas, Pennsylvania, and Oregon – in 1948 cable initially brought distant over-the-air television signals from miles away to mountainous and geographically remote regions. Years later, cable television expanded into bigger cities and major metro areas, giving companies the chance to compete in the cable industry field such as the top three competitors Comcast, Time Warner Cable (now Spectrum), and DIRECTV.

Comcast was the first cable provider and known to be the second-largest pay-TV provider in the U.S.

It is the second-largest pay-TV company after AT&T, largest cable TV company and largest home Internet service provider in the United States, and the nation's third-largest home telephone service provider. Comcast services U.S. residential and commercial customers in 40 states and in the District of Columbia. ... Comcast owns and operates the Xfinity cable/telecommunications service, over-the-air national broadcast network channels (NBC and Telemundo), multiple cable-only channels (including MSNBC, CNBC, USA Network, NBCSN, E!, The Weather Channel, among others).

(Wikipedia, 2018a)

Time Warner Cable is committed to providing its customers with a wide range of TV, internet, and voice services to residential and business customers through the Spectrum brand (the new company name). In 1985 DIRECTV, which is an American direct broadcast satellite provider, was founded by Hughes Communications, a medical research company. DIRECTV provides its customers with a bundle of other AT&T services and provides the consumer with a chance to save money while getting TV, high-speed internet, home phone, and wireless services from the same service provider.

Both DIRECTV and TWC are serious competitors of Comcast. As Comcast Corporation continues to grow, Chairman and CEO Brian L. Roberts is committed to putting his employees through an ongoing extensive training program to be able to stand out from the competition. However, that hasn't always been the case with

Comcast. In 2014, Consumerist named Comcast as the worst company in America. A gold trophy in the shape of a pile of human feces was delivered to Comcast Corporate Headquarters to honor the unmatched level of hostility flowing from its customers to its business. Comcast isn't meeting the needs of its consumers when it comes to treating customer service with the utmost importance. Will this hurt the company in the long run and give its competitors the chance to take its business from it?

History

Comcast is considered a family business. The company dates back to 1963 when Ralph Roberts purchased American Cable Systems Inc., a small cable operator serving 1,200 cable subscribers in Tupelo, Mississippi. At the time American Cable Systems was one of the few community antenna television (CATV) services in the nation. By the early 1970s the acquisition of additional, smaller companies and their subscribers all over the country had taken place. These acquisitions included the purchase of E.W. Scripps, Jones Intercable Inc., and Lenfest Communications. By 1972, Comcast Corporation went public and began trading on the NASDAQ, at a value of $3,010,000 and by 1977 HBO first launched to 20,000 Comcast subscribers. In 1986, Comcast bought 26 percent of Group W Cable, doubling its number of customers to 1 million. That same year, Comcast made a founding investment of $380 million in QVC, further expanding its investor portfolio. After trial and error and losing a bidding war to buy Storer Communications in 1985, it was able to buy a 50 percent share of the company's assets in a joint deal with Tele-Communications Inc. in 1988. Around 1990 Roberts' son Brian L. Roberts was named President of Comcast, and he would eventually become part of the board of directors and control 33⅓ percent of the company's voting rights.

From 1990 to 2000 Comcast experienced a significant increase in market share through an aggressive series of acquisitions under the direction of Brian L. Roberts, In 2001, Comcast acquired a selection of AT&T Broadband cable systems from six states. This acquisition would make Comcast the largest cable television company in the United States with over 22 million subscribers. With the rise of high-definition and high-speed internet, Comcast launched high-definition services and high-speed Internet to remain relevant in the competing market.

As the 2010 Winter Olympics were taking place, Comcast was in the process of merging with media company NBC. Comcast was known as a TV and internet service provider, and company executives felt there was a need to rebrand the cable and internet division to not confuse the diverse portfolio mix of products and services. The answer was a new brand for TV and internet offerings: XFINITY. Comcast unveiled its new brand name logo and thus began renaming Comcast products as XFINITY products. Comcast High-Speed Internet became XFINITY Internet; Comcast TV became XFINITY TV and so on. XFINITY was not just a new name, it also brought with it the ability to get up to 100+ HD channels, nearly 20,000 movies and TV shows online and On Demand with Internet speeds of 50Mbps initially, but even more in the future (Wikipedia, 2018b). Comcast continues with its success and is considered to be one of the nation's leading providers of communications, entertainment, and cable products and services.

Current status of the company

Comcast Corporation is currently the largest broadcasting and cable television company in the world by revenue. This global media technology corporation, headquartered in Philadelphia, has two primary businesses, Comcast Cable and NBCUniversal. The former is one of the largest video, high-speed internet, and phone providers to residential and business customers in the U.S. under the XFINITY brand. The latter provides news, entertainment, and sports cable networks, under the NBC and Telemundo brands. Comcast also invests in the advertising, consumer, hospitality, enterprise, and infrastructure sectors, under Universal Pictures, Comcast Ventures, and Universal Parks and Resorts (Wikipedia, 2018a). The company maintains vertically integrated operations from production to distribution and from communications to broadcasting.

Although the company does not have a clear mission and vision statement, it states on its website that "giving back to the communities we serve is in our DNA. We have extraordinary businesses and game-changing products – but we are at our best when we are using our collective strength to make the world a better place" (Comcast, 2018). Moreover, according to FierceCable (2012), the last slogan trademarked by the company was "The Future of Awesome"; designed to promote its advanced market products such as its XFINITY X1 digital video service.

Comcast's corporate governance practices and policies promote fairness, transparency, and accountability in its dealings with all its stakeholders (Comcast, 2017c). In its corporate responsibility report, it is stated that the company tries to inspire its stakeholders to reach their full potential and shape a world that uses technology and media to improve lives. It invests in local communities by developing programs and partnerships, and mobilizing resources to inspire substantive change (Comcast, 2017a).

From a financial standpoint, 2017 was an outstanding year for the company; it had revenue of $84,526 million, which means an increase of 5 percent from 2016 (Wikipedia, 2018a). Additionally, its year-end stock price was $40.10, $5.57 more than 2016 (Yahoo! Finance, 2018).

It increased its operating cash flow by 7 percent and generated over $8 billion in free cash flow. Comcast also added 858,000 customers (a 29 percent improvement over 2015), and increased its dividend by 15 percent, marking its ninth consecutive annual increase (Comcast, 2017b). That being said, and considering the scope and diversity of Comcast's business, and its subsequent ability to generate cash in various areas, investors can consider Comcast shares a sensible investment.

At first sight, it seems clear to think the company is performing well. With these strong financial results, Comcast should look forward to the future with confidence. However, it seems the company needs to do something about its customer experience woes. In the latest customer experience survey focused on top pay-TV companies by Tempkin Experience Ratings, Comcast had the worst results, with a score of 37 percent. In other words, it ranks last in customer experience. There is no secret that Comcast has a terrible track record with customer service. In fact, by doing a simple online research, you can find a bunch of bad customer experience stories (Brodkin, 2016).

Looking ahead

According to Brian L. Roberts on the Corporate Comcast homepage:

> At Comcast, diversity has always been – and continues to be – an important part of our culture. Since my father founded the company more than 50 years ago in Tupelo, MS, we have been committed to promoting and increasing diversity in our leadership, workforce, purchasing decisions, programming and community investment. Diversity and inclusion is not an initiative or program with an expiration date. It's the right thing to do and also a core principle for the way we do business.
>
> (Roberts, 2012)

Roberts graduated from The Wharton School of the University of Pennsylvania and went to work at Comcast. He became President of Comcast Corporation in 1990 and has grown Comcast's revenue from $657 million in 1990 to $80.4 billion. Roberts has been recognized a number of times for his leadership within Comcast and was even named one of the world's best CEOs by *Fortune* magazine.

In 2015 Roberts unveiled a multi-year plan costing about $300 million that included hiring 5,500 customer service representatives and Comcast began requiring that all employees participate in customer service training. Roberts appointed Charlie Herrin, Senior Vice President of Customer Experience, to help deal with the customer services problems Comcast was facing. Roberts also pledged that Comcast technicians would arrive at their appointments on time and, if the technician was late, the customer would get a $20 credit. Roberts and Herrin understood that customers were not pleased with Comcast as a result of its customer service. Comcast customer service is notorious for making clients wait on hold for extended periods of time, conveying inaccurate information as well as technicians not showing up to scheduled appointments.

Comcast installed a service that allows the customer to track where the technician is and allows them to rate their experience as well. Roberts understood that Comcast's shortcomings were preventing customers from recommending it to friends and family. Roberts was very aware of how Comcast's lack of customer service was affecting its bottom line and he put things in place to make Comcast a company that customers recommend and whose needs are met.

Delivering superior customer service is crucial for Comcast if it wants to remain competitive in the broadcasting and cable television industry. In fact, it would be difficult for any company to survive without a good customer service since customers are the driving force of all organizations.

Roberts has overseen the company for approximately 30 years, and recognizes that Comcast is not providing an outstanding customer service experience. Therefore, he wonders whether his new reinforced customer service staff and $20 credit approach will be a success. Historically, Comcast's closest competitors have scored better in customer satisfaction surveys.

Consequently, there are loyal customers out there, like Carrie, with high levels of dissatisfaction with the service provided by Comcast but wowed by the product it has created. Can Comcast regain customer approval and satisfaction? Will Comcast be able to retain existing customers and possibly attract new customers and increase its market share?

References

AT&T. (2017). History. Retrieved April 4, 2017, from www.att-services.net/

Brodkin, J. (2016, June 24). How Comcast and Charter are trying to fix their awful customer service. *BIZ & IT*. Retrieved April 4, 2017, from https://arstechnica.com/business/2016/06/how-comcast-and-charter-are-trying-to-fix-their-awful-customer-service/

Comcast. (2017a). *2016 Comcast NBCUniversal Corporate Social Responsibility Report*. Retrieved March 21, 2018, from https://corporate.comcast.com/images/2016-Corporate-Social-Responsibility-Report.pdf

Comcast. (2017b, February 6). *2016 Year in Review*. Retrieved April 4, 2017, from http://corporate.comcast.com/news-information/news-feed/2016-year-in-review

Comcast. (2017c). *Corporate Governance*. Comcast Investor Relations. Retrieved April 4, 2017, from www.cmcsa.com/governance.cfm

Comcast. (2018). *Our Values*. Retrieved April 4, 2017, from https://corporate.comcast.com/values

FierceCable. (2012, June 29). Comcast trademarks "the future of awesome" slogan. *FierceCable*. Retrieved April 4, 2017, from www.fiercecable.com/cable/comcast-trademarks-future-awesome-slogan

Roberts, Brian L. (2012, November 26). A message from Comcast Chairman and CEO, Brian L. Roberts. Retrieved April 4, 2017, from http://corporate.comcast.com/news-information/news-feed/a-message-from-comcast-chairman-and-ceo-brian-l-roberts

Time Warner Cable. (2017). About us. *Spectrum*. Retrieved April 4, 2017, from www.spectrum.com/about.html?v=1&cmp=TWC

Wikipedia. (2018a). Comcast. *Wikipedia*. Retrieved March 22, 2018, from https://en.wikipedia.org/wiki/Comcast

Wikipedia. (2018b). XFINITY. *Wikipedia*. Retrieved March 22, 2018, from https://en.wikipedia.org/wiki/Xfinity

Yahoo! Finance. (2018). Comcast Corporation. *Yahoo! Finance*. Retrieved March 21, 2018, from https://finance.yahoo.com/quote/CMCSA/history/

Spirit Airlines

So many issues have surfaced from customers who fly with Spirit Airlines. Of course, consumers love airlines that are cheap or have good deals, but most customers who fly with Spirit are generally disappointed with the service and all the extra fees they have to pay which makes for a higher priced ticket anyway. The tickets, plus the extra fees, would be equivalent to flying with another airline but with all those costs included. These are some of the key problems that consumers have with flying Spirit and customers are very frustrated with its questionable policies and hidden fees. According to Fox News, "Spirit Airlines is the most hated airline in the U.S." (Fox News, 2016).

Other key issues with Spirit include a lack of customer service, oversold boarding, a high cost of carry-ons, whether a customer is part of the "Spirit Fare Club" program or not. The only way to avoid bag fees is to either carry a backpack or small purse that fits underneath the seat in front of you. Also, seat selections can cost up to $200, there is no in-flight entertainment, drinks and snacks come at a cost as well, and if a customer is a "frequent flyer," those miles expire very quickly with Spirits "use 'em or lose 'em" policy (Magaña, 2015).

According to the Department of Transportation, Spirit Airlines had the worst on-time arrival record of 13 U.S. carriers and the highest rate of consumer complaints over that time span. The transportation department's data showed that 11.73 out of every 100,000 customers who flew Spirit in 2015 complained about some aspect of their experience (LeBeau, 2016).

Spirit's latest "Contract of Carriage," updated on February 20, 2018, includes the customer service plan and the tarmac delay plan. Baggage charges will all be nonrefundable and certain countries may require other applicable charges to be collected by Spirit; if there is a modification of the itinerary, the customer has to pay another increased fee in baggage charges. Under this contract, one small carry-on bag will be permitted, with an extra charge, of course. If the small item cannot be safely stowed, there will be an additional charge. As far as its customer service is concerned, Spirit still offers the lowest fares available, ensures responsiveness to complaints, provides refunds, deliver baggage on time, etc. (Spirit Airlines, 2018). Although Spirit has put forth this new contract plan, nowhere in it does it state how it will resolve the specific current issues that its customers are complaining about each time they fly with Spirit. The airline gives general statements about what it will continue to do, but not a plan of execution of how it will deal with disappointed customers. According to its annual report, the only aspect that Spirit is focusing on is price-sensitive travelers. It believes that its growing customer base is more resilient than the customer bases of most other airlines because of low fares and unbundled service offering appeal to price-sensitive passengers (Spirit Airlines, 2013).

Background/company information history

Spirit Airlines is an airline company providing both domestic and international flights. It is known for being an "ultra low-cost" carrier in the U.S. Spirit Airlines started in 1964 as Clipper Trucking Company. In 1980, the airline service was established and known as Charter One. The airline service was based in Detroit, Michigan and provided travel to Las Vegas, the Bahamas, and Atlantic City. In 1992, the name Charter

One was officially changed to Spirit Airlines. Currently, Spirit Airlines is headquartered in Miramar, Florida. The company continued to work on its overall expansion and added additional destinations. It began a Spanish-language customer service plan, the online website, and reservation line. In the early 2000s, the company announced its plans to purchase 30 additional aircraft. Spirit started to branch off into international countries such as Haiti, Costa Rica, Venezuela, and the Netherlands.

The company's overall strategy was to provide "ultra low-cost" services. It started off this strategy by focusing on the baggage fee. Its new pricing was $10 for the first two bags and $5 for bags reserved 24 hours in advance. Lastly, it transitioned the drinks from being complementary to $1 for each drink. Later, it moved to changing the drink fee to $3. In 2007, Spirit revamped its branding strategy and its new aircrafts were updated. A year later the company began to advertise on the side of the aircraft, overhead bins, tray tables, and seatback tray tables. Around this time, it also had to lay off hundreds of pilots and flight attendants as it decided to close off two of its crew base.

Currently, Spirit Airlines travels to 52 destinations in South America, Central America, and the Caribbean. It has the youngest Airbus fleet in America with 49 aircrafts in its fleet. The company is based in Miramar, Florida, with base sites in Chicago, Dallas, and Las Vegas (Spirit Airlines, 2011).

Industry information

The airline industry

Airlines became more mainstream around the beginning of the twentieth century; however, things took a major turn in the sky in 1925 when the risk factor associated with flying became less. Shortly after, the Air Commerce Act allowed the Secretary of Commerce to ordinance a system of certifications and licensing for pilots. This Act also encouraged a system of establishing airways and traffic regulations. Years later, many of the "big players," such as United and American emerged as "heavy hitters" in the industry.

Soon after the establishment of the Air Commerce Act, the Civil Aeronautics Act was established to regulate airline routes and passenger fares. The Air Commerce Act regulated airlines' costs. Since airlines were not able to compete in fares anymore, their points to differentiate would come from their service and offerings.

As competition into the airline market increased, fare prices dropped to remain competitive in the industry. Airlines began focusing significantly on quality service and great associated products. The airline industry took a major hit in its market after the 9/11 tragedies. Business travel took a decline while fuel costs rose. Profitability in the airline industry returned nearly five years later, but only after major reductions. This brought to light the ultra low-cost airline industry, with heavy hitters such as Spirit Airlines (FAA.gov, 2017).

The ultra low-cost airline industry

Miramar, FL-based Spirit Airlines is one of a select few airline companies to offer "ultra low costs." Spirit Airlines' fares are generally lower than other competitors, but come with lots of stipulations that most other industry players do not mandate. This includes random seat selection, increased prices for onboard snacks, or even carry-on luggage. While this is the norm for other competitors such as rival Southwest Airlines, other larger airline companies have begun to explore this fare option. Recently, American Airlines announced its "Basic Economy" fare, which follows Spirit's traditional fare guidelines. Delta Airlines also offers something very similar. Could the Spirit Airlines of the world have been onto a new industry discovery?

Competitors

In such a highly competitive industry, Spirit competes against markets served by traditional network airlines, low-cost carriers, and at times, regional airlines. Despite the fierce competition, Spirit's main competitor is American Airlines with 51 percent market overlap, followed by Southwest Airlines and United Airlines. Additional competitors include Delta Airlines for domestic travel and JetBlue Airways for the Caribbean and Latin American markets (Spirit Airlines, 2015).

American Airlines

American Airlines was founded in 1930 and is now considered to be one of the largest airlines in the world. Together with its regional partner, American Eagle, it is able to offer an average of 6,700 flights per day to over 350 destinations in 50 countries across the globe (American Airlines, 2017). American Airlines is Spirit's single largest overlap with 51 percent of its markets, thus making American its main competitor. In addition, American Airlines is also one of Spirit's principal competitors in the Caribbean and Latin American markets for service from South Florida through its hub located in Miami, Florida (Spirit Airlines, 2015).

Southwest Airlines

Southwest Airlines was founded in 1967; since its inception, it has grown to become a major airline. Today, Southwest Airlines operates more than 3,900 daily flights to over 101 destinations across the United States as well as eight additional countries (Southwest Airlines, 2017). Southwest Airlines is considered to be one of Spirit's main competitors due to its domestic travel routes.

United Airlines

United Airlines was founded back in 1926, making it one of the oldest commercial airlines in the United States. Today, United has one of the "world's most comprehensive route networks" with an average of 4,523 daily departures to 339 destinations across 54 countries around the world (United Airlines, 2017). United Airlines is one of Spirit's main competitors within the domestic travel market.

Delta Airlines

Delta Airlines was founded in 1924 as a small aerial crop dusting operation called "Huff Daland Dusters" (Delta, 2017a), thus making Delta the oldest operating airline in the United States and the seventh oldest in the world. From then to today, it has grown to one of the world's largest global airlines offering an average of 15,000 daily flights to over 322 destinations in 58 countries on six continents (Delta, 2017b). Delta is one of Spirit's main competitors specifically within the domestic travel market.

JetBlue Airways

JetBlue Airways was founded in 1998 making it one of the youngest airlines in the United States as well as the youngest competitor to Spirit. With such great and rapid success, JetBlue became the fifth largest U.S. airline and now offers an average of "825 daily flights to 87 cities in 17 countries, with one-third of its route network in the Caribbean and Latin America" (JetBlue Airways, 2017). JetBlue is one of Spirit's main competitors within the Caribbean and Latin America markets through its operations in Fort Lauderdale, Florida.

Customer/consumer

The majority of Spirit Airlines customers believe in low-cost airfares; Spirit attracts these customers by reducing the service in the aircraft and charging high fees for items such as baggage. Spirit Airlines may offer very cheap airfare deals at times; however, when it comes to customer satisfaction, it does not get good ratings. Spirit gathered negative attention for its strict no-refund policy. According to the U.S. Department of Transportation's Bureau of Transportation Statistics, "Spirit Airlines has seven times more official complaints against them than any other airline operating in the United States" (SpiritAirlinesFacts.com, n.d.).

Whenever there are customer complaints, Spirit Airlines does not respond professionally; company representatives are trained to find excuses and stand their ground. While booking, customers feel as if they've landed a good deal; however, there are numerous hidden costs customers end up paying that typically cost more than elsewhere.

The way forward

Spirit continues to face key issues with its customers' problems, such as low customer satisfaction rates and other charge fees to fly on the airline. Customers are not happy that they pay for every little thing: updating their tickets; luggage and carry-on fees; on-board water and snack fees; and increased baggage costs for traveling over the holidays. Spirit is looked at as taking a quick domestic flight to save money, especially if a customer is traveling by herself for a business or quick weekend trip. Consumers now tend to want the best value for their money, thus customers who fly Spirit should understand that a cheap flight comes at a high cost with no conveniences.

References

American Airlines. (2017). American Airlines Group. Retrieved April 15, 2017, from www.aa.com/i18n/customer-service/about-us/american-airlines-group.jsp

Delta. (2017a). About Delta. Retrieved April 15, 2017, from www.delta.com/content/
www/en_US/about-delta.html

Delta. (2017b). Corporate stats and facts. Retrieved April 15, 2017, from http://news.
delta.com/corporate-stats-and-facts

FAA.gov. (2017). A brief history of the FAA. Retrieved April 15, 2017, from www.faa.gov/
about/history/brief_history/

Fox News. (2016, April 27).Spirit Airlines is the most hated airline in the US.
Fox News. Retrieved March 22, 2018, from www.foxnews.com/travel/2016/04/27/
spirit-airlines-is-most-hated-airline-in-us.html

JetBlue Airways. (2017). The JetBlue focus cities. Retrieved April 15, 2017, from http://
mediaroom.jetblue.com/~/media/Files/J/Jetblue-IR/fact-sheet-documents/
jetblue-focus-cities.pdf

LeBeau, P. (2016). Spirit Airlines triggered the most complaints. *CNBC*. Retrieved April
15, 2017, from www.cnbc.com/2016/02/18/spirit-airlines-triggered-the-most-
complaints.html

Magaña, P. (2015). What you should know before flying with Spirit Airlines. *USA Today*.
Retrieved April 15, 2017, from www.usatoday.com/story/travel/flights/2015/04/02/
spirit-airlines/70774364/

Southwest Airlines. (2017). Southwest corporate fact sheet. Retrieved April 15, 2017,
from www.swamedia.com/pages/corporate-fact-sheet

Spirit Airlines. (2011). Spirit Airlines history. Retrieved April 15, 2017, from www.spirit.
com/Content/Documents/en-US/Spirit%20Airlines%20History.pdf

Spirit Airlines. (2013). *Annual Report*. Retrieved April 15, 2017, from http://ir.spirit.
com/secfiling.cfm?filingid=1498710-14-19&cik=

Spirit Airlines. (2015). Form 10-k. Retrieved April 15, 2017, from http://ir.spirit.com/
secfiling.cfm?filingid=1498710-15-15&cik=

Spirit Airlines. (2018). *Contract of Carriage, Includes Customer Service Plan &
Tarmac Delay Plan*. Retrieved February 20, 2018, from www.spirit.com/Content/
Documents/en-US/Contract_of_Carriage.pdf

SpiritAirlinesFacts.com. (n.d.). Facts about the country's cheapest and most complained-
about airline. Retrieved April 15, 2017, from www.spiritairlinesfacts.com/

United Airlines. (2017). Corporate fact sheet. Retrieved April 15, 2017, from http://
newsroom.united.com/corporate-fact-sheet

Chapter 2

Strategic segmentation

Market definition and market segmentation are concepts of strategic importance to organizations and widely accepted by both academics and practitioners. Segmentation is an important step in strategic marketing as markets impact strategy.

Market definition

Weinstein (2006) developed a new market definition model consisting of three levels and nine components. The first level is the relevant market. This is the market appropriate for an organization given its environment, objectives, and capabilities. Identifying the geographical market the organization serves is the first step. This is the product-market identification. Explicating the generic market is necessary to consider the various and diverse marketing opportunities. The second level is the defined market. The organization is in the position to fine-tune its market definition. It should assess its current customer base or penetrated market, and noncustomers, its untapped market. Level three is the organization's target markets. At this level the organization must apply segmentation bases to identify groups of customers with similar characteristics or needs that will demonstrate similar buying behavior. This will be the segmented market. Lastly, the organization will have to select its specific target markets to pursue differentiated marketing strategies.

According to Sausen, Tomczak, and Herrmann (2005 p. 152),

> strategic market segmentation represents the strategic intent of market segmentation to ensure that the objective of market segmentation is consistent with the firm's overall business and marketing strategy. At the same time, it ensures that a firm's operational capabilities in marketing, sales and market research can fulfil the strategic intent of market segmentation. Therefore strategic market segmentation can be considered as the glue between a firm's marketing strategy and operational segmentation. It ensures a fit between segmentation objectives and a company's competencies, facilitating a successful implementation of market segmentation.

Objectives of market segmentation

Sausen, Tomczak, and Herrmann (2005) suggest that there are five main objectives of market segmentation:

1. Exploitation of new customer potentials. This is a customer acquisition goal and segmentation can be used to identify customer needs that are not satisfied by the organization's current marketing strategy.
2. Developing of existing customer potentials. This is a customer retention strategy and getting penetration into this segment can be achieved through understanding their needs and wants and cross-selling to them.
3. Increasing customer profitability. This is a form of value segmentation whereby the most profitable segments are retained and nurtured and the nonprofitable ones are not supported.
4. Improving targeting of marketing measures. Market segmentation can lead to greater efficiency of marketing activities and lead to better marketing mix decisions.
5. Identification of new submarkets. New product-markets can be identified through market segmentation. It can identify customer groups whose needs are not satisfied by a competitor in the market.

Bases for segmenting product-markets

Segmentation variables include the characteristics of people and organizations. In consumer markets the characteristics of people fall into two major categories: geographic and demographic as well as psychographic. In organizational segmentation, managers need to examine the extent of market concentration and the degree of product customization. In product use situation segmentation, markets can be segmented based on how the product is used. Needs and preferences vary according to different use situations. Mass customization offers a promising means of responding to different use situations at competitive prices. Buyers' needs and preferences and purchase behavior specific to products and brands can be used as segmentation bases and segment descriptors. For example, the customer's loyalty status and benefits sought can be used to segment markets. Consumer needs levels are also important to understand. Organizations will therefore have to understand the demographic and psychographic makeup of the market, consumer and organizational buyer use situations, consumer needs and preferences, and actual purchase-behavior.

Useful criteria for evaluating a potential segmentation strategy include response differences between segments, the existence of identifiable segments and actionable segments, the cost/benefits of segmentation, and the ability to differentiate the product for the resulting market segments.

Segmentation implementation

To implement market definition and segmentation, Weinstein (2006, p. 123) suggests answering the following questions:

1. Is management committed to the process?
2. Are lines of communication open throughout the organization?

3. Do you have a management information system (MIS) in place for gathering marketing intelligence?
4. Do you have sufficient marketing data and internal consensus for logically grouping market subsets?
5. Does the chosen segmentation scheme fit the organization's mission and strategic planning initiatives?
6. Do you have managerial support to provide appropriate personnel and adequate finances for the segmentation initiative?
7. Is communication strategy in place for informing both internal and external constituencies?
8. Are the right people in place and committed to operationalizing the segmentation scheme?
9. Has management shown long-term commitment to segmentation rollout and monitoring?

Target markets

Market targeting consists of evaluating and selecting one or more segments whose value requirements provide a good match with the organization's capabilities. According to Cravens and Piercy (2012), market targeting falls into two major categories: segment targeting when segments are clearly defined and targeting based on product differentiation.

There are situations where an organization can clearly define the different segments in the market but there are also markets where this may be difficult to do. An organization can adopt selective targeting or extensive targeting. There are four possible targeting strategies. When segments are clearly defined, and the objective is extensive targeting, then it can select multiple segments to target. As an alternative, when market segments are clearly defined and there is selective targeting, the organization can select a niche market to target. In situations when the market segments are not clearly defined, and the objective is to extensively target, then product variety is the best targeting strategy. In the other scenario when segments are not clearly defined, and there is selective targeting, product specialization will be a sound targeting strategy.

The factors influencing the organization's targeting strategy include the stage of product-market maturity; the extent of diversity in buyer value requirements; the industry structure; its capabilities and resources; and its opportunities for gaining competitive advantage.

Conclusion

This chapter highlights the strategic importance of market segmentation. It discusses the importance of market definition and structure. It then highlights the objectives of segmentation, the bases for segmenting markets, and the implementation of a segmentation strategy. Last, the choice of target markets is highlighted, which the strategic choices discussed.

References

Cravens, D. and Piercy, N. (2012). *Strategic Marketing*, 10th edition. Englewood Cliffs, NJ: McGraw Hill.

Sausen, K., Tomczak, T., and Herrmann, A. (2005). Development of a taxonomy of strategic market segmentation: a framework for bridging the implementation gap between normative segmentation and business practice. *Journal of Strategic Marketing*, 13, 151–173.

Weinstein, A. (2006). A strategic framework for defining and segmenting markets. *Journal of Strategic Marketing*, 14, 115–127.

Burger King identity crisis: who is it now?

When Burger King was established in the early 1950s, it wanted to attract the families of baby boomers and serve them with affordable and quick broiled burgers. By providing the consumers with the best quality burgers, it was able to achieve great success in a short time and become the second largest fast food chain. Although it achieved great success, because of changing social factors Burger King got caught in an identity crisis. Who is it, what kind of food does it serve, and which market segment is it targeting? Currently, Daniel Schwartz is Burger Kings 21st CEO since the company was founded in 1953. Burger King has suffered from "years of neglect and strategic incoherence" (Leonard, 2014). Burger King needs a strong brand and core values to stand out from all other competition. Fast food sales are declining as more customers are gravitating towards healthier food options. Schwartz is helping Burger King regain its former identity. He started his job as CEO discovering what life was like for the kitchen employees (Leonard, 2014). He has simplified the menu, and also changed the corporate management team so they could work better together on a new tactical plan.

Company background

Burger King is the second largest food chain in the United States, with over 10,400 restaurants. Burger King was originally known as Insta-Burger King and founded in Florida in 1953 by Keith Kramer and Matthew Burns before they had financial difficulties and sold the company to its Miami-based franchisees, James McLamore and David Edgerton in 1954 (Burger King Worldwide, Inc., 2014). Burger King was founded with an idea that was not so unique. Around this time other restaurants, especially drive-ins, were popping up all over the United States. One that stands out in particular is the current number one fast food chain, McDonald's, which started its empire with a California drive-in (Burger King Worldwide, Inc., 2014).

Despite all the competition around it Burger King started out very strong and successful. By 1967 the corporation was acquired by The Pillsbury Co. for $18 million, and it already had about 274 restaurants. Its secret to success was giving its restaurant a special edge. In 1957 the Whopper sandwich – the burger for large appetites – was introduced and from the beginning it was successful. It was also the first chain to offer its customers a sit-in dining room.

Two years later, the company began to expand through franchising. That is when it started having inconsistency in product and service from franchise to franchise. This problem was caused because it used a small field staff for franchise support. Burger King franchisees had varying approaches to the way they implemented the organizational culture in Burger King restaurants (Gibbons, 2000).

Burger King's main competitor McDonald's took a different strategy from the beginning, leasing stores to franchisees and demanding a high degree of uniformity in return (Gale, 2004).

To fix this problem, Burger King hired a strong executive from McDonald's to restructure the company's franchise system. He began by introducing a more demanding franchise contract. This contract stipulated the franchises need to be awarded only to individuals, not partnerships or companies. Another rule was that they may not own other restaurants and must live within an hour's drive of their franchise. These were set in place to stop franchisees from getting too big.

Additionally, he also changed the corporate structure of the company, replacing eight of ten managers with McDonald's people. In order to attack Burger King's inconsistency problem, Smith assigned a yearly two-day check of each franchise and frequent unscheduled visits. All of these strategies worked as planned and by 1979 he had brought the company's share of outlet ownership up from 34 percent to 42 percent (Gale, 2004). Around this time Burger King also started to market its products to kids, making its commercials similar to McDonald's. Using similar tactics to McDonald's, Smith was able to bring up sales for Burger King, but once Smith left the corporation to join another, Burger King's sales started to decline again.

Burger King's organizational culture is based on being friendly and supporting its people for high performance, which is accentuated through meritocracy and empowerment. The primary advantage of Burger King's organizational culture is that people feel comfortable doing what they know how to do. Another characteristic of Burger King's culture is accountability; this ensures that with autonomy and flexibility errors and related unnecessary costs are minimized. However, while Burger King's organizational culture is strongly manifested in its corporate offices, it has only limited implementation in the restaurants.

The fast food industry

The fast food industry is a huge industry in the U.S. With low price points and the emphasis on convenience, fast food restaurants have been a steadily popular option for breakfast, lunch, and dinner in the U.S. for many decades. Many consider White Castle as the first in the business although McDonald's might be the most known as they revolutionized the industry with their effective assembly-line system in the late 1940s. Since then, a huge number of fast food restaurant chains have entered the market and are now battling for market share.

There are about 200,000 fast food restaurants in the United States and it is estimated that 50 million Americans eat at one every day (Franchise Help, 2017). In 1970 the fast food industry generated about $6 billion in revenues. It has been a rapidly growing market with $227.5 billion in revenues and $11.8 billion in profits in 2016.

One of the reasons why these restaurants are wildly popular is mostly because of the convenience, speed, and low prices they offer. The fast food chains have also put a bigger emphasis on the overall restaurant experience over the past few years. The fast food industry has become an industry with a wide variety of food options.

Restaurants that sell burgers make up 42 percent of the products sold in the fast food market. This reflects its biggest player in the market, McDonald's. The menu items are consistent in almost every restaurant which makes it easier for the consumers to pick favorites.

Competitors

The McDonald's way

McDonald's is the largest fast food operation in the world. The first store opened in 1948 in San Bernardino, CA with its first franchise agreement in 1954. By the end of 2015 the company had over 36,000 stores in over 119 countries. By 2018 the company plans to have 90 percent of the stores operated by franchisees. "This is part of a restructuring plan that will give restaurants more opportunities to experiment and better integrate themselves within their core markets" (Alvarez, 2016).

McDonald's restaurants have a marketing strategy in place that is very successful. There are three levels of advertising that McDonald's implements at every location. These are national, regional, and local advertising strategies. McDonald's requires every franchise to give 4 percent of their sales to pay for the national and regional advertisements (Gerhardt, Hazen, and Lewis, 2014). Local advertisements are up to the franchisee to decide on and are separate from the initial 4 percent. According to Business Insider, McDonald's is the most successful food chain in America, compared to Burger King which is in fourth place.

Yum! Brands

Yum! Brands Inc. is a Kentucky-based fast food conglomerate. PepsiCo was the owner until 1997 when it decided to publicly list the company to improve cash flow. "PepsiCo purchased Pizza Hut in 1977, Taco Bell in 1978 and KFC in 1986" (Alvarez, 2016).

In 2003 the company launched WingStreet to co-exist with Pizza Hut locations. Yum! Brands, like many of its competitors, operates under franchises with 80 percent of its stores being franchised. A multibranding strategy is how Yum! Brands believes it is able to offer something for everyone; helping break the family barrier when the kids want to eat different things than their parents. When the company puts two or more of its brands in the same restaurant it is able to increase sales by 30 percent (Enz, 2005). This strategy is believed to offer a chance to leverage its existing assets that have lower volumes.

Wendy's

Wendy's Co. is a fast food burger chain based out of Dublin, OH, operating more than 6,500 stores globally with 85 percent of its stores under franchise agreements. Wendy's also owns a stake of 18.5 percent of Arbys.

Before 2011 Wendy's digital and social marketing was nonexistent. By building a relationship with Facebook and working with its global marketing service group Wendy's was finally using digital and social marketing to reach its target audiences. Wendy's declines to give exact numbers on its digital marketing expense, however, it did spend $290 million in 2013 on media expenses (Morrison, 2014).

Changing factors

The health conscious consumer

Changes in culture and the study of the human body and eating habits have led to a change in the American people (Alvarez, 2016). A common denominator for all restaurant markets is the change of customer eating habits in the United States. Especially in the fast food industry it has been health concerns from customers that have resulted in decreasing sales. The American people have become more health conscious and are demanding alternatives to the traditional greasy food most fast food restaurants serve.

The saturated food traditionally sold at fast food restaurants has helped keep prices low within the industry. Fast food chains have been forced to make drastic changes or additions to their menus to meet customer needs and wants.

These changes mostly consist of healthier options that would appeal to the new trends in eating habits, but still at a very reasonable price. Although the new eating habits have caused changes in strategy and additions in product selection, they have also opened up for chains to market differently with new products or renewing interest in current products.

Threat of fast casual restaurants

As a result of new trends in eating habits, new concepts and hybrids in the restaurant industry have emerged. Fast casual restaurants are one of these new concepts. These restaurants are a hybrid or a mix of a fast food and casual dining place. Basically, they have all the elements of convenience that fast food has like speed and price, but with a more inviting atmosphere like one would find in a sit-down restaurant.

These restaurants focus more on offering healthier, fresher, and higher quality ingredients to attract customers who are health conscious. Fast casual restaurants give off a better impression than most fast food restaurants. Consumers feel they eat healthier and also feel better in a more sophisticated atmosphere (Alvarez, 2016). Fast casual restaurants are stealing market share away from fast food chains. As a counter, many chains are experimenting with their own fast casual concept. If the experiments are a success, this might be the direction fast food chains are going.

However, fast food chains are seeking to offer healthier options and will do so in the years to come. They will also diversify into new areas such as cafes or full-service restaurants but maybe under different names and at new locations (Alvarez, 2016). Fast food chains and fast casual chains will both be investing in further renovations and improving service through technology and the basic aesthetics.

Targeting a market

Since the 1980s, Burger King has been having a difficult time attracting a specific target market. In contrast, some of its competitors such as McDonald's and Wendy's effectively attracted a distinctive target market (Mitchman and Mazze, 1998).

As a result of consumers' concerns about eating healthy food, Burger King decided to be the first fast food chain to include information about calories, fat, salt, and other contents in its menu items. This action was part of a strategic plan to attract new market segments. Likewise, in response to consumers' changes in preferences, McDonald's and other fast food chains deleted sodium from food items, and added healthy options such as salads and baked potatoes (Dugan, 2013).

Daniel Schwartz, current CEO, expressed his concern about the market the company has been historically trying to target, which is males between the ages of 18 and 35, since this market is not representative of the overall fast food market. After realizing this fact, Burger King decided not to target this market's subsets (Kelso, 2012).

In order to make a shift in its demographic, Burger King decided to target not just males but also females in its advertisements. Results were satisfactory; after having the soccer star David Beckham in one of Burger King's commercials, surveys showed higher percentage of females consuming its products.

Baby boomers

This segment of the market, born between 1946 and 1964, is being considered as a powerful consumer of fast food. These members of the population have new habits, they are exercising, traveling, volunteering. Due to this active lifestyle, they need quick meals, and some of them demand healthy meals. Also, grandparents might be involved in their grandchildren's daily lives. By targeting grandparents, fast food chains also gain their family members.

In 1999, the chain released three different advertisements promoting the Whopper; one of them was intended only for baby boomers, the other two for blacks and Hispanics (Albert, 2012). Although it is targeting baby boomers it does not market the brand well to this segment. There are no advertisements that would help them feel connected to the brand, to keep them as returning customers.

Millennials

The population between the ages of 18 and 33 years old are currently the generation that tend to eat out more often. In, fact 53 percent of millennials eat out once a week, compared with 43 percent for the general population in the U.S. However, millennials when being surveyed are embarrassed to say they eat fast food (Lutz, 2015).

The majority of this market segment prefers eating at fast casual dining restaurants when eating out. However, they still consider fast food restaurants as a second option. Recently, the chain reported a decline in 5 percent in traffic of low-income millennials (Forbes, 2017). This decline might be a consequence of not promoting the brand among this market segment appropriately, which is mainly through social media.

Generation X

This generation is the group between baby boomers and millennials, comprising people born between 1965 and 1980. This population is commonly the busiest with work, family, and paying bills. The Generation X segment prefers coupons and special discounts when consuming products. Even though the fast food chain has been doing efforts to broaden its demographic, there is still much to achieve. The brand is constantly launching products for different segments of the market, and it is not adjusting its branding accordingly. Whether Burger King should focus on a specific market segment, or adjust its branding accordingly to each one, is a major concern that the company should analyze, in order to look at solutions for its identity crisis.

Burger King's strategic positioning

When referring to positioning in the fast food industry, McDonald's definitely has the lead. The majority of consumers tend to first think about McDonald's when looking for a fast food option. Burger King has a positioning statement that distinguishes it from the rest, but it has not been enough to achieve a better position in the market.

Burger King, for a long period, was relying on the positioning statement "Have it your way," but recently the senior vice-president of global management decided to sharpen the chain's positioning by first changing the statement to "Be your way" (Parpis, 2016).

However, changing a positioning statement is not enough to gain competitive advantage in the market. In fact, many customers were confused as to why Burger King dropped a 40-year-old slogan, and what it had to do with their food. A food critic summed it up by saying "While the original phrase reminded customers that customizing their food was always on the table, the new phrase seems like a cryptic philosophy a mentor would give a young boy from Jersey right before a karate tournament" (Pham, 2014). Although this critic might have been a little harsh, Burger King gave up part of who it is by changing its slogan.

The company has also decided to advertise without celebrities, and instead focus on the brand's core product, the Whopper. It is making efforts to build an ecosystem of agencies that are constantly aligned. It is also trying to be more unified to achieve brand positioning, by creating an effective advertising campaign and taking in consideration all relevant aspects of Burger King's new marketing strategies.

Burger King is also supporting the LGBT community by launching a campaign called "Proud Whopper." Likewise, the company released a commercial spoken in sign language, and used American Sign Language (ASL) for all the signs located at a store next to Gallaudet University for the deaf. These actions are meant to support the chain's new slogan "Be your way." The company is making efforts to gain a competitive advantage. The significant changes in its marketing strategy have been showing positive results, reporting 4.6 percent growth globally, and 5.4 percent growth in the U.S. in the first quarter of 2016, after implementing the changes.

The way forward

Burger King targets too many market segments, at the same time. However, it does not communicate the same message to all the segments. To do this it creates more than one advertisement for the same product. Burger King is also known to copy many of the methods of its competitors In 2012, Burger King restructured many of its stores with a $750 million investment, to create a more open and inviting atmosphere but McDonald's made the exact same move the year before.

Burger King's menu has also been very inconsistent. A couple years ago it started offering healthier products like salads, smoothies, and new chicken menu items. Analysts said this was a page taken out of the Wendy's playbook. Although this was a move made to target more health conscious consumers, it hurt Burger King's brand identity. Burger King has also brought in some new, wild menu items like the french fry burger. While some of these menu items have brought in more customers to the restaurant, others items have been pulled off the menu before most people even heard about them.

Burger King is having a hard time retaining customers because of its issues with brand identity. It seems a very confused brand to the public. When it first started out it was known for its main product, the Whopper. It offered consumers a great burger at a low price. Burger King needs to restructure its brand image to represent itself and not every other fast food restaurant.

References

Albert, D. (2012). *Geospatial Technologies Advancing Geographic Decision making: Issues and Trends*. Hershey, PA: IGI Global.

Alvarez, A. (2016). *Fast Food Restaurants – US Market Research Report*. Ibis World. Retrieved April 11, 2017, from www.ibisworld.com/industry/default.aspx?indid=1980

Burger King Worldwide, Inc. (2014). *MarketLine Company Profiles Authority, EBSCOhost*. Retrieved April 11, 2017, from http://web.a.ebscohost.com.ezproxylocal.library.nova.edu/ehost/pdfviewer/pdfviewer?sid=5baac5ca-3479-423a-9feb-6ad9154200ee%40sessionmgr4009&vid=4&hid=4114

Dugan, A. (2013). Fast food still major part of U.S. diet. *Gallup*. Retrieved April 11, 2018, from www.gallup.com/poll/163868/fast-food-major-part-diet.aspx

Enz, C.A. (2005). Multibranding strategy: the case of Yum! Brands. *Cornell Hotel and Restaurant Administration Quarterly*, 46(1), 85–91. Retrieved April 11, 2017, from Cornell University, School of Hospitality Administration site: http://scholarship.sha.cornell.edu/articles/360/

Forbes. (2017). The 11 restaurants that need to cater to millennials. *Forbes*. Retrieved April 11, 2017, from www.forbes.com/pictures/gfig45fll/burger-king/#1031254f3231

Franchise Help. (2017). *Fast Food Industry Analysis 2017 – Cost & Trends*. Retrieved April 11, 2017, from www.franchisehelp.com/industry-reports/fast-food-industry-report/

Gale, T. (2004). History of Burger King Corporation. *Encyclopedia.com*. International Directory of Company Histories. Retrieved April 11, 2017, from https://en.wikipedia.org/wiki/History_of_Burger_King

Gerhardt, S., Hazen, S., and Lewis, S. (2014). Small business marketing strategy based on McDonald's. *ASBBS eJournal*, 10(1), 104–112.

Gibbons, B. (2000). Friendly culture. *Executive Excellence*, 17(1), 9–10.

Kelso, A. (2012, June 14). Burger King demographic beginning to shift? *QSRWeb*. Retrieved April 11, 2017, from www.qsrweb.com/articles/burger-king-demographic-beginning-to-shift/

Leonard, D. (2014, July 24). Burger King is run by children. *Bloomberg*. Retrieved April 10, 2017, from www.bloomberg.com/news/articles/2014-07-24/burger-king-is-run-by-children

Lutz, A. (2015). 5 ways millennials' dining habits are different from their parents'. *Business Insider*. Retrieved April 11, 2017, from www.businessinsider.com/millennials-dining-habits-are-different-2015-3

Mitchman, D. and Mazze, E. (1998). *The Food Industry Wars: Marketing Triumphs and Blunders*. Westport, CT: Greenwood Publishing Group Inc.

Morrison, M. (2014). Wendy's has no beef with its latest creative consultant – Facebook. *Advertising Age*, 85(21), 48.

Parpis, E. (2016, May 23). How Fernando Machado is bringing Burger King back to greatness. *US Campaign*. Retrieved April 11, 2017, from www.campaignlive.com/article/fernando-machado-bringing-burger-king-back-greatness/1395717

Pham, P. (2014, May 20). After 40 years, Burger King drops "Have it your way" & adopts cryptic "Be your way" slogan. *Foodbeast*. Retrieved April 11, 2017, from www.foodbeast.com/news/burger-king-passes-on-have-it-your-way-slogan-and-adopts-vague-be-your-way/

Florida Blue: the blues of the Affordable Care Act

A graduate of Colgate, Pat Geraghty spent 18 years with Prudential, before moving on to spend an additional 9 years with the Blue affiliate in New Jersey before being hired in 2008 as Chief Executive Officer (CEO) at the Minnesota Blue. When former Florida Blue leader Robert Lufrano decided to retire in 2011, he advised Geraghty of the position. This was an opportunity Geraghty said he could not pass on; he was excited by the challenges the Florida location would bring, the "size, scope, complexity of the assignment" according to Mark Vogel (2014).

However, as Geraghty took the reins of Florida Blue, the health insurance industry was faced with an important issue that would change the landscape of the company. In 2010, the government passed the Patient Protection and Affordable Care Act (ACA) law, otherwise known as Obamacare. This piece of legislation, which was championed by the president himself, mandates that all citizens be eligible for health insurance. The implementation of the ACA posed a threat to Florida Blue's overall performance in the market, as now there would be an increase in competition, and the lower insurance prices would mean that revenue streams would slow down. That being said, it was up to Geraghty to come up with a solution that would satisfy all parties involved and ensure that the company kept its position as a market leader.

Company information

Florida Blue is a subsidiary of Blue Cross Blue Shield Association, which is a federation of 36 separate health insurance providers in the United States. Florida Blue is one of the providers that cover the whole state of Florida. As currently constituted, Florida Blue is the oldest and largest healthcare provider in the state, with approximately 4.3 million members and 11,500 employees within the state.

Florida Blue was founded in 1944 in Jacksonville, Florida, with a staff of only four individuals. The company was originally called the Florida Hospital Service Corporation (FHSC), but its name was changed to Blue Cross of Florida. Its competition, Florida Medical Services Association, was formed in 1946 with similar goals as FHSC. Eventually, these two companies merged in 1980 to create Blue Cross and Blue Shield of Florida, a name that was kept until 2012, when the company underwent a rebranding campaign and changed its name to Florida Blue in order to make it easier for its customers to remember it.

Florida Blue's organizational structure is divided into three distinct businesses: Health Business, Government Business, and Life and Specialty Ventures. The Health business is the core business, it is the one in charge of the individual insurance policies. With its 4.2 million members, it currently owns approximately 29 percent of the market, more than double that of its nearest competitor. Government business concerns Medicare and the Affordable Care Act, and is administered by a subsidiary called First Coast Service Options. The Life and Specialty Ventures business specializes in selling policies to businesses and other groups, which include dental, health, and life insurance.

Florida Blue's mission statement reads "To help people and communities achieve better health," and its vision states "A company focused primarily on the health industry, delivering value through an array of meaningful choices." These two statements exemplify the core values of respect, integrity, imagination, courage, and excellence. These are values that the company tries to uphold through its services and customer support.

Industry information

In 2014, the insurance industry recorded revenue totaling $1.1 billion. Of this figure, 56 percent was for life and health insurance, while 44 percent accounted for property and casualty. According to a 2015 report by IBIS World Report,

> the Health and Medical Insurance industry, which is made up of carriers of private, group and public health, medical, dental insurance, was characterized by slow growth 5 years ago as a result of reduced employer coverage and continued consumer deleveraging. However, consistent increases in healthcare expenditure and medical cost inflation, as well as a sharp decline in the uninsured rate, have driven industry growth in recent years. Growth is expected to continue in the ensuing years, the assumption is, as the baby boomers aged, their need for more medical coverage will increase. Their retirement will also help to boost Medicare expenditure.
>
> (Ibis World Report, 2017)

To be successful in the health insurance industry, many partnerships and alliances had to be forged. As such, the health insurance market is connected with many sectors of the healthcare system, along with many other private partners. Health insurers act as a third party between the patients and healthcare. The health insurers reimburse the healthcare provider on behalf of the patient for services rendered. The health insurer also provides guidelines on the amount of coverage a patient has available to him/her. Most health insurance plans are managed care plans (Health Maintenance Organizations [HMOs], Preferred Provider Organizations [PPOs]) rather than indemnity or traditional health insurance plans that provide unlimited reimbursement for a fixed premium, according to Austin and Hungerford, 2009.

> The Health and Medical Insurance Industry is in the mature stage of its economic life cycle; this stage is characterized by a slowdown in technological development and wholehearted market acceptance of the industry's products and services. Industry value added (IVA), which measures an industry's contribution to the overall economy, is expected to increase at an annualized rate of 2.7% during the 10 years to 2020. In contrast, US GDP is projected to grow at an annualized rate of 2.2% during the same period. These figures signify that the industry's share of the US economy is holding steady, as the industry is growing at close to the same rate as the rest of the economy.
>
> (IBIS World Report, 2017)

According to Cox, Ma, Claxton, and Levitt (2014),

> The individual health insurance market historically has been highly concentrated, with only modest competition in most states. At the time the Affordable Care Act

was signed into law in 2010, a single insurer had at least half of the individual market in 30 states and the District of Columbia. While a dominant insurer may be able to negotiate lower rates from hospitals and physicians, without significant competitors or regulatory oversight, there is no guarantee that those savings would be passed along to consumers.

The industry products include Pharmacy Benefit Management (PBM), Preferred Provider Organization (PPO), High-deductible Health Plans (HDHPs), Health Maintenance Organization (HMO), Point-of-service (POS), Fee-for-service (FFS), Medicaid (via private firms), and Medicare (via private firms).

Competition

Florida Blue is Florida's largest and oldest healthcare provider notwithstanding the many competitors from both other local brands as well as national brands within the same industry. Florida Blue's top competitors are AETNA Inc., Humana Inc., and UnitedHealth Group Inc. According to Healthpayerintelligence (2016), the top firms in the healthcare industry today are United Healthcare with net sales in 2016 of $184.8 billion, Anthem with $89.1 billion, Aetna with $63.1 billion, Humana with $54.3 billion, and Cigna with $39.7 billion.

Overall, Florida Blue is not ranked in the top ten insurance providers in general; its main competitors are all national providers, and Florida Blue's focus is only in Florida. It has been and remains a leader in Florida since 1944 due to the fact it continuously develops improved solutions that promote more affordable healthcare throughout Florida. Florida Blue has approximately 4 million healthcare members and serves 15.5 million people in 16 states through its affiliated companies. Unlike many other providers, Florida Blue is a not-for-profit, policyholder-owned, tax-paying mutual company.

Although some of its competitors, such as Cigna, have been diversifying their business into overseas ventures, or like UnitedHealth and Aetna, who are into related areas such as health technology, Florida Blue remained committed to its core business, through insurance and new models of care. Florida Blue leads its competition in seeing the need to appeal directly to the people it is covering. Florida Blue has set up 18 retail stores as of today, where customers can come in, shop around, and have the ability to ask questions face to face as opposed to online or over the phone. You will be able to assess and further understand the amount of members the top companies have in Table 2.1.

Table 2.1 shows that Florida Blue has over 310,216 statewide enrollments which was the second highest in 2014 just under Humana Medical Plan. It is a leader due to its reputation along with its principles and the path it follows. Florida Blue is constantly growing, and in 2014 it acquired the Diagnostic Clinic Medical Group located in Key Largo. It has also participated in private sector exchanges, which have been chosen by 90 percent of the full-time Florida employees of Darden Restaurants, owner of Olive Garden.

Over the past two years, Florida Blue has updated its strategy to incorporate campaigns and partnership opportunities that convert social media activity

Table 2.1 Florida Counties: enrollment data are current as of September 1, 2014

Health plan type	Plan name	Statewide enrollment
Commercial HMO	**Humana Medical Plan, Inc.**	377,172
Commercial HMO	**Florida Blue (HMO)**	310,216
Commercial HMO	**Coventry Health Care of Florida, Inc.**	281,663
Commercial HMO	**Aetna Health, Inc.**	205,809
Commercial HMO	**Capital Health Plan, Inc.**	108,537

Source: Florida Office of Insurance Regulation.

into business leads and in return, drive results. Florida Blue has empowered every employee to help drive brand awareness and speak on a personal level with his or her ever-growing online community. It has also been very successful in other areas of driving business such as a campaign it had with the Miami Heat, where Florida Blue offered personalized autographs and in just over a few hours over 2,900 fans received digigraphs, which had the capability to share on social media to help boost brand awareness and spread the brand image. Its campaigns and ability to drive business has not only helped it become the leader in Florida but to also remain the leader in such a competitive industry.

Consumer information

The ACA requires individuals to have health insurance. The law also places stricter guidelines on insurance companies and helps to reduce out-of-pocket expenses. This new law also requires employers with employees working over 30 hours a week to be able to obtain insurance. The law also allows for patients with preexisting conditions to obtain insurance. More information regarding this new law can be found at Department of Health and Human Services (2015).

The new ACA requires the following to be covered under its insurance plans: ambulatory patient services, emergency service, hospitalization, pregnancy and maternal care, mental health and substance disorders services, prescription drugs, rehabilitation services, laboratory work, preventive and wellness care as well as several pediatric care (Healthcare.gov, 2015). These services are considered essential benefits and insurance companies must cover these services according to the ACA.

Having insurance is vital as medical expenses can be very costly. There is also a fee which consumers need to be aware of if they do not have any insurance. This fee is calculated based on household income and tax information. The ACA can help individuals to save money by purchasing a plan that would be cheaper than paying the fee for not having any insurance.

Enrollment period is also an important part of purchasing an insurance plan. The enrollment period to purchase via the marketplace is November 1, 2017–December 15, 2017. This is to purchase plans as well as renew plans for the new 2018 year. Under circumstances there may be times where an individual may be eligible based upon on a life event to obtain insurance while not in the current enrollment period. Insurance can be purchased via the marketplace on the healthcare.gov website. An application must be completed to begin the process; from there many different insurance plans will be shown with coverage options. The individual then can select the plan that is right for them.

Florida Blue, a Florida based insurance plan, offers many plans under the ACA. There are four plans to choose from: Bronze, Silver, Gold, and Platinum. Bronze covers 60 percent, Silver covers 70 percent, Gold covers 80 percent, and Platinum covers 90 percent of medical expenses (Blue Cross and Blue Shield Florida, 2015). Each plan is designed to cover the essential benefits, which is required by the ACA. However, monthly fees and out-of-pocket expenses vary depending on the plan and income level of the individual. In order to choose the plan that suits the individual the best it should be noted that the Bronze plan has the lowest monthly premiums making it the most affordable option; however, it does have significantly higher deductibles as well as the most out-of-pocket expenses. The Platinum plan has the highest monthly premium but has low deductibles as well as fewer out-of-pocket fees. These are important factors when deciding on an insurance policy. Florida Blue also offers an option called catastrophic health insurance plans, which have very low monthly premiums but have a very high deductible of $6,850. This may be a viable option for a healthy individual just needing coverage in case of an emergency and can be used to avoid the fee for not obtaining an insurance plan.

Florida Blue plans can be purchased several ways. One way is through the general marketplace on the healthcare.gov website where multiple insurance carriers can be viewed. Insurance can also be purchased direct through a Florida Blue agent or in one of the 18 retail centers. Insurance plans also must be purchased during the open enrollment period, which is November 1, 2017–December 15, 2017.

The Florida Blue bronze plan for a typical healthy 25-year-old costs $194 a month. This plan also has a deductible of $6,850 and an out-of-pocket maximum of $6,850. Once the deductible for this plan is met, there is no charge for emergency room care, generic prescriptions, doctors and specialists visits (Department of Health and Human Services, 2015). A Silver plan from Florida Blue has a monthly premium of $219, a deductible of $6,100 and an out-of-pocket expense maximum of $6,850. This plan has several co-payments, for an emergency room visit co-payment is $600 after the deductible is met. Generic prescription drugs costs $30 after the deductible is met and primary doctor visits cost $65 and specialists $95 after the deductible is met (Department of Health and Human Services, 2015). Florida Blue's Gold plan has a monthly premium of $290 and a deductible of $1,600 with a maximum out-of-pocket expense of $3,500. This plan has several co-payments, for an emergency room visit, generic drug coverage, and doctors including specialists' visits it is 10 percent of coinsurance after the deductible is met (Department of Health and Human Services, 2015). For a Platinum insurance plan it has a monthly premium of $574, a deductible of $800, and an out-of-pocket maximum of $2,500. There are several co-payments under this plan. for an emergency room visit it is 10 percent of coinsurance once the deductible is met, generic drugs are $10, primary doctors are $15, and specialists are $20 (Department of Health and Human Services, 2015). This is a sampling of the plans and deductibles Florida Blue offers and varies based upon age, income, and other factors. This information was obtained through the health insurance marketplace under the information of a generally healthy 25-year-old non-smoking female. Consumers who want to learn more can visit Floridablue.com as well as healthcare.gov.

The issues

The Affordable Care Act is a law that requires individuals to be covered by health insurance. The law places stricter guidelines on insurance companies and helps to reduce consumers' out-of-pocket expenses. As a result, insurance providers are coming up with new ways to earn a profit. The guidelines enforced directly affect the bottom line of insurance companies and in order to remain successful, plans need to do more than simply sell health insurance.

What did they do?

In August 2013 Florida insurance regulators ruled to allow Florida Blue to restructure into a not-for-profit mutual holding organization (Kennedy, 2013). Florida Blue became public in this transition, but due to several conflicts of interest was not allowed to sell stock to outside investors. The company can, however, transfer assets to its mutual holding company. In September 2014 GuideWell launched as the parent brand over a family of brands, including Florida Blue. According to Chairman and CEO, Pat Geraghty, GuideWell has (Shedden, 2014) "a family of forward-thinking companies focused on helping people and communities achieve better health."

In January 2015 Florida Blue reportedly laid off 150 employees throughout the state. According to Paul Kluding, Senior Director of Public Relations at Florida Blue, "The healthcare industry is undergoing unprecedented change. In order for organizations to adapt, they must tightly manage costs and look for effective solutions that continue to provide customers with the most affordable healthcare choices possible" (Elmore, 2015). This change in the healthcare industry is the Affordable Care Act.

As part of the development of the parent brand, GuideWell went through a reorganization to put leadership in place. According to GuideWell news (PR Newswire, 2014),

> René Lerer, M.D. [was] appointed President of Florida Blue and the GuideWell group of companies which includes GuideWell Health, GuideWell Connect and Diversified Service Options, Inc. Lerer will report to Chairman and Chief Executive Officer Patrick J. Geraghty as part of the newly created Office of the CEO.

Prakash Patel was named Chief Operating Officer (COO) of GuideWell effective January 2015.

The ACA law rules for all citizens to be eligible for health insurance. This transformation in healthcare has allowed low-income families to qualify for subsidies and earn assistance on healthcare plans. These are "highly subsidized" customers. Florida Blue has altered its marketing strategies to target these highly subsidized customers. The company is focusing on grassroots marketing initiatives that target the highly subsidized customer and the Hispanic community. As a result, marketing efforts have shifted from upper-class families to the lower class and highly subsidized, with a strong push towards Hispanics specifically in Miami, Florida.

GuideWell has partnered with a Colombian-based health clinic, Sanitas, to open three initial clinics in Miami, with plans to expand throughout the U.S. in other Hispanic markets. The locations are in Doral, Kendall, and Miami Lakes. While primarily targeting customers seeking care through the ACA individual market, the clinics accept Florida Blue members or cash payments. According to GuideWell (2015),

> The medical center's entire patient experience will be designed to meet the needs and preferences of those in the local markets, including cultural and linguistic aspects that are critical to resonating with a wide variety of Hispanic groups. Furthermore, there will be additional considerations for patient-engagement programs to address country of origin and assimilation differences amongst the targeted Hispanic cultures.

A second clinic platform the brand has developed is GuideWell Emergency Doctors, based in Orlando, Florida. There are currently two locations in Orlando and the business model reflects ER care at urgent care prices. The clinics accept insurance plans from most providers.

Pat Geraghty had to decide what action Florida Blue would take in response to an important issue that would change the landscape of the organization. The ACA posed a threat to Florida Blue's overall performance in the market, and Geraghty's solution to this threat was an organizational restructuring placing GuideWell as the mutual holding company over the family of brands, which included Florida Blue. The restructuring has allowed Florida Blue to maintain its positioning as the market leader and expand its products and services outside of the original scope of the health insurance provider.

References

Austin, A.D. and Hungerford, L.T. (2009). The market structure of the health insurance industry. Retrieved November 16, 2015, from www.fas.org/sgp/crs/misc/R40834.pdf

Blue Cross and Blue Shield Florida. (2015). Health care reform. Retrieved November 16, 2015, from www.floridablue.com/hcr/what-health-care-reform

Cox, C., Ma, R., Claxton, G., and Levitt, L. (2014). Sizing up exchange market competition. *KFF*. Retrieved November 16, 2015, from http://kff.org/health-reform/issue-brief/sizing-up-exchange-market-competition/

Department of Health and Human Services. (2015). The Affordable Care Act. Retrieved November 16, 2015, from hhs.gov/healthcare/about-the-law/read-the-law/index.html

Elmore, C. (2015, January 4). Florida's largest health insurer cuts 150 jobs. *Orlando Sentinel*. Retrieved November 16, 2015, from www.orlandosentinel.com/business/os-mct-florida-blue-layoffs-20150114-story.html

Forbes. (2014). America's biggest health insurance provider. *Forbes*. Retrieved November 16, 2015, from www.forbes.com/pictures/mlf45eljjg/1-unitedhealth-group/

GuideWell. (2015, September 25). GuideWell and Organización Sanitas Internacional establish international joint venture to deliver high-quality and affordable healthcare to the Hispanic market in Florida and beyond.

GuideWell. Retrieved November 16, 2015, from www.guidewell.com/
guidewell-and-organizacion-sanitas-internacional-establish-international-
joint-venture-to-deliver-high-quality-and-affordable-health-care-to-the-
hispanic-market-in-florida-and-beyond/q

Healthcare.gov. (2015). What marketplace health insurance covers. Retrieved
November 16, 2015, from healthcare.gov/coverage

Healthpayerintelligence (2016). Top 5 largest health insurance payers in the United
States. Retrieved March 19, 2018, from https://healthpayerintelligence.com/
news/top-5-largest-health-insurance-payers-in-the-united-states

Ibis World Report. (2017). *Health & Medical Insurance – US Market Research
Report*. Retrieved March 19, 2018, from www.ibisworld.com/industry/default.
aspx?indid=1324

Kennedy, K. (2013, August 19). Florida Blue gets OK to restructure under mutual
holding company. *Insurance Journal*. Retrieved November 16, 2015, from www.
insurancejournal.com/news/southeast/2013/08/19/302117.htm

PR Newswire. (2014). Healthcare executive Dr. Rene Lerer appointed President
of GuideWell group of companies. Retrieved November 16, 2015, from www.
prnewswire.com/news-releases/health-care-executive-dr-rene-lerer-appointed-
president-of-guidewell-group-of-companies-253563391.html

Shedden, M. (2014, September 18). CEO: GuideWell, not FL Blue, our focus. *Health
News Florida*. Retrieved November 16, 2015, from http://health.wusf.usf.edu/post/
ceo-guidewell-not-fl-blue-our-focus#stream/0

Vogel, M. (2014). Pat Geraghty: Florida Blue CEO. *Florida Trend Web*. Retrieved
November 16, 2015, from http://digital.floridatrend.com/article/Pat+Geraghty%3A
+Florida+Blue+CEO+/1583742/190611/article.html

Chapter 3

Competitive analysis and positioning

Competitive positioning is a combination of an organization's choice of target market and the sustainable differential advantage it is seeking to create as a means of securing a place in the market and in the minds of stakeholders. Competitive positioning requires management to make choices that ensure that there is a fit between an organization's resources and the chosen target market. There are three main ways in which an organization can position itself in the market (Porter, 1996). First, variety positioning which is product centered. Second, needs-based positioning where an organization identifies its target market, and then designs its products or services to meet as many of the needs as possible. The third is access-based positioning which is based on the identification of segments through commonality of accessibility.

Price positioning

Positioning can be based on price, quality, and service, a differentiation on benefits, innovation, or corporate citizenship (Hooley, Broderick, and Moller, 1998). Low price positioning is possible provided an organization can reduce costs and have strict cost control systems. IKEA positions itself as a trendy furniture store at low prices because its operations are based on low cost from purchasing through to warehousing and offering minimal services. Price positioning can be very successful when there is a price-sensitive target market. Spirit Airlines is positioned as a low-cost airline as it keeps costs low and charges customers for extra services.

Some organizations price their products and services high to create an image of luxury or exclusivity. Nordstrom is known for high prices, exclusive products, and excellent service. Cars such as BMW and Mercedes-Benz are high priced and are in the luxury segment of the car market. To be successful, high price positioning should be accompanied by high quality, prestigious branding, good reputations, and exclusive images.

Quality positioning requires organizations to have strict quality control, technical competence, and skilled employees. They must understand what the customer and other stakeholders value as far as quality is concerned. Tiffany and Co. has built a good brand reputation based on quality in the jewelry industry. Porsche built its quality reputation on hand-built sports cars. Often customers "see" quality as durability, reliability, and aesthetic appearance. Often high quality is accompanied by high prices.

Innovative positioning

According to Jeffrey Baumgartner (n.d.), innovation is the "profitable implementation of creative ideas." Creativity leads to the development of new product ideas which are then commercialized by the organization. Amazon, regarded as one of the most innovative companies in the world, introduces new goods and services virtually on a weekly basis. While some of these new products have been based on new technology (such as the original Kindle, the Kindle Fire, and, more recently, the Echo), others are new in terms of applying new ideas in a different way. Amazon Key uses well-established processes to deliver products securely *into* your home without you being there.

New technology has been key to the development of new companies for many years, for instance Apple iPod, Microsoft Windows, and Tesla Model S. Organizations adopting innovative positioning are typically associated with genius entrepreneurs and founders – Bill Gates (Microsoft), Steve Jobs (Apple), Jeff Bezos (Amazon), and Elon Musk (Tesla).

Service positioning

Organizations can position on the basis of offering superior service. Emirates Airlines is known for its superior service at reasonable prices which sets it apart from the competition in the airline industry. USAA is regarded as providing exceptional insurance, banking, and investment services to military personnel and their families. It does this at rates well below those of its competitors.

The resources needed for superior service are employees who are skilled in serving customers well. This implies that they need both the equipment, training, and attitude to do the job well. This enables them to live the brand and deliver experience that meets customers' expectations.

Benefit positioning

Organizations that choose benefit positioning strategy need to segment their markets based on benefits valued by consumers. They identify specific needs of customers who require a certain benefit and then they position themselves as the organization that specifically caters to that segment's needs. These benefits can be functional or emotional. Examples of functional benefit position are the Ford Interceptor, a car that caters to the specific needs of police forces as the car is equipped for law enforcement operations, and Crest toothpaste, which has been positioned as a cavity fighter among the toothpaste competitors. An example of emotional benefit positioning is Volvo moving from the functional feature of safety being engineered into its cars to one in which it protects the ones you love most. It is important for organizations to understand their customers in order to have a benefit positioning in the market.

Corporate citizenship positioning

An organization may want to position itself as being a most caring one and would like stakeholders to recognize it as such. For example, since 1946, Target has been committing more and more effort and assents to the communities in which it operates. Each year the company donates 5 percent of its profits to communities to support initiatives such as wellness, sustainability, responsible sourcing, education, civic activity, and several other programs. Zappos is an organization that focuses on the wellbeing of its employees and to make the world a better place for all. Zappos understands that is not only the 9 to 5 work that matters so employees are paid for time off if they want to do volunteer work. Organizations that choose this form of positioning usually have some social or environmental focus and measure themselves using the "triple bottom line" approach (financial, social, and environmental performance). Organizations that adopt this positioning usually make strong statements on social or ethical issues, implement environmentally friendly policies, and have strong corporate social responsibility programs.

Conclusion

This chapter highlights the importance of competitive positioning of the organization. While positioning is usually discussed as a product concept, where the points of parity and points of difference are highlighted, competitive positioning requires the organization as a whole to position itself among the competition. The chapter highlights the different ways an organization can position. This includes price positioning, innovation positioning, service positioning, benefit positioning, and citizenship positioning. The organization then will become known for its "place" in the market.

References

Baumgartner, J. (n.d.). Innovation: back to the basics. Retrieved March 21, 2018, from www.innovationmanagement.se/imtool-articles/innovation-back-to-the-basics/

Hooley, G., Broderick, A., and Moller, K. (1998). Competitive positioning and the resource-based view of the firm. *Journal of Strategic Marketing*, 6(2), 97–116.

Porter, M. (1996). What is strategy? *Harvard Business Review*, Nov–Dec, 61–78.

McDonald's all-day breakfasts

McDonald's is a fast food restaurant chain headquartered in Oak Brook, Illinois. McDonald's had slumping sales in 2014 and 2015. In 2014, "its overall profit plunged to $812 million, or 84 cents per share, from $1.2 billion" (Gensler, 2015). As a result of this downslide, in January 2015 CEO Donald Thompson announced his retirement to take effect in March 2015, when Steve Easterbrook, who was the chief brand officer, took over as CEO. Easterbrook inherited a large number of problems with the company that were difficult, possibly impossible to solve. "Revenue fell 11% in the first quarter, as it experienced across-the-board sales declines" (Gensler, 2015). When taking over, Easterbrook's position for fixing the company's problems was addressed when he made the following statement: "McDonald's management team is keenly focused on acting more quickly to better address today's consumer needs, expectations and the competitive marketplace. We are developing a turnaround plan to improve our performance and deliver enduring profitable growth" (Gensler, 2015). Although Easterbrook wanted to fix the problem, the question remained: How could McDonald's stop the decrease in sales?

Easterbrook wanted to better address customer needs. For years customer feedback has requested all-day breakfasts from McDonald's. Since 2007 tens of thousands of customers had requested all-day breakfasts on McDonald's Twitter page. However, McDonald's has never wanted to do this, stating "limited grill space prevented the company from offering breakfast past a certain time each day" (Geier, 2015). In an attempt to fix slumping sales Easterbrook decided to listen to customer feedback and ran a trial of all-day breakfasts in select stores in the San Diego area in April 2015.

After testing all-day breakfasts in several stores the company announced that it would begin implementing them in all of its stores in October 2015.

The all-day breakfast had a different menu based on region. Some regions would get a McMuffin menu and some regions would get a biscuit sandwich menu, but not both. The decision on which was made at the local level. Both menus had options for hotcakes, sausage burrito, parfaits, and oatmeal. The availability of hash browns varied by location, with some stores having them and some stores not. Easterbrook counted on this limited all-day breakfast menu to fix McDonald's problems, but would it fix McDonald's slumping sales or would it cause more problems?

Background

With the first McDonald's opening in 1955, it has become the favorite of many people from all around the world. As of May 2015, McDonald's is considered to be #6 on the list of the world's most valuable brands (Forbes, 2015). The fast food restaurant was initially opened as a barbecue drive-in but by 1948 it transformed into a walk-up hamburger stand with a limited menu. This limited and simple menu was also a contributing factor for the food being sold for a low-cost price. This strategy ultimately became the catalyst for the fast food chain becoming a successful restaurant, that quickly turned into a franchise across the country and eventually entered the global market.

Not only has it earned its ranking, McDonald's has become a permanent fixture of the world we live in today as 88 percent of people easily identify and recognize the golden arches of McDonald's without the name associated with the brand. But in comparison, only 54 percent of people could recognize the cross that represents religion of Christianity. Another great example of McDonald's and pop culture is the mention in *Bloomberg Businessweek* that McDonald's is like the music industry in which it is inspired by different culture and converts that inspiration into new ideas and product strategies (Helm, 2010). McDonald's has taken cues and analyzed social elements from the African Americans, Hispanics, and Asians to expand their offerings and have executed advertising campaigns in the hopes of encouraging middle-class Caucasians to buy certain food items as they use hip-hop and rock 'n' roll.

Target market

McDonald's holds the leading position in the American fast food industry. Even though it has seen recent slippages in sales and was required to close 700 restaurants around the world in Q1 2015, McDonald's is still well above its second-place competitor in revenues (Gaille, 2015). An interesting statistic provided for McDonald's is that on any given day, it is going to feed 1 percent of the human population which adds up to roughly 70 million people. As of now, there are 119 countries in the world that are selling 75 burgers every second.

With $27 billion in revenues, McDonald's is the 90th largest company in the world. It employs more than 1.7 million people at 350,000 branches as it sits at #2 behind Walmart for number of employees. One of the target markets for McDonald's is the children demographic; 1 in 5 food sales at McDonald's includes a toy, making the company one of the world's largest toy distributors.

In the U.S., 25 percent of Americans eat some type of fast food and 57 percent of the 18–29 age segment have stated that they eat McDonald's at least once per week. Nearly 110 million Americans have visited a McDonald's restaurant in the past month at least once. Of households with an annual income of less than $20,000, 39 percent eat at least once a week at McDonald's.

McDonald's marketing or business model does not officially aim towards a specific audience or consumer segment, in fact, the U.K. company has expressed that McDonald's aims to offer a fun and friendly environment for everyone to enjoy. McDonald's wants to offer and appeal to a wide range of people from families to workers. Yet the customer profile still remains the same – people in the lower-income, lower-middle-income bracket.

McDonald's has tried to be something for everyone as opposed to being everything for some people but it is now starting to change its direction by adding healthier and more expensive options as in salads and quality chicken.

The company

McDonald's divides its revenues into company-operated and franchised. It should be known that McDonald's conventional franchisees make up 57 percent, 24 percent are foreign affiliates, and approximately 18 percent are company operated. Revenue contribution from Europe was at 43 percent, which is under the company-owned business model and highest from the U.S., at 47 percent, which is under the franchise business model. When looking at the operating income, the U.S. is the company's largest segment and it accounts for more than 40 percent of the company's operating income. Outside of the U.S., Australia, Canada, France, Germany, and the U.K represent 40 percent of the company's operating income. The markets with comparatively advanced restaurant expansion and franchising potential include China, Italy, Poland, Russia, Korea, Spain, Switzerland, and the Netherlands. Together these markets accounted for about 10 percent of the company's operating income; India, a country in which the majority of people do not eat pork or beef, has 179 restaurants. (McDonald's Political Contribution Policy, 2016).

In 1965, McDonald's went public and the stock split 12 times. An investment of $2,250 in 100 shares at that time has grown to 74,360 shares worth approximately $7.0 million as of market close on December 31, 2014. McDonald's started to divest itself of other chains it had acquired during the 1990s. The company owned a majority stake in Chipotle Mexican Grill until October 2006, when McDonald's fully divested from Chipotle through a stock exchange and, until December 2003, it also owned Donatos Pizza. McDonald's sold Boston Market to Sun Capital Partners on August 27, 2007 (Horovitz, 2011).

As of December 2016, McDonald's earned total revenue of $24.622 billion. Operating income in 2016 was $7.74 billion (Wikiwand, n.d.).

Political/ legal

As per the McDonald's website, the company has a political contribution policy. As per the policy, McDonald's does not make contributions to any specific political parties or specific candidates for public office or for any political organization. Yet, McDonald's has realized that it is important to support public policies that have the best interest for its business (for its corporate and franchise restaurants), thus in some cases, McDonald's will make contributions (McDonald's Political Contribution Policy, 2016).

The policy also states that any political contribution made by the company is required to be approved by the head of the government relations department of McDonald's Corporation and must support a political candidate, a political party, or ballot that the head of the government relations department determines to be beneficial for the long-term interest of the organization.

Furthermore, if the contribution is more than $100,000 in a calendar year, it should require the approval of the McDonald's world president for that market to agree in addition to the depth of government relations (McDonald's Political Contribution Policy, 2016).

Technological

McDonald's has always been known for its friendly and fun landscape and restaurant design. Yet, that is now going to change as McDonald's is taking the first step in the fast food industry for revamping its interior design. The project started in 2011 with a $1 billion plus budget aiming for a completion in 2015/2016. McDonald's is moving away from its signature Pantone red in favor of yellow, both inside and out. This includes a yellow "eyebrow" detail on buildings and drive-thru that modernizes the traditional golden arch concept (Horovitz, 2011).

The design is also aiming to speed up the drive-thru process as it will offer double lines for fast speed. The fiberglass tables and industrial steel chairs are going away and incoming are wooden tables with comfortable faux leather chairs. The aesthetic is known as McDonald's "Less Is More" (LIM) design. It creates an uncluttered environment with simple, tasteful, and comfortable furniture. It's a European look that will be adopted globally.

In addition to the design and logistics of the restaurants, McDonald's is also taking big steps with technology. In 2014, McDonald's Corporation announced a new payment method in its U.S. restaurants with Apple Pay. As per McDonald's, the Apply Pay will enhance its global digital strategy and aim to provide the McDonald's customer convenience and greater speed. Apple's mobile payments service offers a great convenience to McDonald's customers, as it will allow them to instantly pay and stay, or pay and be on their way. In 2018 McDonald's plans to invest $2.4 billion in capital projects, most of which will go toward ongoing work in converting U.S. locations to the experience of the future model, which includes ordering kiosks, table service, and increasing use of the mobile app. The company plans to convert another 4,000 U.S. restaurants during 2018. The plan is to overhaul most freestanding U.S. restaurants by 2020 (Trotter, 2018).

Company info/organizational analysis

McDonald's has long been a leader in the fast food industry, even boasting on its signage that it has sold billions of burgers. However, in recent years, as the fast food industry has suffered through something of a publicity crisis, McDonald's has implemented various marketing strategies to try to help promotions and bolster sales once again.

Stakeholders

McDonald's has a number of stakeholders to which to answer. Suppliers are stakeholders because without the investment of McDonald's in the products they supply, their bottom line is affected. Employee stakeholders are invested in the brand because declining sales often means hiring freezes, lay-offs, and wage freezes. When the brand is performing well, employee stakeholders receive the trickle-down effect of that success. In that regard, declining sales are not just a problem for the company, but it has an effect on the staff and the suppliers. When the company is not making money, these two groups are not able to benefit.

Investors as stakeholders always have a stake in the company's ability to be successful. When the company isn't doing well from a financial perspective, then stock prices become more volatile and the people that have invested their money in the brand stand to lose that money plus any of the profits they may have made on it. Since the company is making the move towards the all-day breakfast, there are some considerations with regard to marketing strategy as well. For instance, employees will be impacted in the fact that they will need to learn to cook the limited breakfast menu while cooking lunch/dinner. They will need to make sure to include those options when they are upselling menu items or making suggestions to customers. Moreover, those working in the grill areas of the restaurant will need to be prepared throughout the day with the items needed to make breakfast just as they are with lunch-related items.

Customers, as stakeholders, are impacted in that they will now have access to certain breakfast items after 10.30 a.m. Interestingly, customers are also stakeholders in a general sense for McDonald's as they are significantly affected by the quality of food being served by the fast food chain. Finally, there are the suppliers, which stand to increase profits from the restaurants. Suppliers that are offering breakfast supplies will now have a higher demand to meet, which usually means better profits their end.

Business culture

The business culture at McDonald's has changed in accordance with the company's strategy over the years. In the past, McDonald's was considered a wholesome option for a meal, and the business structure reflected that. Franchises were owned by prominent people in the community and there was a family feel within the culture of the company. However, since that time, the culture has changed significantly. Franchisees are completely disconnected from the core of the company and this is somewhat reflected in the inconsistencies in the quality of food and the level of service. Moreover, corporate culture has made it increasingly more challenging for franchisees to grow. More stringent guidelines about what the franchises can and cannot do under the umbrella of the brand have not only left franchisees with an inability to be creative in attracting new customers, but they have not enticed new franchisees to invest in the company.

New leadership has helped in this regard, with the introduction of Steve Easterbrook as the new head of the company in 2015 (Neate, 2015). He has not only asked for more input from the franchisees in terms of improving the brand, but he has implemented some radical ideas of his own, including the all-day breakfast. He is also the driving force behind McDonald's upcoming line of gourmet burgers. The company is now taking a look at the marketplace to determine areas where McDonald's may not have ventured in the past and making it a point to try new things in order to ensure that the brand doesn't stagnate. After all, also at issue has been the fact that McDonald's has somewhat been resting on its laurels. The company has made the incorrect assumption that because of its place in the market, it didn't need to go above and beyond in its marketing endeavors. Anything that the company has tried that hasn't worked in recent years has simply been eliminated from the menu and the company has gone back to its proven strategy of what works.

Organizational structure

The core organizational structure at McDonald's is one typical of the corporate/franchise environment. The company CEO is the head, answering to a board of directors. Under the COO is the executive leadership team and leadership staff. There is a layer of middle management responsible for overseeing the various franchises, which is comprised of regional managers. There are the franchise owners that work directly with the company and from there, store management and beyond.

However, it should be noted that the company has moved to eliminate many of its middle management positions, in order to keep key company leadership in better communication with staff and franchisees (Jargon, 2014b). This change in structure came as part of the company's effort to attempt to stymy the tide of falling profits. Fast casual restaurants and more health food options contribute to lower than ever profits for the fast food giant. The company has been seen as being out of touch as rates of diabetes, heart disease, and childhood obesity continue to be pressing health issues in America, and around the world.

As a result, McDonald's is attempting to make the organizational changes needed to bring in an influx of new ideas meant to revive the struggling fast food chain and help it to recover. This is where the aforementioned change in culture is helping in that the company has had to contend with the public relations crisis of both unhappy franchisees and the unhealthy quality of its food. While it is doing more to address the business culture, it is not doing as much to address the issue of food quality. The company has introduced a few products to make the menu appear healthier, but has done nothing to eliminate some of the unhealthy aspects of the food – such as the hydrogenated oil in which it makes its fries – or the quality of its meat sources.

As such, the company is attempting to distract from these issues by ingratiating itself into the community through better relationships with the franchisees. Moreover, organizational structure has been changed in the last year to cater to regional zones (Jargon, 2014b). This means more offerings that are closer to the local favorites that reflect the communities McDonald's is serving around the country. This focus on more relevant food items by marketplace has not seen huge margins in terms of results just yet, but they are part of a larger organizational reordering that the fast food chain has committed to moving forward (Jargon, 2014b[2]).

Strategies

Given the issues that McDonald's has had with its image as a fast food giant and the business culture that has fostered some resentment among those franchisees considering an investment, it has implemented a few new strategies. The main strategy in place to revive sluggish sales is the McDonald's all-day breakfast venture. The company hopes that this plan will intrigue customers that only eat at the chain for breakfast while capturing some of the market of other fast food brands that offer a full menu any time of the day. Breakfast is the most popular menu item at McDonald's, so the company is hoping to head off further declining revenue by offering this popular choice all day. Additionally, customer polls have consistently revealed that many don't find the choices available at McDonald's to be relevant ones in keeping with the fast casual concept that continues to dominate the market (Jargon, 2014a). McDonald's is hoping that by making the more popular menu items available throughout the day, customers will be willing to come at times of the day when they normally would not. It hopes that customers will eat at McDonald's more than they might throughout the course of an average week.

Additionally, the company is switching things up internally, looking at all internal stakeholders. The company aims to determine what benefits exist – if any – from those that have long tenures on the board and with regard to the investments the company makes. The strategy here is to clean house internally to breathe new life into the company (Neate, 2015). There are also plans to implement new products such as mozzarella sticks, and a line of gourmet burgers. McDonald's is also aiming to include new technology in its new strategy, creating customer-centered portals that make it easier than ever to order and pay for a meal (Jargon, 2014a).

The idea is to streamline the customer experience to the fullest extent possible. Convenience is the name of the game for a company like McDonald's, and it is aiming to capitalize on that. For instance, the company is looking at a system where customers can place an order, customize it, and pay for it using a touch screen that enables them to have full control over the ordering process (Jargon, 2014a). This may eliminate some redundancies in terms of jobs, but create opportunity elsewhere. The strategy here signals that this is the McDonald's of the future, no longer stuck in a 1950s mentality in terms of the way burgers are ordered and served in 2015. The company is taking steps to implement lasting strategies that will help to ensure its survival moving forward.

Restaurant industry info/micro-environment

McDonald's has been the leader of the fast food industry for many years, but its recent sales performance had shown how the competition had affected its sales. McDonald's has had decreasing sales partly because of the emergence of new competitors and the change of customer taste. As Wohl states,

> The world's largest restaurant company has to be more nimble to keep up with competitors that have been quicker to respond to customers' tastes ... That means everything from speeding up internal tests and doing more to appeal to diners who are looking for cleaner labels on what they eat.
>
> (Wohl, 2014)

McDonald's has not been able to grow at the same pace as its competitors. As McDonald's Chief Financial Officer, Kevin Ozan, stated, McDonald's "chain's sales results in the U.S. – [had] a 0.9-percent increase, [however McDonald's is] still 3.2 percentage points behind its immediate quick-service sandwich competitors" (Maze, 2015). In the same way the *Investor's Business Daily* points out that for the first time after at least four decades, "McDonalds had been closing more stores in the U.S. than it is opening" (Investor's Business Daily, 2015). McDonald's has not adapted to the trends of the market and the competitors have taken advantage of this.

McDonald's has been trying to appeal to customers with new menu offers like the McWraps, Buttermilk Crispy Chicken, and others. However, this has not been successful. The market has changed, and consumers are more concerned with taste, quality, and ingredients. "McDonald's has had trouble finding new menu items that diners want" (Derousseau, 2014). Sales have decreased for the past two years. McDonald's does not only compete with its traditional competitors like Burger King and Wendy's, but the growing and trending fast casual dining segment is overtaking

McDonald's customers. In order to avoid losing more market share, McDonald's CEO Eastwood decided to create the all-day breakfast menu.

Quick service restaurants segment

During the last decade, quick service restaurants (QSRs) have grown at a faster pace than any other restaurant segment in the industry. McDonald's, Burger King, KFC, and Wendy's have provided their customers fast food, with average quality and minimal to no table service. The menu in these restaurants is very limited and the prices range from $3 to $6 per person (Trefis Team, 2014). The fast food segment had been led by McDonald's for many years. Nevertheless, its main competitor Burger King had a better year than McDonald's in 2014 (Wong, 2014a). Burger King was more effectively attracting customers to its venues. As Wong (2014a) stated, Burger King has made its menus simpler while McDonald's has make them more complex. In addition Burger King has created very attractive promotions. Burger King has been able to develop and promote more impactful products than McDonald's. In the same way "Burger King is stealing away [from McDonald's] low end customers with hot-selling items like chicken fries and extra-long pulled pork sandwiches" (Egan, 2015).

McDonald's is losing market share to Wendy's as well. "Wendy's is luring customers with higher-priced favorites like the bacon portabella melt on brioche" (Egan, 2015). Wendy's has seen the need to launch new products because customers are more concerned about freshness and quality. Wendy's has been able to reposition itself towards the higher-end market, and McDonald's is losing market share from both ends. While McDonald's sales decrease, Wendy's and Burger King's sales increased. In the U.S., Wendy's restaurant sales increased by 2.4 percent in the second quarter of 2014 (Egan, 2015). Burger King's sales increased nearly 7 percent. The increase in sales is the result of new menu items. Meanwhile, "U.S. sales dipped 2% during the last quarter at the Golden Arches" (Egan, 2015). The fast food segment is being affected by the new trending segment of fast casual dining. For this reason, most of the fast food restaurants are trying to innovate with new menu items and changing their public image, as a more healthy eating option.

Fast casual dining segment

The fast casual restaurant has become more popular in the American market. As a result fast food restaurants are launching new menu items in order to compete with the fast casual market. The fast casual segment is positioned between the QSR and the casual dining segment. This establishment provides a "more customized, freshly prepared and high quality food than traditional QSRs" (Trefis Team, 2014). The fast casual restaurants are characterized by their comfortable and clean ambiance. The consumers feel comfortable and welcome. Nevertheless, the prices are higher than the ones of the QRS. The prices per person range between $8 and $15 (Trefis Team, 2014).

McDonald's is losing market share to the fast casual segment. "A backlash against fatty foods has created an opportunity for so-called fast-casual competitors like Chipotle, a company once owned by McDonald's and whose menu options are perceived as healthier and more authentic" (Allison, 2015). McDonald's has lost market share because of the perception that the public has of their food and because its stores do not have a welcoming ambiance. The fast casual segment is growing. Restaurants like Panera Bread, Chipotle, Starbucks, and Five Guys are becoming more appealing for consumers. In 2014, the fast casual restaurants segment grew by 10.5 percent, while traditional fast food chains grew 6.1 percent. One of the main players in this segment is Chipotle, which had an annual growth rate of 20 percent (Rosenberg, 2015).

The fast casual segment has been able to attract the market because it is perceived as a healthier eating option. Nowadays, people do not see burgers and fries as they used to. Fatty food has become less appealing to customers than before. For that reason "McDonald's shifted to healthier menu items with its new wraps but the products didn't take off as per the company's expectations" (Trefis Team, 2014). McDonald's is trying to enhancing the taste of its products and improve consumer perceptions of quality (Maze, 2015). "McDonald's renaissance will encompass a simplified menu, remodeled restaurants, and modern amenities as Wi-Fi" (Wong, 2014b).

All-day breakfast market

McDonald's is attracting the customers by "adding burgers with lettuce 'buns' and launching all-day breakfast service" (Egan, 2015). McDonald's, with all-day breakfast, is competing with Dunkin Donuts, Panera Bread, Starbucks, and others. McDonald's decided to have all-day breakfasts to increase sales. But the all-day breakfast competition is intensive. As a response to McDonald's all-day breakfast, a Burger King franchise in Garwood, New Jersey decided to serve a few breakfast menu items all day (Nazario, 2015). In the same way the Dunkin' Donuts CEO said, "I think the reality is, if [Dunkin'] executes our plans well, if we go out there and deliver a great coffee experience, a great breakfast sandwich experience, we deliver a variety of donuts and we execute well on our stores, we can fight anybody any day" (Snyder, 2015).

Everyday restaurant war

In the U.S. the customers are pushing the QSR restaurants to have healthier items on their menu. The fast casual segment is growing rapidly but the QSR segment is still growing as well. Rosenberg stated "established fast food companies can maintain healthy margins from their existing footprint, while newer fast casual chains invest billions to build out new locations around the world" (Rosenberg, 2015). In the same way, McDonald's losses from 2013 to 2014 were $664 million dollars but these losses are not dramatic. McDonald's has been able to maintain its expenses relatively flat, generate profits, and provide its inventors with a dividend of 3 percent (Rosenberg, 2015).

Customer/consumer info

McDonald's is the leading worldwide hamburger and food service retailer and holds the leading share (42 percent) of the U.S. fast food market (Trefis Team, 2015). It is said that 8 percent of the American population eat at a McDonald's on an average day and 96 percent eat a meal there at least yearly (Trefis Team, 2015). The U.S. population was McDonald's largest segment accounting for more than 40 percent of the company's 2014 operating income (McDonald's, 2010–2015).

Although the demographics change based on the different markets McDonald's serve, the company bases its segmentation on demographics, with age as a parameter, psychographic (convenience and lifestyle), and behavioral. Kids, students, and family are the main driver of McDonald's segmentation and product positioning. However, the adult target group has yet to be identified. Consequently, its target group for the breakfast model has not been identified either. The chain is trying to adapt to this new consumer. McDonald's recently reorganized marketing to focus on demographic groups – families, millennials, and adults – rather than food groups from its menu (Bertangnoli, 2014).

Millennials

Since the entrance of Fred Ehle (McDonald's first VP-customer officer) McDonald's focus was to enhance the customer experience while visiting the restaurant. McDonald's was facing a millennials (customers in their 20s and 30s) problem and it needed to be addressed. Millennials today are pickier and are more attracted to higher quality offerings of chains such as Chipotle (Anderson, 2014). Mohamed Amer, vice president, global integrated retail unit, said: "The problem is people no longer find novelty in just fast foods as the key convenience marker and do expect fast, tasty (even healthy) and upscale as the new experience and value proposition" (Anderson, 2014). This target group has become more health-conscious. Although price is a driver for them, tastiness, healthiness, and ambiance seemed to be more predominant when deciding their next dining experience (Lutz, 2014). In fact, these same millennials were opting for chains such as Chipotle Mexican Grill Inc. and gourmet-burger chain Five Guys Holdings LLC over McDonald's for their next meal or dine-out experience (Jargon, 2014a). In an effort to regain the millennials market, McDonald's says new items like its McWrap sandwiches – chicken and vegetables rolled in tortillas – are helping to woo millennials. They are also trying to enhance its credibility with the young customer by marketing more through digital channels and testing mobile ordering and payment (Bertangnoli, 2014).

Kids and family

McDonald's has been very predominant in its kids' appeal. Kids and parents of young kids have been heavily marketed with all the different toys and happy meal with toy included promotions. However, in recent years this target market has also been endangered by the millennial parents who are more health-conscious and seek fresher and better options when taking their kids out to eat. This mentality change has driven McDonald's sales to decline as well. By mid-2014, families with a child aged 12 or under accounted for 14.6 percent of McDonald's visitors, from 18.6 percent in 2011, according to Technomic research on the composition of customers of the nation's 100 largest restaurant chains (Bertangnoli, 2014).

Students

McDonald's has done a strong marketing campaign for students offering perks such as being part of the restaurants with special discount cards for food (iConnect Card) (ISSU, 2014), free Wi-Fi, scholarships, internships, students' business studies (offering case studies and real business situations to be analyzed by the students to provide a viable solution) (McDonald's, n.d., 2010–2015), and more. McDonald's advertises its free Wi-Fi at over 11,500 participating restaurants. Now customers can access the Internet using their mobile devices, laptops, or PDAs at no charge. Many students with low-income budgets can benefit from the whole dining experience at McDonald's. They can enjoy an average/low-cost meal and work on their school projects while dining at one of the participating establishments (McDonald's, 2010–2015).

With regards to the scholarships, the organization has been providing various scholarships for aspiring college students and thus helping a number of students in fulfilling their dreams. Apart from this its unique restaurant management curriculum is also been recognized by the American Council on Education and thus enlightening the career path of a number of students in the same field (Scholarship Positions, 2011).

How does McDonald's deliver customer value?

"You deserve a break," "Feed your inner child." This commitment of quality of food and service in a clean, hygienic, and relaxing atmosphere has ensured that McDonald's maintains a positive relationship with its customers. "We remain focused on listening to all of our customers and evolving our menus to meet their expectations and eating habits," Mr. Irwin says in an email. McDonald's "takes our responsibility to children and family very seriously, and we offer food choices that fit within a balanced diet" (Bertangnoli, 2014). McDonald's is responding to the evolving eating habits of its customers and adjusting its menu options to offer healthier choices for the customers it serves. The all-day breakfast was another attempt to show value and to respond to the many requests its customers have made throughout the years requesting extended breakfast hours. However, was this enough? Many customers showed a positive reaction to McDonald's new all-day breakfast as this new model was seen as convenient to people that wanted to have a breakfast McMuffin past 10.30 a.m. However, for true breakfast fanatics, the response was not the same (White, 2015).

Issues/business performance

McDonald's was having many issues with its business performance. In 2015 before Easterbrook took over "Revenue fell 11% in the first quarter, as it experienced across-the-board sales declines" (Gensler, 2015). In the first quarter of 2015 store sales in the U.S. were down 2.6 percent. Some store sales in other regions such Asia, Africa, Pacific, and the Middle East were down 8.3 percent for the quarter (Gensler, 2015). Shares had been "down 5% over the past 12 months" (Gensler, 2015). The company was losing customers to fast food competitors and fast casual restaurants.

McDonald's growth had slowed. In the fourth quarter of 2014 stock closed down 1.5 percent. In 2014, "revenue fell to $6.57 billion from $7.09 billion" (Horovitz, 2015). It will only open 1,000 new restaurants globally in 2015 compared to 1,300 the previous year. "McDonald's will cut its capital expenditures virtually in half in 2015, investing about $1 billion compared with the $2 billion that it spent in 2014 (Horovitz, 2015). McDonald's has always been perceived by consumers as having cheap inexpensive products and customers' perception of cheap products is that they are low quality. However, it had been trying to compete with fast casual restaurants by offering higher-priced items.

> To increase profits and better compete with the likes of Starbucks, Panera Bread, and Chipotle, McDonald's is constantly trying to entice customers into spending more on "gourmet" and "premium" options like espressos and McWraps. As a result, service has slowed, lowering the value proposition at the same time, and McDonald's pricing doesn't make sense to many customers.
>
> (Tuttle, 2015)

Traditionally customers have gone to McDonald's to get inexpensive food, with quick service. The larger menu risked making wait times longer. By offering higher-priced options attempting to compete with other companies like Panera Bread, Starbucks, and Dunkin' Donuts McDonald's was doing the opposite of its traditional market and risked upsetting its traditional market segment. "When there are a bunch of burgers for under $2 in the Dollar Menu & More section, it's puzzling why anyone would pay $5 or so for what seems like a very similar burger on the regular menu" (Tuttle, 2015).

McDonald's has also lost some of its traditional customers to competitors such as Burger King and Wendy's. Both companies offer similar products at similar prices for breakfast, lunch, and dinner. Even with the new all-day breakfast McDonald's faces competition from companies like Starbucks, Dunkin' Donuts, and Panera Bread who also offer all-day breakfast. By adding all-day breakfast, McDonald's will have even more menu items at once and risk making service even slower. It could also cause problems for employees trying to adjust to the new routine. Will the McDonald's all-day breakfast reverse the company's declining sales? Or will it create more problems?

References

Allison, K. (2015, January 30). New McDonald's boss has the right ingredients. *The Business Times*.

Anderson, G. (2014). McDonald's needs millennials and more. *Forbes*. Retrieved November 11, 2015, from www.forbes.com/sites/retailwire/2014/09/23/mcdonalds-needs-millennials-and-more/

Bertangnoli, L. (2014). McDonald's has a new generational problem: kids. *Chicago Business*. Retrieved November 11, 2015, from www.chicagobusiness.com/article/20140906/ISSUE01/309069980/mcdonalds-has-a-new-generational-problem-kids

Derousseau, R. (2014, March 27). McDonald's struggles for growth lead to one place: its menu. *Time*. Retrieved November 9, 2015, from http://time.com/money/2795294/mcdonalds-seeks-to-supersize-growth/

Egan, M. (2015, August 5). Wendy's taking bite out of McDonald's profits. *CNN*. Retrieved November 5, 2015, from http://money.cnn.com/2015/08/05/investing/wendys-mcdonalds-earnings-burger-wars/

Forbes. (2015). Forbes 2015 rankings. *Forbes*. Retrieved November 11, 2015, from www.forbes.com/companies/mcdonalds/

Gaille, B. (2015, April 19). 22 notable McDonalds customer demographics. *BrandonGaille.com*. Retrieved November 11, 2015, from http://brandongaille.com/22-notable-mcdonalds-customer-demographics/

Geier, B. (2015). McDonald's is making a huge change to its breakfast menu. *Fortune*. Retrieved November 11, 2015, from http://fortune.com/2015/03/30/mcdonalds-all-day-breakfast/

Gensler, L. (2015, April 22). New CEO, same problems at McDonald's as revenue falls 11%. *Forbes*. Retrieved November 11, 2015, from www.forbes.com/sites/laurengensler/2015/04/22/new-ceo-same-problems-at-mcdonalds-as-revenue-falls-11/

Helm, B. (2010, July 8). Ethnic marketing: McDonald's is lovin' it. *Bloomberg Businessweek*. Retrieved November 11, 2015, from www.bloomberg.com/bw/magazine/content/10_29/b4187022876832.htm

Horovitz, B. (2011, May 9). McDonald's revamps store to look more upscale. *USA Today*.

Horovitz, B. (2015). McDonald's earnings fall; changes afoot. *USA Today*. Retrieved November 11, 2015, from www.usatoday.com/story/money/business/2015/01/23/mcdonalds-earnings/22179623/

Investor's Business Daily. (2015, June 19). McDonald's to close stores. *Investor's Business Daily*.

ISSU. (2014). Food discounts in Ireland. *ISSU iConnect Card*. Retrieved November 11, 2015, from www.studentcard.ie/discounts/ireland/food/mcdonalds-restaurant

Jargon, J. (2014a, August 24). McDonald's faces "millennial" challenge. *Wall Street Journal*. Retrieved November 11, 2015, from www.wsj.com/articles/mcdonalds-faces-millennial-challenge-1408928743

Jargon, J. (2014b, October 30). McDonald's plans to change US structure. *Wall Street Journal*. Retrieved November 11, 2015, from www.wsj.com/articles/mcdonalds-to-change-u-s-structure-1414695278

Lutz, A. (2014). Millennials are becoming McDonald's biggest threat. *Business Insider*. Retrieved November 11, 2015, from www.businessinsider.com/millennials-eating-less-fast-food-2014–8

Maze, J. (2015). McDonald's works to close gap with competitors. *Nation's Restaurant News*.

McDonald's. (n.d.). McDonald's education. *McDonald's*. Retrieved November 11, 2015, from www5.mcdonalds.com/teachers/home.htm

McDonald's. (2010–2015). Free Wi-Fi @ McDonald's. *McDonald's*. Retrieved November 11, 2015, from www.mcdonalds.com/us/en/services/free_wifi.html

McDonald's Political Contribution Policy. (2016). Retrieved March 19, 2018, from http://stage-corporate.mcdonalds.com/content/dam/gwscorp/corporate-governance-content/political-contributions-and-policy/POLITICAL_CONTRIBUTION_POLICY.pdf

Nazario, M. (2015, October 20). This Burger King had a great response to McDonald's all-day breakfast. *Business Insider*. Retrieved November 6, 2015, from www.businessinsider.com/burger-king-responds-to-mcdonalds-all-day-breakfast-2015-10

Neate, R. (2015, May 19). McDonald's must break "dinosaur" culture in order to stop the rot. *The Guardian*. Retrieved November 11, 2015, from www.theguardian.com/business/2015/may/19/mcdonalds-dinosaur-culture-board- sales

Rosenberg, E. (2015) *Investopedia Stock Analysis: Can McDonalds Survive Against Fast Casual?* Chatham: Newstex.

Scholarship Positions. (2011). McDonalds scholarship program for college, USA. *Scholarship Positions*. Retrieved November 11, 2015, from http://scholarship-positions.com/blog/mcdonald-scholarships-for-college-usa/201112/

Snyder, B. (2015, October 6). This is Dunkin' Donuts' response to McDonald's all-day breakfast. *Fortune*. Retrieved November 9, 2015, from http://fortune.com/2015/10/06/dunkin-donuts-response-mcdonalds-breakfast/

Trefis Team. (2014, July 14). How the fast casual segment is gaining market share in the restaurant industry. *Forbes*. Retrieved November 6, 2015, from www.forbes.com/sites/greatspeculations/2014/06/23/how-the-fast-casual-segment-is-gaining-market-share-in-the-restaurant-industry/

Trotter, G. (2018, January 30). Former rock 'n' roll McDonald's gets new eco-friendly look from riverwalk architect. *Chicago Tribune*. Retrieved March 19, 2018, from www.chicagotribune.com/business/ct-biz-rock-n-roll-mcdonalds-remodel-20180129-story.html

Tuttle, B. (2015). 5 problems that will challenge McDonald's no matter who is CEO. *Time*. Retrieved November 11, 2015, from http://time.com/money/3687899/mcdonalds-problems-new-ceo/

White, D. (2015). Here's what customers had to say about McDonald's new all-day breakfast. *Time*. Retrieved November 11, 2015, from http://time.com/4063699/all-day-breakfast-customers/

Wikiwand. (n.d.). McDonald's. *Wikiwand*. Retrieved March 21, 2018, from www.wikiwand.com/en/McDonald%27s

Wohl, J. (2014, December 10). McDonald's to trim U.S. menu. *Chicago Tribune*. Retrieved March 21, 2018, from www.chicagotribune.com/business/ct-mcdonalds-investor-meeting-1211-biz-20141208-story.html

Wong, V. (2014a, November 5). Hard times for hamburgers hurt McDonald's more than Burger King. *Bloomberg*. Retrieved March 21, 2018, from www.bloomberg.com/news/articles/2014-11-05/hard-times-for-hamburgers-hurt-mcdonalds-more-than-burger-king

Wong, V. (2014b, July). McDonald's gives itself a year and half to get into Chipotle-fighting shape. *Business Week*.

FedEx: how to beat the competition

Introduction

As Fred Smith readied himself for the presentation of the third quarter fiscal earnings for 2017, fleeting thoughts of his competitors nagged at him. Maintaining the position as an industry leader was not enough. The number one long-term goal for the FedEx Corporation was to achieve 10 percent or more operating margin as a whole. Improving cash flows, increasing return on invested capital (ROIC), and increasing returns to shareowners were incredibly important to the company as a whole. Although its 2016 revenue was higher than the previous year, UPS was currently outperforming FedEx with market share. Furthermore, key customer, Amazon, continued to build its repertoire of vehicles making it more of a competitor as well as a customer. Acquiring TNT Express and completely integrating the company into the FedEx Corporation had taken time and money; he had anticipated the investment, and he felt confident that the company was moving in the right direction with the acquisition. FedEx's most recent contract was a 16-year extension of the Express Air transportation relationship with the U.S. Postal Service, and an agreement with Walgreens for easier access to FedEx services (Business Wire, 2017). Were these contracts enough, or were they merely gaining business through mediocre avenues? The key to staying ahead, he thought, was innovation. How could FedEx maintain its current goals while growing its innovative strategies and technology to better compete with the ever-increasing competition in the industry?

Background

According to research, "Federal Express is the world's largest airline cargo carrier. It specializes in delivering parcels of every size and shape" (Wikipedia, 2018). The company began operations in 1973 in the Memphis International Airport. The CEO of the company, Fred Smith, thought to bring a system that could monitor the process of delivering a package from merchant to customer. This system would essentially make logistics less complex for both the customer and the supplier. April 17th, 2017 marks the 44th anniversary of FedEx and when one looks at the history of the company they will notice that the company has made great progress from the day Smith first started it.

In 1973, the company offered both two-day delivery and overnight delivery for its courier pack and its envelope delivery. The company was also able to connect with about 25 cities in the country with the use of the Dassault Falcon 20s, which is a French jet that was primarily used for the French navy and the United States coast guards. In two short years in 1975 FedEx tried to make sending parcels easier for customers by placing parcel drop boxes in major localities so that they would not have to go to the company's office. Customers got used to this method of parcel sending and by 1976 FedEx was carrying an average of nearly 20,000 parcels a day (Wikipedia, 2018). FedEx in many ways has been able to offer solutions to improve the ways in which companies handle logistics. FedEx was the first to pioneer tracking and tracing capability so customers would know where their shipments were. Over more than four decades, FedEx has built a portfolio of innovative solutions that connect customers to more than 220 countries and territories which consists of 99 percent of the world's global gross domestic product. In 1980, it introduced COSMOS (Customers Operations and Services Master Online System), which enabled the company to track every single package and document that it transports on a day-to-day basis. It also introduced DADS (Digitally Assisted Dispatch System) which is a system that enables monitoring of on-call pickups for customers. In 1983, the company exceeded one billion dollars in revenue. Starting in 1994 FedEx acquired air routes in the Asia, Pacific, and European hubs and thus began expanding its operations worldwide. As of 2018 it has 660 planes in its fleet reaching 375 destinations every day. In 2017 its revenue was $60.3 billion and it had more than 400,000 employees (Wikipedia, 2018). As the timeline of the company is examined, it is easy to see the evolution of the company from the time it started to the point it has reached now.

Services of FedEx Corporation

FedEx Corporation provides its services through a wide range of portfolios that consist of e-commerce, transportation, and business services. The business strategy of the company focuses on providing services to both individual customers and businesses worldwide. It maintains an integrated business application with a network of collaboratively operating companies under the brand name of FedEx. The company inspires more than 400,000 employees to uphold the professional and ethical standards at the highest level by maintaining a positive attitude in order to provide its services to the customers. The company's ultimate goal is to provide high value-added transportation, logistics, and related business services. All operations give the priority to safety of team members and service receivers currently known as FedEx Express, FedEx Ground, FedEx Freight, and FedEx Services are the main operating segments of its operations that provide the needed logistical and strategic support (FedEx, 2017b).

All these operating segments operate relatively independent to each other while ensuring the maximum level of coordination to deliver quality services to customers on time. The segment division of FedEx Express covers more than 220 countries and territories with its time-certain delivery service consisting of FedEx Trade Networks, Inc. which is responsible for providing international trade services. In addition, it specializes in global ocean and air freight forwarding and customs brokerage. FedEx Supply Chain Systems, Inc. also comes under the division of FedEx Express, and its main operations focus on offering supply chain solutions to the customers. The FedEx Ground segment includes FedEx Ground Package System, Inc., and is responsible for providing small-package ground delivery services. FedEx acquired Parcel Direct, a parcel consolidator, in 2004 and renamed it as FedEx SmartPost, Inc. It also operates under the FedEx Ground Package System, Inc. division. This operating segment specializes in the consolidation and delivery of low-weight, less time-sensitive business-to-consumer packages. It operates jointly with the United States Postal Service (USPS) which makes the deliveries to the final destination.

The third main operational division, the FedEx Freight segment includes FedEx Freight, Inc. which is responsible for providing freight services of less than a truck-load. Its main operations cover most geographical regions in Mexico, Canada, the U.S. Virgin Islands, and Puerto Rico. FedEx Custom Critical, Inc. also comes under the

FedEx Freight segment which is responsible for providing critical and time-sensitive shipment services.

The FedEx Services division consists of FedEx Corporate Services, Inc. which is mainly responsible for providing the services on information technology, sales, marketing, communications, and support for the FedEx Group's other companies. FedEx TechConnect, Inc. also operates under the division of the FedEx Services which provides services that include billings and collections for U.S. customers while providing the technical support. FedEx Office & Print Services, Inc. is another segment which comes under the FedEx Services division. The main services of FedEx Office & Print Services, Inc. include document and business services while providing access to its package transportation businesses. After FedEx Corporation made the $2.4 billion acquisition of Kinko's Inc. in 2004, the company has been able to expand retail access to FedEx Kinko's locations. One of the latest acquisitions made by FedEx is the acquisition of GENCO which is one of the largest third-party logistics providers, and it now provides the services on reverse logistics, the marketing and product liquidation solutions, and test and repair (FedEx, 2015).

Competitive positioning

FedEx prides itself on superior service, innovation, and speed advantage (FedEx, 2017a). The company claims this element of focus is driving its growth. For FedEx Ground, building a better ground business is the ultimate goal, and through its speed advantage on the ground, it claims to be 26 percent faster than UPS Ground as of October 2016. FedEx Express is where the company excels, as it remains the industry leader in the express transportation market (FedEx, 2017b), a market it claims to have created 40 years ago.

The Courier and Local Deliveries industry has a high level of concentration, as exemplified with the top four companies accounting for 86.3 percent of the market share (Kalyani, 2016). Traditionally, FedEx, United Parcel Service (UPS), United States Postal Service (USPS), and Deutsche Post AG (DHL) have been household names for individuals and companies looking to transport packages. Companies like FedEx and UPS have dominated the industry in the past due to the strong brand names they created and resources they have established over the past decades (Kalyani, 2016, p. 14). According to Williams (2014), USPS is no longer a contender in the market. Despite the reduced rate it gives government agencies, USPS only managed to win 2 percent of all federal shipments; the other 98 percent of parcels were sent through either UPS or FedEx. Kalyani (2016) adds that USPS does not maintain the "value-added services" like the other leading industry operators, such as express shipment and package tracking (p. 10).

One area of concern in the industry is the potential threat that could come from the key customers of such parcel delivery companies, such as Amazon (Kalyani, 2016, p. 10). FedEx CEO, Fred Smith, maintains that FedEx isn't at any risk of being disrupted by new competitors to the business, as the system, that consists of thousands of facilities and the ability to pick up, transport, and deliver packages in one to two business days, has been decades in the making (Rocco, 2017). Smith adds that the real story behind e-commerce is behind mobile phones in the forms of trucks, airplanes, and facility team members which are something FedEx has in enormous quantities

(Rocco, 2017). Industry leaders like UPS, DHL, and potential newcomer, Amazon.com, remain the current competitive leaders for FedEx.

Competition

UPS

Headquartered in Atlanta, GA, UPS is currently the world's largest packaging delivery company, with its brown trucks running the streets globally. UPS has been in business since 1907 and maintains its Main Global Air Hub in Louisville, KY. It also serves over 9.8 million customers daily (UPS, 2017). The UPS company divides its organization into two segments: Package Operation and Supply Chain & Freight. In 2016, the UPS Package Operation maintained revenue of $51 billion in 2016. The UPS Supply Chain and Freight brought in $10 billion, and asserts the following key services: logistics and distribution; transportation and freight (air, sea, ground, and rail); freight forwarding to 195 countries and territories; international trade management, and customs brokerage (UPS, 2017). Its specialty services include service parts logistics; technical repair and configuration; supply chain design and planning; returns management (UPS, 2017). UPS currently maintains 57.1 percent of the market share, followed by FedEx, which maintains 25.2 percent (Kalyani, 2016). With the industry services segmented into Ground delivery, Air Transit services, & Other, it is unsurprising that UPS maintains the number one spot as 56.8 percent of the industry consists of ground deliveries.

Where FedEx's superiority is the functionality of its air fleet, UPS's lies in its ground delivery, where it operates more than 108,000 package cars, vans, tractors, motorcycles, and alternative fuel and advanced technology vehicles (UPS, 2017). In the shipping industry, the pressure is to keep margins low and prices attractive and consistent to maintain a delivery guarantee; the differential, however, lies in customer loyalty (Williams, 2014). UPS delivers 91 percent of express packages on time, versus a still impressive 88 percent for FedEx Express.

Perhaps one of the biggest elements of differentiation between FedEx and UPS is the number of stores they operate. According to FedEx (2017b), the company operates over 1,800 office locations across the United States. On the contrary, UPS operates "4,756 UPS Stores, about 1,000 customer service centers, 13,000 authorized outlets, and 40,000 drop boxes" (Williams, 2014). In 2016, its UPS Stores ranked #1 in the Postal and Business Centers category for the 26th consecutive year.

DHL

DHL is a company based in Germany that refers to itself as the leading global brand in the logistics industry (DHL, 2017). In 2015, the company boasted revenue over $59.2 billion, securing it as one of the largest global players in the logistics industry (Kalyani, 2016). DHL has operations segmented into four different areas: mail, express, global forwarding, and supply chain. The biggest drawback as a competitor is that its presence is relatively small in the United States. Although it offers shipments internationally to and from the United States, DHL discontinued its ground and air services inside the United States in 2009 (Kalyani, 2016, p. 31).

Though DHL does not deliver within the United States, it still provides steep competition with FedEx globally. One of the major areas in which DHL excels is through innovation; it has become a thought-leader in the logistics field (DHL, 2017). From the utilization of robots in the supply chain to Unmanned Aerial Vehicles (UAVs) in the delivery field, DHL is committed to seeking out the areas of innovation and trends that can enhance current logistics techniques. It is collaborating with customers, research and academic institutions, industry partners, and logistics experts (DHL, 2017) in order to engage stakeholders in a central platform.

One area in which DHL has been able to expand its brand is through corporate responsibility. DHL makes a name for its brand through the charity organizations and green opportunities in which it takes part. It has established a coordinated effort to give back to the communities in which it serves as an integral part of its corporate strategy. The partnership with the United Nations spreads not only the good it does, but also the brand DHL. It is also designating investments into innovations to decrease its CO_2 emissions (DHL, 2017). Its GoTeach initiative partners with two world organizations that provide teaching opportunities for volunteers in the organization. One last notable initiative is the DHL Express Operation Holiday Cheer, which is now in its 14th year. This initiative provides U.S. troops serving our country overseas the opportunity for deliveries of fresh-cut Christmas trees, thousands of holiday letters, menorahs, decorations, and gifts (Helping holidays, 2016). While these partnerships and initiatives do not directly contribute to the bottom line, they inadvertently provide an image of a brand that strives to do more for its community than just make money. It signifies an investment in a sustainable, better, future; a brand image that consumers like to support.

Amazon

Amazon, a company that boasted a 55 percent profit growth in Q4 2016, has been a long-time partner of FedEx (Wolf, 2017). Rocco (2017) points out that the executive leaders at FedEx view Amazon.com as a "friend, not a foe" despite its movement in the last few years in taking a "more active role" (Szakonyi, 2016) in transporting its own shipments. Global shippers like FedEx, DHL, and UPS have watched over recent years as Amazon has moved toward creating its own logistics network (McFarland, 2017).

In 2015, it purchased over 4,000 trailers to make deliveries in the United States (Wolf, 2017). It also released an application called Amazon Flex, where individual drivers can sign up, be vetted, and make local deliveries (Wolf, 2017) in a sort of "Uber of logistics" role. In 2016, Amazon made a move to increase its presence in air cargo by entering into agreements with both Atlas Air Worldwide Holdings (AAWW) and Air Transport Services Group (ATSG) to lease 40 freighter aircraft (King and Woods, 2017). Not only were these formal agreements beneficial, Amazon also invested with a voting stake in both companies (2017). In January 2017, Amazon announced its plans for the future, painting a clearer picture of the transition. It released a statement that it would be shifting away from its current air hub in Ohio to the Cincinnati/Northern Kentucky Airport in the spring (King and Woods, 2017). Amazon plans to build a 3-million square foot hub to sort e-commerce traffic and aims to also increase delivery speeds to customers at an investment of $1.5 billion.

Amazon claims that these new investments and shifts were made to supplement its current carrier partners; however, Wolf (2017), and many other experts, claim that these moves will further lessen Amazon's dependence on traditional carriers ... and continue a logistical buildout that extends to trucking and ocean freight (p. 6). Raj Subramaniam, executive vice president of global strategy, explained that Amazon is a long-standing partner which still relies a great deal on USPS, UPS, and FedEx for the delivery of its packages (Rocco, 2017). The threat of customers like Amazon turning into competitors will be the biggest challenge for major players in this industry within the next few years (Kalyani, 2016, p. 10).

How should FedEx evolve?

FedEx has invested in innovation efforts in creating technological advancements in order to expand its services to its customers domestically and internationally. By initiating this strategic orientation to target customers in a global perspective, it allows FedEx to connect with companies and search for global opportunities through investments. For example, the organization opened an operations facility in Mexico making it the largest logistics company in the country and attaining a large portion of the Mexican market share. FedEx is also researching where to position more of its facilities in the Caribbean and Latin American countries to enhance its infrastructure.

Mr. Smith straightened his tie and walked toward the board room, prepared to make his presentation. He knew his company was making some necessary improvements in terms of logistics, but he also thought it needed to expand its strategies in terms of innovation in order to evolve and grow in this highly concentrated industry.

References

Business Wire. (2017, March 21). FedEx Corp. reports third quarter earnings. Retrieved April 16, 2017, from https://seekingalpha.com/pr/16777561-fedex-corp-reports-third-quarter-earnings

DHL. (2017). Our vision, our mission, our strategy. Retrieved April 6, 2017, from www.dhl.com/en/about_us/company_portrait/mission_and_vision.html

FedEx. (2015). Company overview – acquisition history. Retrieved April 6, 2017, from http://investors.fedex.com/company-overview/Acquisition-History/default.aspx

FedEx. (2017a). About FedEx. Retrieved April 14, 2017, from http://about.van.fedex.com

FedEx. (2017b). Company overview – mission and goals. Retrieved April 6, 2017, from http://investors.fedex.com/company-overview/mission-and-goals/default.aspx

Helping holidays feel like home for troops. (2016). *The Lane Report*, 31(12), 43.

Kalyani, D. (2016). Couriers & local delivery services in the US (IBISWorld Industry Report, pp. 1–41, Rep. No. 49222). IBISWorld, Inc.

King, L. and Woods, R. (2017). Amazon, FedEx throw down gauntlet over e-commerce fulfillment. *Air Cargo World*, 107(2), 10.

McFarland, M. (2017, February 7). FedEx's new service takes aim at Amazon. Retrieved April 5, 2017, from http://money.cnn.com/2017/02/07/technology/fedex-fulfillment-amazon/

Rocco, M. (2017, March 22). FedEx CEO shrugs off competition from Amazon. Retrieved April 4, 2017, from www.foxbusiness.com/markets/2017/03/22/fedex-ceo-shrugs-off-competition-from-amazon.html

Szakonyi, M. (2016). Amazon opens doors with NVO status. *Journal of Commerce* (1542–3867), 17(3), 24.

UPS. (2017). UPS fact sheet. Retrieved April 10, 2017, from https://pressroom.ups.com/pressroom/ContentDetailsViewer.page?ConceptType=FactSheets&id=1426321563187-193

Wikipedia. (2018). FedEx. *Wikipedia*. Retrieved March 21, 2018, from https://en.wikipedia.org/wiki/FedEx_Express

Williams, S. (2014, May 9). UPS or FedEx: which company is best at keeping its customers loyal? Retrieved April 5, 2017, from www.fool.com/investing/general/2014/05/09/ups-or-fedex-which-company-is-best-at-keeping-its.aspx

Wolf, A. (2017). Do Amazon's disruptions know no bounds? *Twice: This Week in Consumer Electronics*, 32(3), 6.

Chapter 4

Strategies for growth

Markets are constantly changing, complex, and challenging. Managers need to constantly monitor markets and develop and alter strategies as markets change. They need to constantly monitor competitors' change in positioning, the changing needs of customers, and identify opportunities in the market as the environment of business changes. For example, the two major supermarket retailers in Florida were Publix and Winn-Dixie selling a full range of grocery items ... However, in recent years there have been a number of new competitors selling groceries in South Florida, including mass merchandisers Walmart and Super Target stores. Trader Joes and Amazon's Whole Foods Market are also major competitors.

Many forces are changing markets resulting in the industry structure changing and the players in an industry are also changing. As a result, organizations will find both opportunities and threats in their markets. New players in an industry are bringing disruptive innovation and doing things in different ways. The Internet and social media have also changed the way some competitors do business. As a result, new market space is being created in fast-changing markets. Amazon's dominance in the retail industry is a case in point. Many of the traditional retailers are closing stores and are developing their online offerings in order to survive.

Types of product-market structures

Organizations will have to evaluate their product-markets on a continuous basis. There are generally three types of product-market structures:

1. Generic product-market. These are a broad group of products that satisfy a general, yet similar, need. For example, when a consumer needs something to drink, they could purchase water, soda, wine, beer, tea, or coffee.
2. Product-type product-market. These are brands of a particular product type, such as cell phones for use by consumers. Samsung competes with the Apple iPhone, for example.
3. Product-variants. These are created by differences in the products within a product-type product-market. For example, Samsung offers a variety of cell phones in the market, all with different features.

In the generic product-market, if a consumer is wanting some food, they can buy food from a supermarket, a restaurant, a convenience store, or microwave some food from their fridge. They will all satisfy the same need. In the product-type product-market, consumers can choose between a BMW, Mercedes-Benz, Audi, and Lexus as these cars are in the same luxury market and satisfying similar needs. There are many product-variants, with BMW offering a 1, 2, 3, 5, 6, 7 series and other variants among its product mix.

It is important for marketers to understand how consumers make choices. It is also important for organizations to understand their competitive position in relation to the other players in the industry.

Sources of organizational growth

According to Treacy and Sims (2004), there are five sources of growth in the organization. They are all centered on customers. The first is continuing sales to established customers (base retention); the second, sales gained from the competition (share gain); third, sales in an expanding market (market positioning); fourth, moves into adjacent markets where core capabilities can be leveraged; and fifth, new lines of business unrelated to the core. According to Zook and Allen (2003), there are six ways to grow into adjacent markets. The first is to expand along the value chain, for example, a manufacturer extending into the wholesale or retailing businesses. The second is to enter new geographic areas, either within a country or in global markets. The third is addressing new customer segments, often by modifying a product or technology. For example, Porsche, a traditional sports car manufacturer developed SUVs and sedans for families and soccer moms. The fourth is to grow new products and services, for example, IBM moved from a major computer supplier into a global services company. The fifth way is to use new distribution channels, for example, Wal-Mart and other brick and mortar retailers are developing online sales and distribution (etailing). The last way to grow into adjacent space is to move into new businesses built around a strong capability. One of the best known examples of this is American Airlines creating the Sabre reservation system which, in turn, went on to create an online travel agent Travelocity. The success of all these strategies depends on the organization's understanding of buyer behavior.

One way to grow is to recognize the need for a few key strategic processes and a few simple rules to guide organizations according to Eisenhardt and Sull (2001). In strategy as simple rules, advantages come from successfully seizing fleeting opportunities. They contend that rather than picking a position or leveraging a competence, managers should select a few key strategic processes and craft a few simple rules. "The simple rules provide the guidelines within which managers can pursue opportunities. Strategy, then, consists of the unique set of strategically significant processes and the handful of simple rules that guide them" (Eisenhardt and Sull (2001, p. 109).

Strategy by simple rules

These authors suggest five categories of simple rules, namely, how-to rules; boundary rules; priority rules; timing rules; and exit rules. How-to rules spell out how a process is accomplished. For example, rules for customer service processes could include that every customer question must be answered on the first call or email. Boundary rules focus managers on which opportunities can be pursued and which are outside the boundary. For example, companies that are to be acquired should be small with no more than 50 employees. Priority rules help managers rank the opportunities. For example, manufacturing capacity allocation must be based on a product's gross margin. Timing rules synchronize managers with the pace of emerging opportunities and other parts of the company. For example, project teams in the new product development process must know when the product has to be delivered to the customer and development time must be less than 24 months. Exit rules help managers decide when to pull out of a project or withdraw a product. For example, if a leading member of the project team leaves the company, the project is dropped. Simple rules are not broad, vague, or thoughtless. Simple rules are created from past experience and by previous mistakes.

All this requires sound knowledge of the competition. The organization must identify its key competitors as well as potential new ones. An evaluation of each competitor's core competencies, target markets, marketing strategies, and key resources and skills are necessary. It is also important to anticipate its future strategies. This will enable the organization to develop growth strategies of its own that will enable it to stay ahead of the competition.

Conclusions

This chapter highlights the fact the markets are dynamic and constantly changing. Thus industries are constantly changing with new players entering the market and old ones exiting. Under these conditions there are many opportunities for growth. The types of product-market structures are discussed, and then the sources of organizational growth are highlighted. Last, the concept of strategy by simple rules is presented as a way organizations can grow.

References

Eisenhardt, K.M. and Sull, D.N. (2001). Strategy as simple rules. *Harvard Business Review*, January, 107 116.
Treacy, M. and Sims, J. (2004). Take command of your growth. *Harvard Business Review*, April, 1–8.
Zook, C. and Allen, J. (2003). Growth outside the core. *Harvard Business Review*, December, 2–10.

Twitter

Despite all that we have accomplished, Twitter still has huge unmet potential.

Jack Dorsey – Twitter/Square CEO

You can sense the tension in the room just by the demeanor of both Jack Dorsey and Anthony Noto. There was an awkward silence that lingered for a few minutes before the calls were taken. It's the summer of 2015 and Twitter is currently in disarray. Effective July 1st, Dick Costolo will step down as CEO and Jack Dorsey will become the interim CEO. Jack Dorsey is the co-founder of Twitter and was the CEO back in 2007 when the firm first emerged onto the social scene. For many users including the co-founders it was love at first tweet.

> During a conference call with shareholders, it was important that we expressed our true feelings in regards to the state of the firm. Both Anthony and I agreed that we do not see any changes in strategies and direction to shareholders. After the conference, the uncertainty of the firm's future plagued Jack. Twitter may be struggling to a certain degree but the platform has a significant importance in our society. It's a part of our culture. Social media has opened so many doors for countless individuals, breaks the latest news, and has captured some of our greatest moments in recent history. Our only dilemma is how we can show our users Twitter's value. How can we enhance the quality of the user experience without losing the core essence of Twitter's purpose? Most importantly how can we increase user engagement?

In the beginning of 2016 Twitter shares hit an all-time low. They were just under $20 at $19.26. Executives were scrambling to figure out how they could introduce new changes to improve the current financial position. New features for users were introduced in the hope that it would generate more user engagement. Twitter abandoned its favorites and stars for likes and hearts which is similar to Instagram. They also introduced moments which are big news events and trending topics in real time. Moments included both pictures and video content. Users also had the option of creating their own moments as well for events in their life. Periscope – which is the video streaming application Twitter acquired – will no longer require a link; it will auto play in newsfeeds. Although these features are a step in the right direction, many investors don't believe they will have a powerful impact on Twitter's financial performance.

Competition

When it comes to social media, competition is fierce among the biggest platforms. Facebook, Instagram, and Snapchat are just a few of Twitter's biggest competitors. Facebook is an application that allows users to share their thoughts and content without a 140 character limit. Facebook has over 1.5 billion monthly active users. This greatly exceeds Twitter's 325 million monthly active users. Year after year Facebook has seen enormous growth and engagement. In 2015 Facebook saw an average of

15 percent growth while Twitter only experienced a mere 1.4 percent. Annual revenue for Facebook has been strong and increasing over the last few years and it currently holds the biggest market share in the industry.

Instagram is a visual app that allows users to post beautifully filtered photos and videos. Instagram, which is owned by Facebook, boasts an impressive 500 million monthly active users. The aesthetically pleasing platform was bought by Facebook in 2012. Over 80 percent of Instagram's active users are outside of the United States. This is good for global advertising revenue. It is estimated that by 2019 Instagram's global advertising revenue will be $6.84 billion (Johnson, 2017). Snapchat, which is fairly new to the social media arena, is a platform that allows users to post and send 10-second videos and photos that disappear. Your photos or videos can be enhanced with beautiful, fun, and whimsical filters. The application is wildly popular among teenagers and young adults. The young firm has a very active 150 million users. In 2016 the company hit a milestone when it was reported that it exceeded Facebook's daily video views by 2 billion.

The history of Twitter

Jack Dorsey, Twitter co-founder, had an idea in 2006 of an SMS-based communications platform. Groups of friends could keep tabs on what each other were doing based on their status updates (MacArthur, 2016). Jack sent the first message on Twitter on March 21, 2006 at 9.50 p.m. It read, "just setting up my twttr."

When it started, Twitter was referred to as "twttr." Software developer Noah Glass is credited with coming up with the original name twttr as well as its final incarnation as Twitter (MacArthur, 2016).

The initial concept of Twitter was tested at Odeo, but that company's business model failed with the release of the Apple podcasting platform. Odeo's founders decided to buy their company back from the investors. They acquired the rights to the Twitter platform. Obvious Corporation was created after the investor buyback of Odeo in order to house Twitter (MacArthur, 2016). There is a 140-character limit on Twitter since it was originally designed as an SMS mobile phone-based platform. 140 characters were the limit that mobile carriers imposed with SMS protocol standard. Twitter eventually grew into a web platform and the 140-character limit remained.

The 2007 South By Southwest Interactive conference saw a huge explosion of Twitter usage. More than 60,000 tweets were sent per day at the event. The Twitter team had a huge presence at the event and took advantage of the viral nature of the conference and its attendees (MacArthur, 2016). It's safe to say that Twitter had its fair share of growing pains during its formative years. Twitter's user base grew at astounding rates and quite frequently the service would be over capacity. As Twitter's user base started growing users created new jargon and different ways to use the service. Examples include users adding an "@" symbol before their username to identify another user within a tweet to facilitate replying to others. This functionality was then added to the Twitter platform. The use of hashtags was also created by a user in 2007 and became part of Twitter (Twitter, 2017).

In October 2010, Dick Costolo became the CEO replacing Jack Dorsey. In 2011, Twitter acquired TweetDeck, teamed up with Apple to integrate Twitter into IOS 5, and allowed users to share photos via SMS. In 2012, Twitter was able to offer self-service advertising for small businesses, in partnership with American Express. In 2013, Twitter filed an IPO and in November, it made news with one of the biggest IPOs of all time for a U.S. internet company, and shares soared more than 70 percent after they debuted on the New York Stock Exchange (Tsukayama and ElBoghdady, 2013).

Twitter's growth has come from what it has launched and what it has acquired. In 2013, Twitter launched Vine, which is a short-form video hosting service where users could share 6-second-long looping video clips. In 2014, Twitter acquired Gnip (an enterprise application programming interfaces [API] platform, delivering real-time and historical social data to power businesses), Namo Media (a specialist in "native ad" content that integrates with the site where the ads that are being viewed), Snappy TV (the service for clipping, editing, and sharing clips from live broadcasts in near real-time), Tap Commerce (mobile retargeting and reengagement advertising), and CardSpring (API that makes it easy for developers to link digital applications to credit or debit cards). In 2014, Twitter launched Promoted Videos and Fabric (Twitter, 2017).

In 2015 Twitter acquired ZipDial, Niche, Periscope, TellApart and launched direct messages and mobile video, highlights, birthday features on profiles, an event targeting tool for advertisers, moments, polls, and hearts (Twitter, 2017).

Since its inception, Twitter has gained almost 200 million users worldwide. About 460,000 new Twitter accounts are opened daily. More than 140 million tweets are sent daily which translates to one billion weekly (Picard, 2011). Twitter impacted media by enabling people to tweet about the news including disasters, politics, sports, and celebrities (Picard, 2011). Many people were following news via the tweets from people they followed on Twitter. Twitter has affected businesses as it is used increasingly by business to communicate with employees and customers. Business can communicate real-time messages to the customers they want to reach. Conversely, when customers are unhappy with a product or service, they can spread the word quickly – and do damage – with a few tweets (Picard, 2011).

By 2015, Twitter's stock plunged from $40 billion at the time of the IPO in 2013 to as low as $16.5 billion in August of 2015 (Bilton, 2015). Investor confidence was declining and Twitter faced competition from Facebook and other social media companies. The board of directors was fragmented and employee morale was at a low. Original CEO and founder Jack Dorsey was brought back to Twitter to take over leadership as CEO and resolve the many troubles facing it.

Current status

Twitter has hit a few roadblocks along the way. Though it made some right decisions, it is just not being able to generate revenue consistently. While monthly user growth remains slow, Twitter has the lowest advertising spending compared to its competitors. International strength helped user growth to stay ahead of expectations, though it had a decline from 307 million users to 305 million active by the end of 2016 (Guynn, 2016).

According to the COO Anthony Noto, Twitter is welcoming lost users as well as new ones by improving confusing rules that drive users away. The problem is that many people do not understand how or why to use the platform and as a result the company has been losing users to other apps. Since Microsoft's purchase of LinkedIn, experts speculate that Twitter will be the next acquisition. It is believed that Twitter may live on in a whole new form if acquired by successful companies like Google or Disney. But the number one priority to Jack Dorsey is recruiting and innovation around the core product experience. S&P Global Market Intelligence analyst Scott Kessler points out that one of the most difficult things for Twitter now is "seeing the turnover in terms of product leadership … and what they really lack is their ability to really change and improve their product experience which has led to flattish user engagement numbers" (Guynn, 2016).

According to Q4 2016 reports, Twitter was expecting to reduce its staff by as much as 8 percent, which means approximately 300 jobs. It has considered selling itself but experts wonder who would be the best candidate. Though the company reported its total user base at 307 million users, up from 305 million, Twitter reported the stock down nearly 11 percent in Q2 2016. The revenue miss was because the brand marketers did not spend as quickly. While Twitter is today the most popular app it can also be a marketer's worst fear. The issue Dorsey is committed to is to find the strategy to attract the right type of followers and keep them engaged. A year after Dorsey returned with live-streaming and new products, Twitter is still not showing signs of growth. Twitter's stock dropped 20 percent in 2016 before news began to surface about a possible sale. The question that keeps popping up is should Twitter continue as an independent company or consider the benefits of getting acquired (Frier, 2016)?

Jack Dorsey – background and influences

Jack Dorsey, founder and current CEO of Twitter, was born in St. Louis, Missouri in 1976. Growing up, Jack had an obsession with cities and maps. He also had an interest in coding and computer programming. Starting off with a Macintosh computer given to him by his father, Jack created a program where he could track vehicles moving around St. Louis in real time (Statt, 2015). As a self-taught college programmer bored with his schooling in Missouri, he set his sights on a job with Dispatch Management Solutions in New York. With no contact information on its website, Jack hacked into it, in order to create an email to the company's founder (Parnell, 2016). The email let Greg Kidd know about a security breach on its website and he explained that he could write dispatch software. He was hired one week later and it was a dream come true. His employer allowed him to see (and work) first hand with a company that kept track of public transit, emergency vehicles, and taxis which took him back to his childhood and obsession with cities; who is doing what and when they are doing it.

Jack had first begun a college career at the Missouri University of Science and Technology, left for his position at Dispatch Management Solutions and later enrolled at NYU. He dropped out before graduating, later moving to Oakland, California along with Greg Kidd. Jack moved to be closer to where technology and business was booming.

In 2005, Jack was hired as an entry level coder at the podcast startup Odeo (Statt, 2015). With Apple's podcasting taking off around the same time, Odeo was done for. Jack was able to bring his ideas to life with the support of Odeo's cofounder Noah Glass.

Twitter started as an idea for a way to keep in touch with your friends, sharing short messages online. Twitter 1.0 began as a simple website where users were able to post 140-character messages that Jack called "tweets." Twitter Inc. was officially founded on March 21, 2006 (MacArthur, 2016).

Twitter's problem

The main problem that Twitter has been facing throughout the years is the ability to monetize its platform and grow its user base. "Twitter has been looking for newer ways to figure out how to monetize its user base if it isn't going to be able to rapidly grow it" (Lynley, 2017). One way it has tried to increase engagement has been through live-streaming as it says that "video is its largest revenue-generating ad format," but it still struggles with seeing the numbers it desires (Lynley, 2017). It has also released many new product updates and has increased character limits, but it seems like these updates have had no effect on its expected growth. "After a wildly successful IPO in 2013, Twitter quickly began to struggle with life as a public company. Gone were the cushy days of being a well-funded private start-up; the reality of pleasing shareholders began to set in" (Alba, 2017). It seemed like it was very difficult for it to figure out exactly what kind of service it was trying to provide to its users while also being able to meet its shareholders' expectations.

Advertising revenue totaled $638 million in the fourth quarter of 2016, which has actually been down year after year. "Advertising revenue growth may be further impacted by escalating competition for digital ad spending and the re-evaluation of their revenue product feature portfolio, which could result in the de-emphasis of certain product features" (O'Brien, 2017).

> Twitter needed to show that it could have a strong fourth quarter given that the 2016 U.S. presidential election, probably one of the most Twitter zeitgeisty moments of all time, happened. Beyond that, President Donald Trump is also an active Twitter user, giving it additional strength as a go-to platform for news.
>
> (Lynley, 2017)

Despite all of that, Twitter's revenues were still down and it seemed like it was not able to capitalize in a way that could benefit it.

User growth is another significant challenge that Twitter has been facing for years. Unless people use Twitter for their job or "have become familiar with it over a long period of time, there may not be a good reason to sign up and continue using it day in and day out" (Statt, 2015). This is the major obstacle Twitter has been facing and even with added product features and a strong engagement from its core users, new users are not really interested when they have other social platforms as options. While Twitter makes the case of everything being in real time on its platform to be an advantage, it is still not enough to grow that number. With Dorsey's return as CEO in 2016, the company was expecting him to execute the kind of plan and results that only a founder can. "Twitter is live," Dorsey said decisively during a Twitter earnings call at the top of 2016. "Live commentary, live conversations, and live connections" (Alba, 2017). "Twitter wants to be the digital, forward-thinking equivalent of live television, and it's been scooping up select streaming rights to make this transformation" (Statt, 2015).

Harassment is also an issue the company faces within the platform which may be contributing to the slow growth in numbers. This issue seems to be intimidating potential new users. Twitter "has started making some moves toward silencing abuse in order to curb the harassment problem that plagues the platform throughout its existence" (Lynley, 2017). However, it has not been enough to see the positive turn-around it would expect.

"While Twitter is still a platform with hundreds of millions of users, Wall Street may find itself too impatient to wait for Dorsey and his team to figure out where to take the company and start with some fresh eyes" (Lynley, 2017).

References

Alba, D. (2017). 2017 is the year that Twitter learns to thrive or dies. *Wired*. Retrieved April 13, 2017, from www.wired.com/2017/01/2017-year-twitter-learns-thrive-dies/

Bilton, N. (2015, October 5). Jack Dorsey returns to a frayed Twitter. *New York Times*. Retrieved April 15, 2017, from www.nytimes.com/2015/10/06/technology/jack-dorsey-returns-to-a-frayed-twitter.html

Frier, S. (2016, October 5). Jack Dorsey is losing control of Twitter. *Bloomberg*. Retrieved April 15, 2017, from www.bloomberg.com/features/2016-twitter-dorsey-strategy/

Guynn, J. (2016, February 10). Twitter growth grinds to a halt. *USA Today*. Retrieved April 15, 2017, from www.usatoday.com/story/tech/news/2016/02/10/twitter-fourth-quarter-earnings-user-decline/80178140/

Johnson, L. (2017, October 2). eMarketer drops Snap's global ad revenue estimates by $126 million, citing slow growth: meanwhile, Instagram will roar. *AdWeek*. Retrieved March 20, 2018, from www.adweek.com/digital/emarketer-drops-snaps-global-ad-revenue-estimates-by-126-million-citing-slow-growth/

Lynley, M. (2017). Twitter's advertising business is stalling. *Tech Crunch*. Retrieved April 13, 2017, from https://techcrunch.com/2017/02/09/twitters-streamlining-efforts-still-arent-fixing-its-core-business-problems/

MacArthur, A. (2016). The real history of Twitter, in brief: how the micro-messaging wars were won. *Lifewire*. Retrieved April 16, 2017, from www.lifewire.com/history-of-twitter-3288854

O'Brien, C. (2017). Twitter posts big revenue miss for Q4 2016 despite user growth of 4%. *Venture Beat*. Retrieved April 13, 2017, from https://venturebeat.com/2017/02/09/twitter-posts-big-earnings-miss-for-q4-2016-despite-users-growth-of-4/

Parnell, B. (2016). Jack Dorsey broke the law? *Medium*. Retrieved April 15, 2017, from https://medium.com/making-waves/jack-dorsey-broke-the-law-1c00b3995a06

Picard, A. (2011). The history of Twitter, 140 characters at a time. *The Globe and Mail*. Retrieved April 15, 2017, from www.theglobeandmail.com/technology/digital-culture/the-history-of-twitter-140-characters-at-a-time/article573416/

Statt, N. (2015). To Twitter CEO and back again: a timeline of Jack Dorsey's rise. *The Verge*. Retrieved April 15, 2017, from www.theverge.com/2015/10/5/9457277/jack-dorsey-twitter-ceo-timeline

Tsukayama, H. and ElBoghdady, D. (2013). Twitter opens at $45.10 a share, valued at about $25B. *The Washington Post*.

Twitter. (2017). Twitter milestones. *Twitter*. Retrieved April 14, 2017, from https://about.twitter.com/company/press/milestones

CrossFit SOFLA: growing pains

CrossFit SOFLA was started in August 2012 by Josh and Stephanie Thompson. The business began very humbly, offering workouts in the park from August 2012 through April 2013. It opened its first brick and mortar location in April 2013. For the first year, it ran a business model called the "closed class model." The closed class model was a model that had each client commit to two things: the number of times per week they trained (either two, three, or four times per week) and the time of day they trained (either 5.30 a.m., 9.30 a.m., 5.30 p.m., or 6.30 p.m.). The client was required to follow a set schedule, much like you would for a college course, allowing the client to always train with the same coach and the same fellow athletes. From a business perspective, this maximized the space. From a client perspective, it minimized their flexibility. They were locked into the same class which proved to pose a difficulty for many prospective clients. They found the model to be limiting, and SOFLA realized it was not working. The adoption of the closed class model caused disparity for the business and stunted its growth. A change needed to be made, and in April 2014, it shifted the business model to a more traditional model: the "open class model." This allowed for more freedom for the clients, as they were now allowed to come as often as they want and come to any class time that fit their schedule. After this shift, the gym started turning around. In January 2015, CrossFit SOFLA rebranded with a new logo and website. After the rebrand and the change in business model, there was slow but steady growth.

CrossFit SOFLA is known in the community for providing an excellent experience and superior coaching. It offers a high-quality product, and is respected in the local CrossFit community.

The retention rate is high, and customer satisfaction is high as well. Overall, the service is top notch. This is clear through the reviews on Google, Yelp, and Facebook, the responses to random surveys, and the positive reputation buzzing in the community.

In spite of the obvious quality and superior customer experience, CrossFit SOFLA has not found the kind of traction that it needs to become profitable. The problem is that CrossFit SOFLA does not have nearly enough people actually coming out and trying the service. The good news is that when people do venture out, CrossFit SOFLA is very successful in converting potential clients to paying members. They typically love their experience. This problem is crushing the business, keeping it at breakeven status and away from profitability.

- In the first year there was little to no growth.
- After the business model shift, there has been slow but steady growth.
- It offers a very high-quality product.
- Once a potential client tries out classes SOFLA has a high rate of converting them to members and a high retention rate.
- SOFLA's physical space is one of the nicer CrossFit gyms in South Florida but it doesn't have air conditioning or locker rooms (which is almost standard for CrossFit gyms across the world).

CrossFit headquarters and CrossFit's position in the fitness industry

Challenging the paradigm of fitness

In 2000, CrossFit was founded by Greg Glassman and Lauren Jenai in Santa Cruz, California. The concept of CrossFit is to offer a general and inclusive fitness regimen, which all begins in the belief of fitness. This program was built in order to prepare members for any unpredictable situation. By offering such a broad range of fitness skills, CrossFit believes that all these skills will be easily transferable and adaptable to any physical situation providing a performance advantage over others. In short, CrossFit boasts a General Physical Preparedness, or GPP, strength and conditioning program.

Glassman's fitness regimen has changed the way people think of fitness. The protocol calls for constantly varied, functional movements, performed at high intensity. What that means is that the client is exposed to several different components of fitness (weightlifting, throwing, gymnastics, running, jumping, etc.) all of which are movements that you would find in the real world. And to make the most impact, these varied, functional movements are performed at a very high level of intensity, allowing for incredible fitness gains over time. Another huge component of CrossFit has been the creation of a strong, unbreakable community, leading the company to impressive growth and success. Glassman contends that the combination of these standards is what leads to fitness and health:

CVFM @ HI + Communal Environment = Health

A regimen of Constantly Varied (CV), Functional Movements (FM), performed at High Intensity (@HI) in a communal environment leads to health and fitness (CrossFit, n.d.).

The affiliate model

> We want to fuel a revolution in fitness that advocates the pursuit of function, not form – that measures performance, not anatomy. We want rings and bumper plates in our gyms, not machines. We believe that where you train is less important than how you train and that who you train with matters more than what gear you have. We know this can be done in little boxes and we've proven that the garage is as good an environment as any for Forging Elite Fitness®.
>
> (Glassman, 2005)

CrossFit is now a movement that has provided an alternative to commercial gyms with its "big box," machine-based, bodybuilding approach to fitness. CrossFit's garage gyms have proven a success as they focus more on the fitness than the aesthetics of the actual location. Along with its communal environment mentality, CrossFit has taken this advantage by developing affiliations with this fitness concept. The first affiliated gym was CrossFit North in Seattle, WA. By 2005, there were a total of 15 affiliated gyms and in 2015 there were over 12,000 affiliates worldwide.

CrossFit is not a franchise and never will be. Under a franchise, the franchisee must follow the rules and regulations of the franchising company. Unlike a franchise, an affiliation of CrossFit only pays for the right to use the CrossFit name and to be listed on crossfit.com. Each affiliate owner has the freedom to control all their business decisions to run and organize their gym.

Becoming a CrossFit affiliate is a simple process. An applicant must submit their application online, as well as submit the appropriate paperwork and payment. Along with all the paperwork and payment that must be filed the interested affiliate must provide an essay explaining why they are interested in affiliating, explaining what CrossFit means to them and why they would like to affiliate, and what they wish to achieve as an affiliate. This essay is critical in the application process as it can indicate if the applicant aligns with CrossFit's mission and business model.

Business culture

To sum up the overall business culture, CrossFit SOFLA is built around excellence. Its coaches work hard on continued education and personal development, and on providing a high-quality coaching experience for their athletes. They are out in suburbia where their athletes consist of young families between the ages of 30 and 40 looking to be fit for life, not for competing. Their fitness is measured by whether or not they can do cool things with their kids and not get out of breath. They have an inclusive, open community with a laidback atmosphere, and low drama. Coaches are extremely helpful and are always going out of their way to assist customers. Their mission is to use fitness to improve lives. The best part about CrossFit SOFLA's cultural environment (something that would not necessarily be able to be seen from just a walk around the gym) is the high level of coaching. Coaches are well educated who have chosen coaching as a profession and career, not just a hobby. The coaches love working with and helping people. The goal of the coach is to help clients reach their potential. The coach guides them and they start seeing changes in their life physically, which then turns into changes in their mentality, which ultimately leads to them living healthier lifestyles.

Based on strongly encouraged feedback provided by customers, CrossFit SOFLA's clientele are highly satisfied. There are, however, some types of clients that would not thrive as well at CrossFit SOFLA. The highly competitive athlete or a young millennial looking for party friends will not necessarily fit in at CrossFit SOFLA, as the majority of clients are working professionals and moms and dads. CrossFit SOFLA also works diligently to provide special conflict resolution training to employees in an effort to prevent and eliminate drama. A strong, positive, and drama-free culture is important to the leadership team, so they work hard to maintain a great culture.

Services offered

CrossFit SOFLA offers three different kinds of services: group classes, personal training, and CrossFit for kids. Group classes are simply personal training sessions in a group setting. The advantage of group classes is that the athletes get personal coaching in a competitive and motivating environment that pushes them to achieve their goals. Each class is structured to have two workout options – fitness workouts

Table 4.1 Service prices

CrossFit adults	Price
8 Group Class Card	$120
Unlimited Group	$145/month
Personal Training	$220+/month
8 Class Card	$100
	50% off for any additional kid
	50% off if the parent is a member

Source: Price List (CrossFit SOFLA, n.d.).

and performance workouts – to fit every athlete's needs and physical capabilities. Fitness workouts are customized to be beginner-friendly for CrossFit SOFLA's athletes that don't have a lot of experience. Fitness workouts help the athletes build a strong CrossFit foundation through the use of lighter, progressive weights that correspond to the athlete's boundaries. Performance workouts are targeted for CrossFit veterans who have experience and are proficient in the more complex movements. Athletes can attend any class offered by CrossFit SOFLA and choose the option that best fits their experience level. An experienced coach helps and motivates the athletes throughout the session. CrossFit SOFLA offers high-quality personal training for those athletes that feel more comfortable working out alone and getting complete, one-on-one attention from their coach. The experienced CrossFit SOFLA coach will design a workout program with the athlete based on their current fitness level and desired goals. The coach then trains, guides, and supports the athlete to help them achieve their individual goals in a safe, timely manner. CrossFit Kids is a unique class for kids, ages 6–12, that teaches them the basics of how to squat, jump, climb, run, push, pull, lift, and throw, all while developing mental strength and willpower in a fun, focused, and education-orientated manner.

Table 4.1 illustrates the membership fees CrossFit SOFLA charges for its athletes. CrossFit for adults offers an eight-group class card for $120 and unlimited group class access for $145 a month. Personal training costs $220 or more in a month depending on the number of visits per month and coach. A kids' eight-class card costs $100 and CrossFit SOFLA offers 50 percent off for the final price on any additional kid or if the parent is already a member.

Service strategy

The CrossFit SOFLA team understands that the biggest determinant for success is consistency. Most people who are out of shape start going to the gym 2–3 days per week, then they might add a day. Over time, the changes will come. What deters success is inconsistency such as when a customer goes for 5 days, then skips a week. Inconsistency is where success is missed. In order to address the issue of inconsistency, CrossFit SOFLA has built its service strategy on three major points: make things simple, make them smile, and give them hope. The CrossFit SOFLA customer is between the ages of 30 and 40, and they live in suburbia with their family. They are not looking for a competitive atmosphere as much as they are looking to be fit for life so they can do fun, active activities with their kids. They are looking for an inclusive, open community with a laidback atmosphere, and low to no drama. CrossFit SOFLA has successfully created this atmosphere by providing an encouraging, positive, and helpful environment that focuses on teamwork and the customer's ongoing progress. All that being said, just in case there is an unsatisfied customer, CrossFit SOFLA has a strong conflict resolution policy that focuses on sincerely listening and sympathizing with disgruntled clients, and then including them in the solution.

Most contact with customers is conducted on a face-to-face basis at the gym either in casual conversation, or announcements after class. For those who are in a rush, there is a board in the gym that posts the same announcements. In addition, customers are contacted via email, and through a weekly newsletter where CrossFit SOFLA communicates anything new it will be working on, any changes, and/or events. It also communicates with its customers on a more personal level by mailing hand-written birthday cards. CrossFit SOFLA has a very active and successful Facebook page with over 700 followers and boasting a 5.0 rating, which it uses to communicate with its followers/customers.

Type of customers SOFLA is trying to attract

CrossFit SOFLA's ideal target market consists of four different types of client segments. One of the segments is working parents who have a lot going on and are trying to find a work/life balance. Their goal is to excel at work, live a fit life, and have time for their family. Young professionals aged 28–35 with an active lifestyle living in suburbia make up another segment. Their goal is to lose weight, feel better physically, have more energy, be around healthy people, and increase their quality of health. Experienced CrossFitters who want to compete in CrossFit, look good, improve their own results, and learn from the best available coaches are another segment. Parents looking for kids; programs to help teach their kids an active lifestyle early on make up the last client segment. These personas represent the desired CrossFit SOFLA customers.

Current marketing efforts

CrossFit SOFLA's marketing relies strongly on word-of-mouth promotions. However, CrossFit SOFLA has a solid social media presence on Twitter, Facebook, and Instagram. The company's social media posts focus on athlete success stories, events, and workout tips. It has one sponsored ad on Facebook every week to tell a success story of one of its own athletes. CrossFit SOFLA's marketing focuses on highlighting its athletes' achievements as much as possible. Facebook ads allow CrossFit SOFLA to target people who are in CrossFit groups, like CrossFit pages, and write posts about CrossFit. CrossFit SOFLA is very engaged within the community. CrossFit SOFLA's staff meets potential new athletes and hand out flyers every two weeks at local farmers' markets. This has been very successful in recent years to get close to the community and has provided a great opportunity to meet new potential athletes. CrossFit SOFLA also takes part in local 5k runs and provides nutrition seminars. The company sends out an email newsletter once a week to its email list providing content in three different categories: knowledge, care, and fun. CrossFit SOFLA offers a "bring a friend" promotion on the first Wednesday of every month to increase the awareness of the sport and CrossFit SOFLA. Both the inviting member and the guest will get $20 off from their membership fee if the guest decides to purchase a membership. CrossFit SOFLA's coaches also write a blog on the company's website. Blog posts consist of workout tips, nutrition, upcoming events, success stories, and the sharing of related articles. Also on the blog, Workout of the Day adds value by allowing members to check the day's workout schedule and routine online. CrossFit SOFLA's ongoing challenge is to create and deliver high-quality content across all platforms at all times to increase engagement of current members and to attract new members.

Competition

The marketplace is currently very congested with other CrossFit gyms, big box gyms, yoga studios, spinning studios, boot camps, and any other business that is charging the consumer for fitness. There is not one gym or set of gyms that currently stands out as a major competitor because there happen to be hundreds of these establishments within a 20-mile radius. The challenge has become differentiating themselves as a jewel instead of just a face in the crowd. It is becoming increasingly clearer, however, that Orange Theory is positioning itself as the major potential competitor. Upon receiving feedback, most customers usually say they are deciding between CrossFit SOFLA and Orange Theory. They are similar in the sense that they are both group classes, start to finish. They are different in the sense of method and foundation. Essentially, there are two types of thought structures for fitness. The traditional thought structure, carried out by Orange Theory, speaks from conventional wisdom and is followed by the majority of the industry. This is the traditional box structure that focuses on bodybuilding, cardio, and weights for the purpose of such activities as long metabolic workouts. Specifically, the physiological theory behind the Orange Theory workout is known as "Excess Post-Exercise Oxygen Consumption." By providing the client with a heart-rate monitor, it can monitor the five-zone interval training sessions that it calls the Orange 60. During the 60-minute workout, clients will perform multiple intervals designed to produce 12–20 minutes of training at 84 percent or higher of their maximum heart rate, which translates to Zones 4/5. This program design produces a workout "after burn" effect, which is an increased metabolic rate for 24–36 hours after the workout. CrossFit, on the other hand, runs on a more unconventional functional fitness thought framework. The idea is how to make someone the fittest person possible across several measurements so that they are as fit as possible for any task, also known as General Physical Preparedness. Its total body exercises are designed to help the client run a marathon, deadlift a ton of weight, knock out a bunch of unbroken pull-ups, sprint fast, swim a mile, back squat really heavy weight, and do a variety of other total body-involved activities.

In addition to catering to the majority of the population in terms of fitness mentality, Orange Theory has air-conditioned facilities with locker rooms. Although CrossFit SOFLA is nicer than most CrossFit gyms, it is not too polished, is not air conditioned, and it does not have locker rooms. Despite all of this, the real difficulty lies in the fact that not only does CrossFit SOFLA have to think about how to attract people to its gym, but it also has to shift its customers' vision about fitness as a whole; a worthy yet daunting task.

CrossFit SOFLA wants to be aware of what is going on in the marketplace, and what Orange Theory is doing, but that is not the basis for the decisions that are made. For instance, if Orange Theory is focusing on rowing, it is not just going to focus on rowing, or if StrikeFit is kickboxing, it is not going to be focusing on kickboxing. In essence, it is not necessarily trying to compete head to head with potential competitors, although it is aware of the changing trends.

Demographics of the area around the gym

CrossFit SOFLA is located in the city of Coral Springs, Florida. As of 2015, its total population consists of an estimated 354,511 people, of which 47.9 percent are males and 52.1 percent are females (within a 5-mile radius) according to the *Demographic Detail Summary*. Of this population, the race breakdown is as follows: White (67 percent), Black (20.5 percent), Hispanic (22.6 percent), or non-Hispanic or Latino (77.3 percent). Within these demographics, there are a total of 137,851 households, which is expected to have a 3.2 percent change from the year 2015 to 2020 (DemographicsNow, 2015). The average household income is about $74,305 and it is expected to increase by 15 percent between 2015 and 2020. Coral Springs estimates that of the total population, the majority of the residents range from 25 to 64 and the average age is approximately 40½ years of age (DemographicsNow, 2015).

Within a mile of CrossFit SOFLA's facility, slight changes were shown. The total population consists of 51.1 percent of females and 48.8 percent of males, which intends to grow 7.7 percent by 2020, according to the *Demographic Snapshot Comparison*.

The future

CrossFit is very polarizing. The ones who love it really love it, and the ones who hate it really hate it. It challenges everything we have ever known about fitness, and change, as we know, is not always easy for people to deal with. With the Thompsons' dedicated team, they strive to change the stigma behind the CrossFit methodology and show their community its superiority to other methods of training. However, since CrossFit SOFLA is at the breakeven point after three years in business, it has to make some changes. How can this family-owned CrossFit gym increase profits and increase membership? What is considered to be the underlying issue that this gym is facing that can cause a detrimental impact on the future of this establishment?

References

CrossFit SOFLA. (n.d.). Retrieved November 14, 2015, from www.crossfitsofla.com
DemographicsNow. (2015). Library edition.
Glassman, G. (2015, July 1). Garage Gym II: the revolution. *CrossFit Journal*.
    Retrieved March 20, 2018, from http://journal.crossfit.com/2005/07/
    garage-gym-iithe-revolution-by.tpl

Chapter 5

Corporate branding and internal brand management

The corporate brand reflects the organization that will deliver and stand behind the product or service offering that a customer will buy and use as well as provides value to other stakeholders in different ways. Corporate brands are important to different stakeholder groups because they play a role in constructing identities by many groups, including employees, governments, and suppliers. Employees, for example, develop esteem from working for a company like American Express, Miami's self-image is enhanced by being an international gateway for business in Central and South America, and local farmers pride themselves as being suppliers to supermarkets like Publix. Corporate brands apply to for-profit and nonprofit organizations, like IBM and Nova Southeastern University, cities, like Fort Lauderdale, and regions like South Florida or Napa Valley. Abratt and Kleyn (2012) define a corporate brand as expressions and images of an organization's identity. For organizations, it is the mechanism that conveys the elements and builds the expectations of what the organization will deliver for each stakeholder group. Core elements of its corporate identity include corporate affinities, products and services, and social responsibility programs.

Corporate brands are different from product brands. According to Balmer and Gray (2003) the chief executive is responsible for the management of the corporate brand and all the departments have functional responsibility for its implementation, so one can conclude that every employee has a role to play in corporate branding. The corporate brand also reflects the real values of the organization which are converted into a brand covenant or brand promise to stakeholders. Corporate communications are responsible for communicating the brand covenant to the various stakeholders. The brand covenant is often encapsulated in the form of a brand mantra. For example, Publix stores' mantra is "where shopping is a pleasure."

Most corporate brands share the following characteristics (Aaker, 2004):

A corporate brand most often has a rich heritage

The reason companies with heritage should use it is to take advantage of differentiation that is valuable for all stakeholders. For example, the McDonald's Corporation is the world's largest chain of hamburger fast food restaurants, serving around 68 million customers daily in 119 countries. Headquartered in the United States, the company began in 1940 as a barbecue restaurant operated by Richard and Maurice McDonald; in 1948 they reorganized their business as a hamburger stand using production line principles. Businessman Ray Kroc joined the company as a franchise agent in 1955.

He subsequently purchased the chain from the McDonald brothers and oversaw its worldwide growth (www.aboutmcdonalds.com/mcd/our_company/mcdonalds_history_timeline.html).

A corporate brand has a main set of assets and capabilities

Assets can include something unique that gives the company a sustainable competitive advantage. For example, the Coca-Cola Company is a U.S. multinational beverage corporation headquartered in Atlanta, Georgia. The company is best known for its flagship product Coca-Cola, invented in 1886 by pharmacist John Stith Pemberton in Columbus, Georgia. The Coca-Cola formula and brand was bought in 1889 by Asa Griggs Candler, who incorporated the Coca-Cola Company in 1892. The Coca-Cola Company only produces syrup concentrate which is then sold to various bottlers throughout the world who hold an exclusive territory. While many others have tried to copy this secret formula, they have been unsuccessful, and it remains an asset until this day (www.coca-colacompany.com/brands/the-coca-cola-company/; www.whoinventedit.net/who-invented-coca-cola.html).

A corporate brand can have a strong people element in its founder

For example, Apple was founded by Steve Jobs, Steve Wozniak, and Ronald Wayne on April 1, 1976 to develop and sell personal computers. It was incorporated as Apple Computer, Inc. on January 3, 1977, and was renamed as Apple Inc. on January 9, 2007 to reflect its shifted focus towards consumer electronics. (www.gartner.com/newsroom/id/2017015).

A corporate brand always has a particular set of values and priorities

Values should be built into the brand, expressed through behavior and communications to stakeholders. Some have a cost-driven culture, like IKEA, others have a culture of innovation, like 3M and Apple.

While some companies have a local frame of reference, some have a global frame of reference as well

For example, Coca-Cola has a strong U.S. presence but also a strong global brand available in over 200 countries in the world. McDonald's also is the leading hamburger chain in the United States but is also the world's largest chain of hamburger fast food restaurants, serving around 68 million customers daily in 119 countries. (www.aboutmcdonalds.com/mcd/our_company/mcdonalds_history_timeline.html).

Some companies have strong citizenship programs

An example of strong citizenship is McDonald's.

> As part of a global network of local family restaurants, McDonald's and our owner operators are proud to give back to the communities we serve. Whether it's supporting a local sports league, helping talented young athletes, or taking steps to improve our neighborhoods, our support reflects our commitment to you and our communities.
>
> (www.mcdonalds.com/us/en/our_story/our_communities/inspiration.html)

Lastly, a good performance record will enhance a good corporate brand

All the corporate brands should have a good performance record which has led in part to high brand equity. This is often reflected in brand equity valuations like Interbrand (see Interbrand.com).

Advantages of the corporate brand

A corporate brand provides an umbrella of trust for the organization and also provides a seal of approval. For example, companies like P&G and Unilever are best known by their product brands but the corporate brand always stands behind the products that they sell. Corporate brands are transferable assets and can be bought and sold. Strong corporate brands can obtain investors easier than weak ones. Amazon's investment in Whole Foods is a case in point. Corporate brands can reduce the organization's costs by exploiting economies of scale in advertising and other forms of marketing communication. Corporate brands also give customers and other stakeholders a sense of community. The Apple logo for example is a simple one that makes users of Apple products feel part of a brand community. Corporate brands also attract good people to work for the organization as many employees want to work for strong corporate brands. For example, companies like Facebook and Google have no trouble attracting top talent to work for them.

Internal brand management

The positive interactions between employees and customers are said to be crucial in building customer satisfaction and loyalty. This is particularly true in service organizations like airlines and hotels as well as in retailing where frontline employees are constantly interacting with customers. Employees have a key role in brand-building activities. While there are many different definitions of internal branding, Saleem and Iglesias (2016, p. 50) provide a comprehensive one.

> Internal branding is the process through which organizations make a company effort within a supportive culture to integrate brand ideologies, leadership, HRM, internal brand communications and internal brand communities as a strategy to enable employees to consistently co-create brand value with multiple stakeholders.

Internal branding is therefore a process through which brands aim to facilitate the internalization of brand values by employees. The behavior of employees must align with the organization's brand values when delivering the brand covenant or brand promise to customers and other stakeholders. The outcomes of internal branding include the identification with the corporate brand, brand commitment, job satisfaction and the intention to stay in the job, and brand citizenship behavior.

Saleem and Iglesias (2016) suggest that the components of internal brand management are brand ideologies, brand leadership, brand-centered human resource management, internal brand communication, and internal brand communities. Brand ideologies provide focus to employees because they incorporate the mission, vision, goals, and shared values of the brand. Internal brand management also includes the organizational structure and culture which guides employees to behave in a certain manner in order for them to deliver on the brand promise. Strong brand leadership has an impact on brand commitment because it leads to increased identification with brand values. When employees internalize the brand values it should increase their in-role and extra-role brand-building behavior. It is important for top management to make the mission and values of the organization clear to employees and live by these values by setting an example for the rest of the staff. Brand-centered Human Resource Management involves recruiting and selecting individuals with values that are in alignment with the organization's values. There are many other policies and procedures that fall under HRM, including training and development as well as internal communication. They need to work closely with the marketing department in order to deliver brand-centered communication and training. Internal brand communication is essential for employees and must be aligned with external communication because employees are exposed to both. Du Preez and Bendixen (2015) found that internal brand communications is the most significant contributor of internal branding. Internal brand communities are physical or virtual brand communities within an organization that could lead to employee identification with the brand. Social networking sites enable employees to add value to the brand.

According to Du Preez, Bendixen, and Abratt (2017), there are two forms of service behaviors that employees can exhibit; in-role and extra-role behaviors. In-role behaviors are specified in job descriptions and extra-role behaviors are discretionary in nature. This extra-role behavior has led to the concept of brand citizenship behavior in internal brand management. The dimensions of brand citizenship behavior include helping behavior, sportsmanship, self-brand development and brand endorsement. A study by Porricelli, Yurova, Abratt, and Bendixen (2014) demonstrates that by increasing effective internal brand management, retailers will increase brand citizenship behavior.

Conclusion

This chapter discusses two important elements of strategic marketing, the corporate brand and internal brand management. The corporate brand reflects the organization and its values to stakeholders. The characteristics of corporate brands are highlighted and the advantages of a corporate brand are discussed. Internal brand management is highlighted and the key roles employees play in an organization in brand building are discussed.

References

Aaker, D. (2004). Leveraging the corporate brand. *California Management Review*, 46(3), 6–18.

Abratt, R. and Kleyn, N. (2012). Corporate identity, corporate branding and corporate reputations: reconciliation and integration. *European Journal of Marketing*, 46(7/8), 1048–1063.

Balmer, J. and Gray, E. (2003). Corporate brands: what are they? What of them? *European Journal of Marketing*, 37(7/8), 972–997.

Du Preez, R. and Bendixen, M.T. (2015). The impact of internal brand management on employee job satisfaction, brand commitment and intention to stay. *International Journal of Brand Marketing*, 33(1), 78–91.

Du Preez, R., Bendixen, M.T., and Abratt, R. (2017). The behavioral consequences of internal brand management among frontline employees. *Journal of Product and Brand Management*, 26(3), 251–261.

Porricelli, M., Yurova, Y., Abratt, R., and Bendixen, M. (2014). Antecedents of brand citizenship behavior in retailing. *Journal of Retailing and Consumer Services*, 21, 745–752.

Saleem, F.Z. and Iglesias, O. (2016). Mapping the domain of the fragmented field of internal branding. *Journal of Product and Brand Management*, 25(1), 43–57.

Cadillac: the battle to recapture the luxury car market

When Johan de Nysschen was asked to lead Cadillac, General Motors' (GM) luxury brand, he was skeptical. After all, he was having great success at Infiniti growing the company's profitability and developing the Japanese brand. He wondered why he should join an automaker which despite aggressive efforts could not make a significant impact on the luxury car industry.

De Nysschen knew Cadillac needed to go through major changes if it wanted to grow and regain its relevance. Thus, he spent many hours on the phone talking to GM President Dan Ammann before he accepted the position; he made sure that GM would be willing and able to provide Cadillac with the resources necessary to make the changes the company desperately needed (Welch, 2015). Because GM depended on Cadillac to drive its future profit growth, it agreed to de Nysschen's conditions. And so, de Nysschen was appointed CEO of Cadillac in July 2014.

When he took over, Cadillac's new CEO expected to find a brand with no clear direction and limited resources. However, what he encountered surprised him more than he thought. The number of people in his product planning, marketing, and sales teams were less than optimal. In fact, very few were dedicated to Cadillac.

In addition, he was baffled to find out that German automakers, the competitors Cadillac wanted to topple, were not used as points of reference when developing product and marketing strategies. The brand was also suffering from deep-rooted image problems and declining sales, issues that needed immediate attention. This is when he knew he had a great challenge in front of him.

Thankfully, GM kept true to its word. It budgeted $12 billion to be used through 2020 to overhaul the Cadillac brand. As part of the changes, Cadillac's headquarters were moved to Manhattan and dedicated teams of marketers, engineers, product planners, and designers were hired to help make the brand relevant again.

Furthermore, plans were made to develop eight new car models, Cadillac's logo was enhanced, and a new advertising campaign was created to convey a new and improved brand image. Roughly one year after assuming his role as Cadillac's CEO, de Nysschen sat in his new SoHo corner office looking out the window. He wondered whether his efforts would be enough to put Cadillac back on the radar of luxury car buyers. Would Cadillac's new and redesigned models appeal to Millennials and Generation X buyers? Could the new brand positioning and advertising campaign create a brand image strong enough to compete with the likes of BMW and Mercedes-Benz? Could he and his team bring the former American icon back to greatness?

The automotive industry

The automotive industry faced great challenges during the global recession that began at the end of 2007. During this time, automakers around the globe endured declining revenues due to weak sales. The overall automotive industry is dependent on consumer spending, employment rates, financing rates, government regulations, and oil prices, which make it vulnerable to economic and political changes. However, as conditions began to improve in 2009, the auto industry started to recover from the economic crisis. Thanks to improving economies, the decline of interest rates, and the rise in consumer confidence, car sales started to pick up. Generating $1.1 trillion in revenue in the U.S. alone in 2014, which translated into 54 million new and used units sold, the global car industry enjoyed record-breaking growth from 2009 through 2014 (Eisenstein, 2014). Analysts expected sales and profits to continue growing through 2020, with most of the growth fueled by emerging economies like China and India which enjoyed rapid economic growth and increases in consumers' income (Mohr et al., 2013).

Technological trends

Since the emergence of the automotive industry in the 1880s, the automobile has under gone several changes. From the inside out, many of its features changed throughout the years as the industry responded to consumers' needs and aligned with the innovation and advances of the field. The twenty-first century, especially, has been one of the most relevant times for this industry as technology became a necessity for most people and the driving force behind efficiency and competitive advantages.

Since the early 2000s, hybridization became a prominent area of development. The hybrid vehicle became an important alternative due to the changes in government regulations for motor vehicles. Legislation limiting emissions of fuel-generated gases propelled by environmental concerns have pushed technological advances forward (Albulescu, Dascalu, and Niculescu, 2015). This has caused the competition amongst manufacturers to increase, starting a race to produce cleaner and more efficient vehicles. According to a KPMG report (2014), many premium car manufacturers decided to introduce hybrid engines in higher-end models. Some of the pioneers in this concept included the Mercedes S500, BMWi8, and Lexus CT200h and GS450h, which transformed the utilitarian look of the first hybrids. The hybrid cars also opened a door for the idea of e-cars, which have grown in popularity in both luxury and nonluxury segments. Electric vehicles represent an opportunity to reduce carbon use and global warming by reducing emissions. This trend began to take place worldwide, with the Leaf and Volt models from Nissan and Chevrolet respectively leading the movement in the nonluxury sector. In addition, vehicles such as the Porsche Panamera E-Hybrid, the Audi R8 e-Tron, and the Tesla Model S demonstrated that power and luxury did not have to be compromised to get efficiency, but that all characteristics could happen at the same time.

A trend in connectivity also encouraged automobile manufactures to connect with technology companies, engineers, designers, and dealers in order to create data and deliver a product that would lead to customer loyalty and profits. As a result, digitalization became an important player, with vehicles becoming dependent on software to meet customers' expectations. In-vehicle interactive features started to include internet connection, smartphone syncing functions, a series of help sensors, and the collection of data to offer a more personalized, safe, and efficient experience to each driver. This concept generated the idea of "self-driving vehicles," which could increase in availability and popularity in the near future (Albulescu, Dascalu, and Niculescu, 2015). Totally autonomous vehicles are not expected to be seen on the road until 2020 (Albulescu, Dascalu, and Niculescu, 2015).

Population and demographic trends

Car sales have been positively affected by worldwide population growth, posing a great opportunity for car manufacturers in the U.S., Western Europe, and Japan as industrialization and incomes rise around the world. The global population is expected to increase by 38 percent in the next decades, going from 6.9 billion in 2010 to 9.6 billion in 2050 (Albulescu, Dascalu, and Niculescu, 2015). Hand in hand with urbanization is the mobility trend that Millennials have brought upon the market. With cities becoming more congested over time, mobility as a service has become a reliable option that this generation has started to strongly rely upon. Studies showed that Millennials "are more in favor of ride-sharing and other services such as Uber" than they are interested in buying cars (Castillo, 2016). These unusual car buying habits have made Millennials a difficult demographic to reach, posing a challenge to manufacturers.

Although Millennials are often believed not to have the financial capital to buy new cars, "a study by J.D. Power & Associates showed that Millennials bought 27 percent of the new cars in 2015, making them the second-largest car buying group after baby boomers" (Castillo, 2016). Industry leaders recognize that both Millennials and Generation X buyers would make up 80 percent of car buyers between 2020 and 2025, showing the importance of these consumer segments for all car manufacturers moving forward.

The luxury car segment

The luxury car segment grew by 6.4 percent in 2014, growing faster than the overall automotive industry (Wernle, 2015). This growth was fueled by more flexible and appealing financing options as manufacturers and dealerships sought to open the market for as many buyers as possible. The sales of luxury autos were also positively affected by increases in income with the end of the recession and the affordability provided by leases; nearly half of all new luxury vehicles were leased (Plache, 2014). According to IHS Automotive, the luxury car segment was 12.7 percent of the automotive industry in 2016, growing from 11.4 percent in 2014 (Wernle, 2015). Therefore, the stakes for aspiring luxury brands were high. Although the luxury segment accounted for only a small fraction of overall auto sales, this category made up half of the industry's profits due to its high margins (Ulrich, 2015).

In 2014, the luxury category also experienced a shift in consumer preferences. Thanks to lowering gas prices and increased efficiency of newer models, consumer started to trade compact cars for small SUVs. In fact, compact luxury SUVs and small luxury SUVs increased 25.8 percent and 19 percent respectively (Statista, 2015). When asked why they were changing cars for small SUVs, consumers said that small SUVs "are a desirable size, but concede very little in efficiency and are comparably priced with models in other popular segments" (Aubernon, 2015). Small SUVs provided a new middle for consumers.

As in many other sectors of the automotive industry, luxury vehicles also entered in the electric vehicles category. According to CBC News, "U.S. subsidies for EVs [Electric Vehicles] probably helped drive the new luxury electric car programs" (Burns, 2015). As a result, electric car buyers started to experience a wider range of options available to choose from as Tesla was no longer the only make offering this alternative. Porsche, Audi, and others were already fighting for their share in this growing segment of the market.

Competition in the luxury segment

As of 2015, there were a large number of brands competing in the automotive industry worldwide, but Cadillac was concerned with the brands within the luxury car segment. Over the years, the company had been losing market share to major luxury brands such as BMW, Mercedes-Benz, Lexus, and Audi, which led the category (Nilsson, 2015). It was important for de Nysschen, Cadillac's CEO, to evaluate the strategies and success points of Cadillac's competitors to have a better course of action for success in the luxury automobile market. BMW, Mercedes-Benz, Lexus, and Audi enjoyed the biggest portion of the U.S. luxury segment, with the top three accounting for more than half of all the sales within the category (Wernle, 2015). BMW, Mercedes-Benz, and Lexus had been the top three brands in the U.S. luxury market since 1998, with Audi being a close follower in fourth place (Wernle, 2015). In addition, in 2015, BMW sold close to 2 million new units worldwide, while Cadillac only sold 250,000 units (DeBord, 2016). In fact, in 2015, Lexus, BMW, and Mercedes-Benz sold more new units each in the U.S. alone than Cadillac did in the entire world (IHS Market, n.d.). Cadillac was not even among the top ten best-selling luxury cars in the first quarter of 2015.

Over the years, Cadillac's rivals developed multiple product lines, a strategy that was key to their success (Levin, 2015). Looking at the variety of models of the top brands in 2015, it was evident that the four most successful brands stood out in comparison to the others. While Cadillac only had 8 models in 2015, BMW had 35, Audi had 29, and Lexus and Mercedes-Benz both had 19 models each (Wernle, 2015). In addition to a great array of models, brands like BMW, Lexus, and Audi separated product lines according to sizes, body styles, and engines, which prevented customers from defecting to rival luxury brands (Levin, 2015). Ludwig Willisch, CEO of BMW of North America, said, "We don't ever want our customers to grow bored" (Levin, 2015). The variety of products allowed the customers of the top brands to have multiple options when making the decision to purchase a car, which helped them maintain a competitive edge over Cadillac and other competitors in the category.

Another key point of success for Cadillac's competitors, especially its German rivals, was their highly regarded brand image. Industry experts agreed that German brands "sell not just on design or performance, but also on their badges and status" (Ulrich, 2015). German luxury automakers like BMW, Audi, and Mercedes-Benz have consistent brand elements that are recognized all over the world. BMW's emblem, which incorporates the Bavarian state colors, as well as Mercedes-Benz's three-pointed star emblem and Audi's four interlaced rings were symbols of prestige in every corner of the globe. Furthermore, these brands counted with impressive levels of brand loyalty. In 2014, Mercedes-Benz had the highest brand loyalty level in the luxury category with 58 percent, and BMW was second with 53 percent, which reflected their strong residual values; Cadillac ranked seventh with 44 percent customer loyalty. For these reasons, despite strong competition from Japan's Lexus, de Nysschen was focused on his German counterparts.

General Motors: the parent company

Organizational and strategic issues

General Motors (GM) was founded in 1908 by President Pierre DuPont and CEO Billy Durant. Durant was famous for being a risk taker and a dreamer. He was known for being driven by instincts and not always a prudent manager, which eventually led to him being replaced by Alfred Sloan. In 1920, Sloan presented an organizational chart where he suggested a new organizational structure for GM. Under this structure, top management would hold strong central financial controls and division managers would have the freedom to make their own decisions. Eventually, Sloan's plan was enacted, becoming the basis of modern corporate America. "The premise of Sloan's organizational plan was decentralized operations with coordinated financial controls" (LaReau, 2008). This organizational structure worked until GM lost its leadership in the market in the late 1970s. Inconsistent objectives and overlapping market segments throughout divisions plagued the company with problems (The Week, 2009). This led GM to tighten controls and increase centralization of decisions in an effort to remain competitive.

GM lost its direction in the last few decades of the 1900s due to managerial and cultural issues within the company. In the early 1980s, GM was led by its most notorious CEO, Roger Smith. He combined six of GM's distinctive car brands into two generic groups following a ruthless cost-cutting strategy aimed to achieve more efficient production (Wilson, 2013). Under this strategy, GM's car brands, which were supposed to be targeted at different market segments and had particular characteristics they were known for, started being manufactured with interchangeable parts. This killed demand for GM's entire portfolio, and the brands' design heritage was lost (Wilson, 2013). All cars started to look alike; designs were a bland and a homogenous mix of several brands combined. In addition, in 2009, GM went bankrupt after 101 years in the business, which was followed by a $49.5 billion government bailout (Cohan, 2014).

Overcoming these setbacks was a challenge for the American car manufacturer.

Due to its leadership, which tended to ignore competitive threats and manage in a bubble, GM's organizational culture suffered greatly. An isolated approach to business and a fear amongst its employees to speak up propelled GM into a massive dark hole. Mary Barra found herself in this chaos when she became CEO in 2014. She recognized the magnitude of the company's dysfunction when she was tasked with the challenge of fixing the public's perception of GM after the infamous ignition switch fiasco in 2014, which caused the company to recall vehicles worldwide. However, with shifts in organizational structure and strategies spearheaded by Barra, the company took steps to regain its leadership in the market. Among these changes was Cadillac's company reinvention.

GM and the luxury car segment

To ensure the survival of the company, GM recognized that it needed to give the luxury market the importance it merited. Thus, it decided to turn its attention to Cadillac, its only luxury brand. Experts have said that without adequate sales of luxury cars, which yielded high profit margins, "G.M. will struggle to fund critical technology and the low-margin economy cars that it must sell to meet rising fuel economy standards" (Ulrich, 2015). With tightening emission regulations that could push production costs up, GM would be less able to rely on just the high truck margins to stay profitable (Welch, 2015). Cadillac provided roughly 30 percent of the company's global profits.

Things were not as easy as they seemed, however. Cadillac had problems of its own, many of which had been caused by GM's negligence. Throughout the years, GM erred by giving its luxury line little importance and differentiation within the company due to its low sales. GM produced 13 brands in 37 countries, Chevrolet, Buick, GMC and Cadillac being the most known in the U.S. (Automotive Database, n.d.). It was typical for brands that yielded the highest sales to take priority. As a result, GM did not equip Cadillac with the resources necessary to compete with its German and Japanese competitors, exemplifying GM's insular management structure and lack of attention to the external environment.

Cadillac's history and the start of its uphill battle in the luxury category

Cadillac is one of the oldest car manufacturers in the United States and the world. Founded from the ruins of the Henry Ford Company in Detroit 1902 by William Murphy, Lemuel Bowen, and Henry Leland, Cadillac established a brand reputation of luxury, innovation, and quality from its very beginnings and quickly became a market leader in the luxury car segment (History, n.d.). After seven prosperous years in the business, GM bought Cadillac for $4.5 million in 1909. It became GM's prestige division in charge of producing commercial and institutional vehicles (Global Cars Brands, 2015). During the first few decades of the twentieth century, Cadillac enjoyed tremendous success by pioneering several automotive technologies. The company introduced "the first car to ever be built with a closed frame body-style" in 1910 (Global Cars Brands, 2015), it introduced the world's first successful electric self-starter in 1912, and in 1954, "it was the first automaker to provide power steering and automatic windshield washers as standard equipment on all its vehicles" (History, n.d.). For years, Cadillac was seen as aspirational and cool, which made it "the most iconic American car brand this side of the Mustang" (Geier, 2014).

Things started to change for Cadillac in the late 1970s, however. The brand and the rest of the American luxury automakers were taken by surprise by the changing consumer preferences in the category. John Grettenberger, the general manager of Cadillac at the time, said in an interview with *The New York Times*: "We didn't recognize as early as some other parts of the world that the market for luxury vehicles was changing in terms of what it wanted in addition to the traditional elements of comfort, image and prestige" (Holusha, 1984). Despite Cadillac's accomplishments for most of the early 1900s, its top-of-the-market position was challenged in the 1980s by the German luxury automakers (History, n.d.). Emphasizing engineering advances and top-of-the-line performance, the European imports started to chip away at Cadillac's leading market share. By the time Cadillac reacted to the competitive threats, German luxury brands had already gained a following from the young Baby Boomers who, at the time, where in their 30s and 40s; meanwhile, Cadillac's average customers were in their mid to late 50s (Holusha, 1984). To make things worse, in an attempt to compete with Mercedes-Benz, BMW, and Audi, which were taking over the growing compact luxury segment, Cadillac rushed to introduce the Cimarron in 1982, which backfired greatly on the company (Ernst, 2013). The Cimarron provided neither the performance of the European luxury imports nor the quality and look of Cadillac, tarnishing Cadillac's already eroding brand image. In 2007, the Cimarron was named by *Time* magazine "one of the 50-worst cars ever built" (Seetharaman and Klayman, 2012). Cadillac's inability to attract younger consumers, coupled by the failure of the Cimarron and other later projects, initiated an image problem that Cadillac is still trying to come back from.

Cadillac in the twenty-first century

Since the German luxury automakers entrenched themselves in the hearts of American consumers, especially the younger generations, Cadillac has had a tough time regaining its prestige and market leadership. In 2014, Cadillac's share of luxury autos was 9.1 percent, well behind BMW's 18 percent, Mercedes' 17.5 percent, and Lexus' 16.5 percent (Mie, 2015). In fact, Cadillac sales in 2014 fell 6.5 percent, making it one of only three luxury brands to lose ground (Welch, 2015). Despite design improvements, Cadillac's sales were slow and declining in a market segment where sales were on the rise and where German competitors were breaking one record after another. Furthermore, "Cadillac's residual values were among the lowest in the luxury segment, ranking near the bottom with Ford Motor Co's Lincoln and Jaguar" (Lienert and Klayman, 2015). This resulted in Cadillac having to close a Michigan assembly plant in 2014 to try to reduce inventories; even after reopening six weeks later, the plant had to operate with a reduced schedule (Ulrich, 2015). To increase the demand for Cadillac vehicles, the company also had to offer subsidized leases, discounted financing, rebates, and price cuts (Lienert and Klayman, 2015).

Cadillac had made efforts to become a more powerful player in the luxury arena, but progress had stalled. The company redesigned its vehicles in 2012 to better compete with the German automakers. The reengineered Cadillac sedans were praised by critics and believed to have a sporty feel and handling similar to that of BMWs and Audis. In 2013, the CTS was named *Motor Trend's* car of the year, and the ATS compact car won North American Car of the Year at the Detroit auto show (Higgins, 2014). Thanks to product enhancements, Cadillac enjoyed sales growth in 2013, becoming the fastest-growing luxury brand in America. However, these results were short-lived. By August 2014, U.S. sales were down 4.7 percent, with the new CTS and ATS dropping 6 percent and 20 percent respectively (Burden, 2014b). Luxury buyers did not follow the buzz generated by Cadillac's new award-winning models, and the sedans did not move off the lots for long. The fact that they were priced anywhere from $50,000 to over $70,000 did not help the matter either. People just did not think a Cadillac commanded such premium prices. At this point, the only car Cadillac was selling successfully was the Escalade, the one Cadillac product that still carried some prestige. In August 2014, Escalade sales were up 23 percent year over year (Burden, 2014b).

Cadillac's problems stemmed from several issues that had been affecting the company for years. First of all, the brand suffered from an image problem. "There was a time when Cadillac symbolized the American dream, a status symbol and a coveted choice by movie stars like Elvis Presley," but that was no longer the case (Mie, 2015). According to a San Diego consulting firm called Strategic Vision Inc., Cadillac appealed to an older demographic, with the average customer hovering around 60 years of age; that is 15 years older than the average BMW owner (Welch, 2015). Despite its heritage and high level of brand awareness, Cadillac did not attract Millennials or Generation X customers, which were the demographic segments that would be fueling the luxury car sales during the upcoming decades. These customers were "looking for a more modern, progressive, contemporary expression of luxury" (DeBord, 2016). However, they viewed Cadillac as a car their parents or grandparents would buy and not as a brand they aspired to own, much less pay large amounts of money for. This posed a major problem for the company's long-term growth plans. As Kelly Blue Book's automotive analyst Tom Libby said to USA Today: "Once you get labelled as [a brand] associated with the older buyer, you're really in a bind with younger buyers" (Frohlich, 2014).

Not only was the brand associated with older generations, but a few years ago the Escalade was adopted as a symbol of the hip-hop culture. This further confused the brand's identity in the minds of consumers. Cadillac lacked the solid image and positioning that its German counterparts possessed. American car brands in general did not carry the same perception of high quality as their imported rivals, especially in the luxury segment. As a result, Cadillac had not been able to gain the worldwide recognition that its German and Japanese counterparts had. As mentioned in an article, "while an American Cadillac owner will happily consider a BMW or a Mercedes, drivers of those famous German cars just won't put a Cadillac on their shopping list" (Lienert and Klayman, 2015).

Another issue hindering Cadillac's success was GM's organizational structure. Under GM's centralized system, Cadillac did not have a dedicated product planning or marketing team. The employees in these departments worked for not just Cadillac, but also for Chevrolet, Buick, and GMC (Welch, 2015). Moreover, engineers and product planners did not use the German automakers as reference when designing upcoming Cadillac models. When comparing engine options for a future model, for example, product planners looked at charts of motors used by Chevy rivals, not Cadillac rivals (Welch, 2015). This left the brand unable to compete efficiently with its German and Japanese counterparts in the luxury segment. Cadillac constantly got overshadowed in GM's automotive empire, where brands that produced higher volume sales, such as Chevy, received the bulk of the resources from the parent company. GM had a history of making half-hearted efforts to help its prestige division. In 2000, GM provided Cadillac with $4.3 billion, which helped the brand gain momentum with the Escalade SUV and the first CTS sedan. However, after the increase in gasoline prices and the onset of the financial crisis in the United States in 2005, GM reduced its spending, which halted any progress Cadillac could have had (Welch, 2015).

Cadillac also counted with a limited product portfolio. Cadillac only had 8 models to sell, whereas German competitors like BMW and Audi sold 35 and 29 different models respectively (Wernle, 2015). In addition, Cadillac was not well equipped to meet the demand for luxury crossover SUVs, a segment that was experiencing exponential growth. In an interview with The New York Times de Nysschen lamented: "How is it possible that we have so few crossovers from this iconic American luxury brand?

The Germans have more than I can count on two hands" (Ulrich, 2015). As of 2015, Cadillac had only one crossover SUV to compete with, the Cadillac SRX.

Paving the road to change

Bringing Johan de Nysschen on board as Cadillac's CEO was just the first step of a sequence of changes that GM was committed to making in order to help its prestige brand recover its status. De Nysschen brought with him more than 20 years of experience in the luxury car industry. He worked for Audi from 1993 through 2012, where he held several management positions. De Nysschen was general manager of Audi South Africa, president of Audi Japan, and president of Audi America, where he helped the brand increase its U.S. sales by 42 percent during his term (Higgins, 2014). Then, in July 2012, he became president of Infiniti where he laid down the foundation for the brand's entry into China and helped increase sales by 30 percent during the first half of 2014 (White and Murphy, 2014). Because of his successful track record, de Nysschen was recruited by Dan Ammann, GM's president, in July 2014 (General Motors, 2015b). As part of the business arrangement, GM gave de Nysschen full authority to reorganize Cadillac and provided the company with an investment of $12 billion to overhaul the brand. This sizable investment, which was more than a quarter of the sum being spent on new models companywide, was to be spent in a period of five years, from 2015 through 2020 (Welch, 2015).

One of the first things de Nysschen did as CEO was relocating Cadillac's headquarters from Detroit to Manhattan during the second quarter of 2015. This was done in an effort to move the brand away from the shadows of GM's other car brands and gain more autonomy from the parent company. De Nysschen justified his plan saying that "by changing geography, you force a change" (Ulrich, 2015). In Detroit, there were few product planning and marketing employees dedicated to Cadillac's tasks. This personnel, was for the most part, spread thin working for Chevy, Buick, GMC, and Cadillac (Welch, 2015). He told Detroit News: "We want to put a little bit of distance between Cadillac and the rest of the General Motors entity so that we can begin to put together a team that is able to give 100 percent mindshare to meeting the challenges of the premium market" (Burden, 2014b). De Nysschen also hoped that establishing the company's headquarters in Manhattan would help attract young and talented employees who were otherwise difficult to entice to work in Detroit. Furthermore, being the epicenter of global trends, New York City would hopefully help Cadillac's team to better understand the sophisticated lifestyles of the customers Cadillac wished to target.

De Nysschen hired 40 people in New York who would be solely dedicated to Cadillac. The team included engineers, designers, product planners, and marketers. He expected to have 150 people working at the new headquarters by the end of 2015 (Welch, 2015). Many of these employees would come from Detroit, but the majority would be new hires (Burden, 2014b). De Nysschen wanted to make sure to bring in people with fresh and innovative ideas and to establish a culture where taking risks was encouraged and failures were accepted. "If you punish setbacks, you stifle innovation," he said (Ulrich, 2015). Cadillac's CEO wanted a cohesive team with consolidated leadership.

With the $12 billion provided by GM, Cadillac focused on improving the quality, performance, and technology of all its products. Design also took center stage; efforts were made to give Cadillac cars a personality with sleeker and more sophisticated looks. As de Nysschen put it, the strategy of the manufacturer was "built around producing the type of car Cadillac drivers have never seen before. A car driven, not only by advances in traditional automotive technology, but also by connectivity" (Geier, 2014). The company also planned to add eight new car models to its lineup by 2020 in order to seize market opportunities, give customers more options, and better compete with the variety of cars offered by competitors. In first quarter of 2016, de Nysschen arranged to introduce the XT5, a midsize crossover, to replace the existing SRX and keep up with what buyers were asking for. The XT5 would follow the CT6, a full-size luxury flagship similar to the Mercedes S-Class, Audi 8, and the BMW 7 series. There were also three additional SUV models in the pipeline as well as three other cars, including one model bigger than the CT6 and a convertible. All new models were intended to target several different market segments, especially Millennials and Generation X buyers (Ulrich, 2015). The existing CTS, ATS, and XTS models were scheduled to be discontinued at the end of their seven-year life cycle, being replaced by the newer cars in Cadillac's growing product portfolio (Eisenstein, 2015).

Expanding Cadillac globally was also among de Nysschen's priorities, as it could eventually drive profit growth for the brand in upcoming decades. Cadillac's plan was to make designs more globally appealing, yet instantly recognizable. China, the Middle East, and Russia would be the focus of the growth efforts through 2020. De Nysschen's goal was to establish China as a second sales volume hub for the brand behind the United States (Burden, 2015). China held great potential for Cadillac as it was "the world's largest market for new cars and the industry's brightest hope for the last 15 years" (Bradsher, 2016). Expansion to Europe was part of a future growth plan beyond 2020 for when Cadillac had more status and was better prepared to face the German automakers in their backyard.

Helping de Nysschen on this journey was Uwe Ellinghaus, a former BMW marketing executive, who was named Cadillac's chief marketing officer (CMO) in November 2013 (Higgins, 2014). Having led BMW as well as Mini and Rolls-Royce's marketing initiatives, he had many years of experience in the luxury segment. Thus, GM put him in charge of creating a consistent image for Cadillac around the world. With de Nysschen's support, Ellinghaus set in motion a plan to redefine Cadillac's identity and to put the brand in a position where it could rival German and Japanese luxury automakers.

Rebranding Cadillac

Cadillac's brand overhaul had several components. It included a change in the products' naming scheme, a change in the brand's logo, and a revolutionary advertising campaign to reposition the brand and appeal to younger and more diverse consumers.

Alphanumeric naming scheme

Following cues from Mercedes-Benz, Audi, Infiniti, and BMW, Cadillac started using an alphanumeric naming convention with the introduction of its new sedan and crossover models, the CT6 and XT5, in 2015 and 2016 respectively (Lienert, 2014). The changes, according to de Nysschen and Ellinghaus, were meant to give clues to consumers about what each model was. CT would be used for sedans and XT for the SUVs; numbers would identify the size and position of the models. Ellinghaus said that the names of existing sedan models would be kept and slowly phased out as the cars were redesigned over the years. The decision was made to preserve the name of the Escalade (Burden, 2014a).

Logo redesign

Customer feedback showed that the brand's logo felt old and outdated. The wreath around the logo almost always tested negative in consumer surveys and focus groups (Meiners and Colias, 2013). And so, with the introduction of the 2015 year models, Cadillac did away with the wreath. The change was intended to streamline the logo and match the sleeker designs of the company's new cars.

Daring greatly: brand repositioning

Cadillac wanted to be the premium American luxury car brand. De Nysschen's team wanted the company to be perceived on the same level as its German counterparts. To do this, however, the brand had to gain acceptance from the younger generations who had grown up thinking of a Cadillac as their grandfather's road yacht. In order to be able to grow, Cadillac had to appeal to Generation X and Millennials as well as shed its outdated image. It also had to attract a more diverse customer base. Thus, Ellinghaus launched the "Dare Greatly" campaign to reposition Cadillac as a sophisticated, modern, provocative, and technologically driven brand that is different from anything else in the market. In Ellinghaus' words, "Cadillac wants to attract buyers who are passionate, entrepreneurial, and unwilling to settle for an obvious choice" regardless of their background, gender, or age (Mie, 2015). He added: "This is for people who simply dare great things." The campaign made no mention of luxury and focused very little on the features offered by the cars. Instead, it emphasized the lifestyle of its target market and the aspirational aspect that the brand now stood for. Ads used taglines like: "Only those who dare move the world forward." They showed several prominent leaders in different industries as well as spokespeople that were early in their careers and that were between 15 and 25 years of age. In addition, many of these spokespeople were women and had visible multi-cultural backgrounds (Castillo, 2016).

The "Dare Greatly" campaign was launched during the 2015 Oscars, where Cadillac bought four commercial spots. The goal was to associate the brand with the glamour represented by the event. Besides TV, the marketing efforts also included large online components, including search ads, social media, a brand new website, and a "Dare Greatly" landing page. Print advertising on lifestyle magazines instead of on automotive publications was part of the plan too, as "young people are less interested in technical details" (Mie, 2015). Cadillac also pursued out-of-home displays and creative partnerships to show off the company's new cars in unconventional places, such as inside Saks Fifth Avenue stores in New York City. There was no call to action on any of the advertisements or promotions. Ellinghaus hoped that the tactics would be intriguing enough to entice consumers to go online and learn more about the cars, eventually driving them to the showrooms. With this new campaign, Cadillac wanted to sell an image, a status, not just a car.

Will Cadillac's turnaround efforts be enough?

GM and Johan de Nysschen were betting on their new marketing strategies to bring the Cadillac brand back to greatness. De Nysschen's goal was to make Cadillac "a powerhouse global luxury brand that will command the respect of its peers" (Welch, 2015). He wanted to attract younger car buyers and carve out a fresh identity for Cadillac that would help the company grow not only domestically but also globally. However, changing consumer perceptions and taking on well-established brands like Mercedes-Benz and BMW were long and grueling tasks. Furthermore, the threat of an economic downturn was always lurking, especially with the increase in political and social unrest around the world. Gas prices were also volatile, and significant changes could halt the growth of the SUV segment. Finally, the growth of many international economies had stalled. The Chinese economy had slowed down to its lowest rate in 25 years, exports in the country were falling, and pollution had forced the implementation of policies limiting the number of new cars that could be registered (Bradsher, 2016).

It was still too soon to tell whether de Nysschen's strategies would move the needle for Cadillac in the luxury segment. It could take years to see the results, and stakes were high. Still, the Cadillac team was hopeful. Ellinghaus told Ad Age: "Hopefully in 20 years we [will] sit here together and 'Dare Greatly' will [have] become, as I call it, the ultimate driving machine" (Mie, 2015). But, as de Nysschen looked at the New York City landscape from his office on the 16th floor of a SoHo building during the fourth quarter of 2015, he questioned whether Cadillac's turnaround plans would be enough. Will Cadillac succeed and rival its German and Japanese competitors in the luxury category? Will GM be able to depend on Cadillac to drive the company's profits in the next decades? Will the brand be able to attract younger buyers and successfully expand globally? The verdict was still out.

References

Albulescu, S., Dascalu, O., and Niculescu, A. (2015). Trends in the automotive industry. FAIMA Business & Management Journal, 3(1), 38–49.

Aubernon, C. (2015, March 27). Compact SUVs gain popularity at the midsize, compact cars. The Truth about Cars. Retrieved March 20, 2018, from www.thetruthaboutcars.com/2015/03/compact-suvs-gain-popularity-expense-midsize-compact-cars/

Automotive Database. (n.d.). General Motors. Automotive Database. Retrieved March 20, 2018, from www.autocarbase.com/2015/09/general-motors.html

Bradsher, K. (2016, March 28). Automakers expanding in China may soon face weakening demand. The New York Times. Retrieved March 20, 2018, from www.nytimes.com/2016/03/29/business/international/china-automakers-cars-demand.html

Burden, M. (2014a, September 24). Big Cadillac named CT6, starts new naming strategy. The Detroit News. Retrieved March 20, 2018, from www.detroitnews.com/story/business/autos/general-motors/2014/09/24/gm-cadillac-name/16169489/

Burden, M. (2014b, September 29). Cadillac brand to move headquarters to New York. *The Detroit News*. Retrieved March 20, 2018, from www.detroitnews.com/ story/business/autos/general-motors/2014/09/23/gms-cadillac-brand-open- headquarters-new-york/16084371/

Burden, M. (2015, August 11). Cadillac pushes back Europe expansion plans. *The Detroit News*. Retrieved March 20, 2018, from www.detroitnews.com/story/ business/autos/general-motors/2015/08/11/cadillac-delays-europe-expansion/ 31479997/

Burns, M. (2015, September 28). New luxury cars trend: going electric. *Benzinga*. Retrieved March 20, 2018, from www.benzinga.com/15/09/5870040/ new-luxury-cars-trend-going-electric

Castillo, M. (2016, March 4). Cadillac dares to reach a younger consumer. *CNBC*. Retrieved March 20, 2018, from www.cnbc.com/2016/03/04/cadillac-dares-to- reach-a-younger-consumer.html

Cohan, P. (2014, June 6). Six hard steps to fix GM's culture. *Forbes*. Retrieved March 20, 2018, from www.forbes.com/sites/petercohan/2014/06/06/six-hard-steps-to- fix-gms-culture/#74512fa358ee

DeBord, M. (2016, January 21). Cadillac has a bold plan for the future – now it just needs the right cars. *Business Insider*. Retrieved March 20, 2018, from www. businessinsider.com/cadillac-is-being-reinvented-2016-1

Eisenstein, P. (2014, December 19). U.S. auto industry generates record $1.1 trillion in 2014 sales. *The Detroit Bureau*. Retrieved March 20, 2018, from www.thedetroitbureau.com/2014/12/ u-s-auto-industry-generates-record-1-1-trillion-in-2014-sales/

Eisenstein, P. (2015, April 8). Cadillac planning to replace ATS, CTS, XTS models. *The Detroit Bureau*. Retrieved March 20, 2018, from www.thedetroitbureau.com/2015/ 04/cadillac-planning-to-replace-ats-cts-xts-models/

Ernst, K. (2013, November 4). Lost cars of the 1980s – Cadillac Cimarron. *Hemmings Daily*. Retrieved March 20, 2018, from http://blog.hemmings.com/index.php/2013/ 11/04/lost-cars-of-the-1980s-cadillac-cimarron/

Frohlich, T. (2014, October 4). Cars with the oldest buyers. *USA Today*. Retrieved March 20, 2018, from www.usatoday.com/story/money/cars/2014/10/04/24-7-wall-st- cars-oldest-buyers/16587437/

Geier, B. (2014, October 29). Cadillac wants to take back luxury. *Forbes*. Retrieved March 20, 2018, from http://fortune.com/2014/10/29/ cadillac-wants-to-take-back-luxury/

General Motors. (2015a). About our company. Retrieved March 20, 2018, from www. gm.com/company/company-overview.html

General Motors. (2015b). Leadership: Johan de Nysschen. Retrieved March 20, 2018, from www.gm.com/company/leadership/corporate-officers/johan-de-nysschen. html

Global Cars Brands. (2015, March 11). Cadillac logo, history timeline and latest models. *Global Cars Brands*. Retrieved March 20, 2018, from www.globalcarsbrands.com/ cadillac-logo-history-and-models/

Higgins, T. (2014, July 11). GM names Infiniti CEO DeNysschen president of Cadillac. *Bloomberg: Business*. Retrieved March 20, 2018, from www.bloomberg.com/news/ articles/2014-07-11/gm-names-infiniti-ceo-de-nysschen-president-of-cadillac

History. (n.d.). General Motors buys Cadillac. *History.com*. Retrieved March 20, 2018, from www.history.com/this-day-in-history/general-motors-buys-cadillac

Holusha, J. (1984, November 1). Boom in luxury car imports. *The New York Times*. Retrieved March 20, 2018, from www.nytimes.com/1984/11/01/business/boom-in- luxury-car-imports.html?pagewanted=all

IHS Markit. (n.d.). Automotive. *IHS Markit*. Retrieved March 20, 2018, from https://ihsmarkit.com/industry/automotive.html

KPMG. (2014). Global Automotive Executive Survey. *KPMG*. Retrieved March 20, 2018, from https://home.kpmg.com/ru/en/home/media/press-releases/2014/02/kpmg-presents-global-automotive-executive-survey-2014.html

LaReau, J. (2008, September 14). After the frenetic Durant era, Sloan brought order to chaos. *AutoNews*. Retrieved March 20, 2018, from www.autonews.com/article/20080914/OEM02/309149952/after-the-frenetic-durant-era-sloan-brought-order-from-chaos

Levin, D. (2015, May 12). This is how BMW became the top selling luxury car company in the U.S. *Fortune*. Retrieved March 20, 2018, from http://fortune.com/2015/05/12/bmw-luxury-sales/

Lienert, P. (2014, September 24). GM's Cadillac adopts new naming scheme as part of brand overhaul. *Reuters*. Retrieved March 20, 2018, from www.reuters.com/article/us-gm-cadillac-idUSKCN0HJ2B020140924

Lienert, P. and Klayman, B. (2015, February 10). GM is having trouble getting luxury car buyers to look at Cadillac. *Business Insider*. Retrieved March 20, 2018, from www.businessinsider.com/r-exclusive-gms-barra-faces-roadblocks-in-rebuilding-cadillac-brand-2015-2

Meiners, J. and Colias, M. (2013, July 23). Cadillac plans to rest its laurels in logo redesign. *AutoNews*. Retrieved March 20, 2018, from www.autonews.com/article/20130723/RETAIL03/130729973/cadillac-plans-to-rest-its-laurels-in-logo-redesign

Mie, A. (2015, February 2015). Cadillac unveils new brand image on Oscars night. *Advertising Age*. Retrieved March 20, 2018, from http://adage.com/article/cmo-strategy/cadillac-unveils-brand-image-oscars-night/297182/

Mohr, D., Müller, N., Krieg, A. (2013). *The Road to 2020 and Beyond: What's Driving the Global Automotive Industry?* McKinsey & Company. Retrieved March 20, 2018, from www.McKinsey.com

Nilsson, J. (2015, February 13). Top 15 best-selling luxury car brands in the US. *The Richest*. Retrieved March 20, 2018, from www.therichest.com/rich-list/most-popular/top-15-best-selling-luxury-car-brands-in-the-us/?view=all

Plache, L. (2014). Autoeconomy trends: leasing goes mainstream. *Edmunds*. Retrieved March 20, 2018, from www.edmunds.com/industry-center/analysis/autoeconomy-trends-leasing-goes-mainstream.html

Seetharaman, D. and Klayman, B. (2012, January 8). GM challenges German brands with small Cadillac. *Reuters*. Retrieved March 20, 2018, from www.reuters.com/article/us-gm-cadillac-idUSTRE8070RF20120109

Statista. (2015). Luxury car sales growth in the United States in 2014, by category. *Statista*. Retrieved March 20, 2018, from www.statista.com/statistics/287760/luxury-vehicles-united-states-premium-vehicle-market-share/

The Week. (2009, June 11). The rise and fall of General Motors. *The Week*. Retrieved March 20, 2018, from http://theweek.com/articles/504619/rise-fall-general-motors

Ulrich, L. (2015, August 20). Cadillac has new boss, new address, and big plans. *The New York Times*. Retrieved March 20, 2018, from www.nytimes.com/2015/08/21/automobiles/cadillac-has-new-boss-new-address-and-big-plans-for-a-revival.html?_r=1

Welch, D. (2015, March 31). How a former Audi guy plans to spend $12 billion reviving Caddy. *Bloomberg: Business*. Retrieved March 20, 2018, from www.bloomberg.com/news/articles/2015-03-31/how-a-former-audi-guy-plans-to-spend-12-billion-reviving-caddy

Wernle, B. (2015, March 16). "Tier 2" luxury brands struggle to compete with elite Germans, Lexus. *Automotive News*. Retrieved March 20, 2018, from www.autonews.com/article/20150316/RETAIL01/303169995/tier-2-luxury-brands-struggle-to-compete-with-elite-germans-lexus

White, J. and Murphy, C. (2014, July 11). GM hires Infiniti chief de Nysschen to head Cadillac. *The Wall Street Journal*. Retrieved March 20, 2018, from www.wsj.com/articles/gm-hires-infiniti-chief-de-nysschen-to-head-cadillac-1405099203

Wilson, M. (2013, June 18). How Cadillac designed a comeback. *FastCo Design*. Retrieved March 20, 2018, from www.fastcodesign.com/1672830/how-cadillac-designed-a-comeback

Uber Technologies Inc.: managing the repercussions of #DeleteUber

Uber cofounders Travis Kalanick and Garrett Camp first envisioned the revolutionary ridesharing mobile app in December 2008. Kalanick and Camp were in Paris attending the LeWeb European technology conference, when they realized the complications in finding transportation to and from the event (Hartmans and McAlone, 2016). Upon returning to their hometown of San Francisco, Camp insisted on pursuing the idea of the on-demand car service and purchased the domain name UberCab.com. Originally, Camp hoped to provide a limo-service business. However, Kalanick eventually agreed to collaborate with Camp to create an on-demand black-car service. Kalanick later became the company's CEO (Swisher, 2014).

The initial UberCab engineers and employees sought to perfect Kalanick and Camp's vision before pushing it onto the App Store. Engineers worked on sign-up flow as well as integrated credit card payment systems. Employees also met and interviewed cab drivers to better understand the industry (Lashinsky, 2015).

The duo officially launched the prototype application in San Francisco during the summer of 2010. The service had a small operational structure with a handful of employees and few cars. Users would enter their credit-card information into the app, and were then able to request cars on-demand through their smartphones. The GPS function allowed drivers to find the users' locations. The cost was automatically charged on user's credit cards, with tipping already accounted for (Lashinsky, 2015).

In October of 2010, UberCab faced its first setback when San Francisco Municipal Transportation Agency, as well as California Public Utilities Commission, sent the company cease-and-desist orders. Both objected to UberCab's use of the word "cab" in its company name, since drivers were operating without taxi licenses. Despite the opposition from local officials, UberCab continued operations and changed its name from UberCab to Uber. In order to do so, the domain name Uber.com was purchased from Universal Music Group (Lashinsky, 2015).

Despite controversy, Uber managed to raise capital from several investors. In October 2010, the company received its first major funding of $1.2 million by First Round Capital. Later in early 2011, the company raised $11 million in Series A round funding led by Benchmark Capital. The increasing influx of funds allowed Uber to expand into New York, Seattle, Boston, Chicago, Washington D.C., and overseas into Paris. In 2011, at the LeWeb Conference, three years after the inception of the ridesharing app, Kalanick announced an additional $37 million in Series B funding from Menlo Ventures, Jeff Bezos, and Goldman Sachs. Such funding allowed for further international expansion (Blystone, 2017). Uber also broadened its service offerings and in 2012 launched Uber X. Uber X aimed to provide customers a less expensive hybrid car option as an alternative to the black-car service (Alpe, 2015).

Uber's operational practices encountered criticism in December 2013. Uber's surge pricing, the increasing of price during peak times, came under fire when New York rates were massively increased during a snowstorm. The prices skyrocketed to eight times the regular rate. CEO Kalanick responded to criticism stating, "You want supply to always be full, and you use price to basically either bring more supply on or get more supply off, or get more demand in the system or get some demand out" (Alpe, 2015).

Meanwhile, Uber continued to face rising resistance from the taxi industry and government regulators. CEO Kalanick directly taunted his rivals who questioned his company practices. He commented via videos, speeches, and Twitter. As a further response to growing opposition, the company hired David Plouffe, a high-profile political strategist who was responsible for Barack Obama's 2008 presidential campaign. Plouffe was hired to lead Uber's public policy and communication. Plouffe claimed that, "I don't subscribe to the idea that the company has an image problem ... I actually think when you are a disrupter you are going to have a lot of people throwing arrows" (Alpe, 2015).

Uber initially intended to be a disrupter in the taxi industry, and as such, created controversy. However, growing negative public image and ongoing critique of CEO Kalanick may risk customer loyalty. Loss of customers may result in continued loss of revenue, as at the end of 2016, it was reported that Uber was projected to lose $3 billion (Marks, 2017). Kalanick now faces the task to revamp not only the Uber brand image, but also his own brand image.

The ridesharing industry

The ridesharing industry has grown to become a billion-dollar industry from 2011 to 2016. Real-time ridesharing is composed of three technological tools: the GPS navigation, smartphones, and social networks. These three elements combined provide a network service that handles payments and enhanced carpool.

Uber emerged in 2008 as a technological start-up aiming to provide consumers a simple and more convenient mode of transportation by using a mobile application. This idea of ridesharing apps rapidly grew because of the wide acceptance of the audience and by 2013, the industry was controlled by three main competitors: Uber, Lyft, and Sidecar (Sekar, n.d.).

In 2011, Sidecar was the first ridesharing transportation company in California. However, Sidecar went out of business in 2015 due to the aggressive competitors in the industry. Uber's rapid expansion and exponential growth included 50 countries and 334 cities, while Lyft focused on the American market and achieved presence in 61 cities (Dogtiev, 2015). Uber was valued at $68 billion (net value) and rapidly gained more than 8 million customers worldwide. Furthermore, Lyft has grown to be worth $5.5 billion (net value) with approximately 630,000 followers (Buhr, 2016).

The ridesharing market response reflects that the app usage has made the life of customers easier, allowing those that do not own a car the chance to move around without solely depending on public transportation. Ridesharing offers many benefits compared to taxi transportation. Ridesharing is timely, the customer can share the transportation charge, and it is also cost efficient due to the low rates. Consequently, private and public transportation has been impacted by the ridesharing industry because of the upward trend and advantages that ridesharing offers. Additionally, the ridesharing entities did not comply with any of the public/private transportation regulations that taxis or other modes of transportation have to follow (Helling and Ajma, 2017).

Political factors

Ridesharing businesses operate under a number of legal rules and government operations. Among these factors is the required Federal Motor Carrier Registration requested by law and the background checks and consultations that are completed by the employer. The private transportation industry also establishes a number of guidelines. However, ridesharing entities like Uber and Lyft seem to work at the borders of these regulations because the companies do not fit into this category.

Economic factors

After the 2008 economic recession, income and unemployment have gradually improved. This definitely affects purchasing power of customers. The GDP growth rate has been increasing by 2 percent per quarter. The GDP per capita of the United States was $52,194 in 2016 (Trading Economics, n.d.). Moreover, with growing disposable income, consumers will have more power to utilize private transportation since customers perceive it as a luxury/comfort service. Then, the ridesharing industry has a great opportunity for growth and development. Nevertheless, fuel is another important factor that depends on the economy and drives the ridesharing industry. Therefore, the price and availability of fuel are important criteria to obtain results in the car transportation industry.

Social factors

Social factors such as population size and growth rates in cities highly affect the ridesharing industry. With highly populated areas, more people can be targeted due to broad target audience and the variety in the demographics of Uber and Lyft customers (gender, nationality, language, culture, age, income, profession, preferences, etc.). Consumers in the ridesharing industry have an accelerated lifestyle and look forward to working with convenient, speedy, safe, and environmentally friendly businesses.

Technological factors

The ridesharing industry works on technology with its three-tool approach to ultimately provide a supreme service. Ridesharing works on mobile connections amongst the drivers and the customers in order to optimize the process of the carpool. The ridesharing industry relies on new technology like GPS, apps, and mobile connections to secure a service and process payments in an effective and efficient manner.

Uber's competitive positioning

The most important asset for Uber being so successful has been its competitive positioning. In order to compete with taxis, Uber has detached its business from the category of public/private transportation. It has created its own category of "Information Content Providers" to avoid legal and political transport regulations and have further autonomy in its operations (Zhang, 2014). Furthermore, in order to differentiate itself from its competitors and create greater value, Uber offers different alternatives in car sizes and rates in order to better meet the needs of its different customers. Among the options Uber provides are:

1. Uber X – the car is generally a minivan that seats four passengers. This is the most common and affordable alternative for transportation on a daily basis.
2. Uber Pool – known for being inexpensive as it is a shared ride with a total of four people that are migrating in the same direction.
3. Uber XL – this rate is a little higher because the car is an SUV and it seats up to six people.
4. Uber Select – known for being a luxurious car (BMW, Audi, Mercedes-Benz) that seats up to four individuals.
5. Uber Black/Uber SUV – the elite service with the highest rates and this alternative is offered to customers that desire a luxury travel experience in a black extravagant SUV/sedan (DougH, 2016b).

On the other hand, Lyft also offers a couple of options for customers. Among these alternatives are:

1. Lyft – four-passenger ride at the lowest price.
2. Lyft Plus – six-passenger ride at a moderate price.
3. Lyft Premier – luxury sedan, four passengers (option only available in LA, SF, NYC) at a high price.
4. Lyft Line – shared ride with passengers going on the same/similar route (DougH, 2016a).

However, even though Uber's pricing strategy seem similar, Lyft's fare prices are actually different from Uber's rates. Lyft rates also vary from city to city depending on the local market prices. In addition to the various options, Lyft also takes into consideration other cost breakdowns. First, it encounters a base charge, cost per mile, cost per minute, applies a service charge and even toll ride fees (DougH, 2016a).

In terms of market share, Uber and Lyft have an ongoing conflict due to certain matters in the U.S. First and most importantly is the fact that Lyft lacks presence in a number of cities leading to Uber's monopolization of these cities and ultimately to the increase in Uber's total U.S. market share. Nevertheless, the Lyft community insists that Uber's superiority in terms of market share is misleading because in cities like San Francisco and Los Angeles, Uber and Lyft closely compete with market share (Hartmans, 2016).

Uber's target market

Uber varies throughout the world as it has different services that it offers in each region. The company itself has broken into different service offerings, from basic to luxury cab models, to be able to cater to the vast majority of market segments. Each segment is characterized by the need of the customer as well as the different economics (IRR Labs, n.d.).

Uber not only markets for the riders to go into these vehicles but also the drivers or "partners" they need to be able to match the riders' requests and the segmented areas the app will do well in. Even with all the different services, however, the company has a common trend of users that it targets.

About 15 percent of Americans have used ridesharing apps such as Uber. Out of the consumers who use the app, the majority fall within the age range of 18–49 with the median age being 33. There are no specific gender or racial lines outlined for the riders of the app – the application is used by both males and females and races of every type (Smith, 2016).

Early adopters

Considering the application originated in San Francisco, the original target market was tech savvy users that lived in the San Francisco area who were willing to utilize a new tool or service that helped improve their quality of life. San Francisco at the time was going through issues in having enough taxi drivers available for customers, which helped it adopt easily to the new Uber platform. With the new platform being easy and convenient in San Francisco the app went "viral" – which helped Uber gain momentum (Jain, 2015).

Primary target

Aside from San Francisco, Uber has targeted specifically urban and suburban areas to release its app. The app also focuses more on young adults that are tech-savvy or technologically advanced. The majority of advertising for Uber is done online through Facebook ads, PPC, and online streams to help get to its target users (Nickel, 2016). Another major push that Uber tends to do is special events to help correlate riders with the events they attend. An example would be in Miami, March 2016. Uber promoted Steve Aoki, a famous DJ and star performer for major event Ultra, to drive a random ride requester. This helped gained popularity of the app and built correl--ation around the big event for consumers (Aoki, 2016).

Specialized target markets

Uber itself started with an Uber Black-like service where it used luxury black vehicles to pick up customers on-demand. Uber has since then expanded allowing for discounted trips through its Uber X and Uber Pool programs; however, it still has a target for consumers who wish for that luxury experience on-demand. The Uber Black, Uber Lux, and Uber SUV programs allow customers to ride in that luxury. The target market for these segments is working professionals, and young wealthy people looking for indulgence (Medium, 2015).

Drivers/partners

Uber chooses mostly large publishers that appeal to general audiences when it comes to its digital ad spend; however, looking closer to see its ads it is noted that the majority are on career-driven websites. As Uber continues to expand and recruit new riders, the company aims to recruit new drivers to match those requests (Medium, 2015). The company's target market for drivers are those who are looking to gain an extra income or are seeking full autonomy over their income and schedule. Drivers are even eligible without a car through the Uber Xchange program (Chapin, 2015). Uber drivers are targeted mainly through digital ad or through word of mouth.

Will Uber ever regain its market share?

In January 2017, President Donald Trump issued an immigration order to ban the entrance of Muslim immigrants. The New York City Taxi Alliance called to stop pick-ups at JFK Airport in solidarity with Muslim-ban protesters. Uber, nonetheless, continued operations and suspended surge pricing, lowering the cost of rides. Backlash ensued, as Uber's business practices were perceived as undermining and profiting off the taxi strike. Many consumers began believing that Uber was more focused on making a profit by promoting the ban rather than promoting what is deemed as morally right. Furthermore, Kalanick's prior connection to President Trump, as economic advisor in the business advisory council, caused greater uproar. This revolutionized the company's brand image as #DeleteUber began to trend on Twitter and over 200,000 users deleted their Uber accounts (Carson, 2017). Due to this negative publicity, the ridesharing company was further scrutinized on unrelated issues that were not previously relevant. Some of the named issues are a sexual harassment claim by a female employee, minority discrimination and lack of diversity, and the CEO's behavior towards his employees (Smith, 2017).

Uber's challenges

Uber is now faced with the challenge of overcoming its poor brand image, which has resulted in a drop in market share, a significant decrease in customers, and a high employee turnover rate in key cities and states such as California, New York, Pennsylvania, and North Carolina (TMZ, 2017). With the loss of more than 200,000 customers (TMZ, 2017), Uber lost a portion of its market share to its main competitor, Lyft, which overtook its rival in total app downloads. To counter Uber's practices, competitor Lyft publicly pledged to donate $1 million dollars to the American Civil Liberties Union (ACLU) (Bomey, 2017).

The #DeleteUber movement left the company vulnerable to further financial loss as Uber not only lost customers, but it also began losing its employees to Lyft. Uber was under media attention for its treatment of employees, namely immigrants, who believed their voices were not being heard by management. Uber's CEO, Travis Kalanick, has also received quite a number of backlashes due to his leadership style and quality. The public began questioning his character after an incident in February 2017 where he was said to have had a verbal dispute with one of his employees, which was caught on video. In the video, driver Fawzi Kamel intended to inform Kalanick of the difficulties faced by Uber drivers, specifically falling fares. After the release of such footage, Kalanick emailed Uber staff stating,

To say that I am ashamed is an extreme understatement. My job as your leader is to lead … and that starts with behaving in a way that makes us all proud. That is not what I did, and it cannot be explained away. It's clear this video is a reflection of me – and the criticism we've received is a stark reminder that I must fundamentally change as a leader and grow up. This is the first time I've been willing to admit that I need leadership help and I intend to get it.

(Newcomer, 2017)

Kalanick further stated that "I want to profoundly apologize to Fawzi, as well as the driver and rider community, and to the Uber team" (Smith, 2017). The lack of a marketing communications management team has resulted in the company not being able to respond effectively to negative publicity received (Dua, 2017).

In March 2017, claims of sexual harassment at Uber were brought to light. Susan Fowler, a female employee, had made sexual harassment claims that were ignored by the Human Resource Council (Isaac, 2017). This speaks to the culture of the work environment, which supports minority discrimination and creates an unhealthy working condition (Kraemer, 2017). To counteract the allegations, Mr. Kalanick said in an emailed statement:

What she describes is abhorrent and against everything Uber stands for and believes in. We seek to make Uber a just workplace for everyone, and there can be absolutely no place for this kind of behavior at Uber — and anyone who behaves this way or thinks this is O.K. will be fired.

(Kraemer, 2017)

Reports stated that human resources did not effectively intervene amid allegations. Again, Kalanick's leadership was scrutinized due to negative company culture.

With Uber experiencing a high employee turnover rate in key cities and states such as California, New York, Pennsylvania, and North Carolina, the company is now faced with instability as it is uncertain whether or not it will regain this human capital. Given that many of the Uber drivers are immigrants, there is a risk of diminished goodwill that will directly decrease the value of the company.

Attempts to mend the damage

Kalanick recognized his error that caused the #DeleteUber backlash, and attempted to do damage control by publicizing a mandate sent to his employees on the subject of speaking up for what is right, where he reached out to employees that were affected by the travel ban. Kalanick also stated his action plan to overcome the remnants of the travel ban. The company will be offering legal support for the affected drivers, compensating drivers for their lost earnings due to the ban, creating a $3 million legal defense fund, and urging the government to reinstate the right of U.S. residents to travel, regardless of their country of origin (Lekach and Flynn, 2017).

To publicize its efforts, Uber invested in sponsored ads on social media platforms such as Facebook and Instagram that spoke on the company's action plan, in order to increase awareness among its targeted consumers (Lekach and Flynn, 2017). In an effort to further eradicate the effects of #DeleteUber, Kalanick removed himself from

President Trump's advisory council as an act of solidarity with Uber's stakeholders (Buxton, 2017).

Uber has dominated the ridesharing industry with a market share of 84–87 percent, which differs in any given state. It is able to monopolize the market in certain cities, as it is the only ridesharing app available there. The company views its loss in market share as a temporary issue that will be overcome by its superior target segment and positioning, where Uber has a higher number of drivers and availability (Hartmans, 2016).

Plans for the future

In light of the recent challenges, Uber is faced with the risk of never regaining its loss of market share if it does not reposition itself. This can be executed by making a change in brand management through marketing communication and leadership style and quality.

Travis Kalanick announced his resignation as CEO in June 2017 but will remain a director of the company. Will Uber ever regain its market share? Does the company need to take further steps to overcome the backlash? Can Uber regain trust among its target customers? Are the initiatives taken enough to overcome the negative brand image?

References

Aoki, S. (2016). Request an Uber ride. *Facebook* video. Retrieved March 21, 2018, from www.facebook.com/Steve.Aoki/videos/10153325558052461/?fallback=1

Alpe, L. (2015, November 3). The history of Uber. *The Telegraph*. Retrieved March 21, 2018, from www.telegraph.co.uk/technology/uber/11962859/The-history-of-Uber.html

Blystone, D. (2017, April 14). The story of Uber. *Investopedia*. Retrieved March 21, 2018, from www.investopedia.com/articles/personal-finance/111015/story-uber.asp

Bomey, N. (2017, January 30). #DeleteUber? Trump ban stirs Lyft to ACLU donation as Uber takes heat. *USA Today*. Retrieved March 21, 2018, from www.usatoday.com/story/tech/2017/01/29/deleteuber-trend-erupts-lyft-backs-aclu-amid-trump-ban-fury/97214078/

Buhr, S. (2016, January 4). Lyft, now worth $5.5 billion, hops into the autonomous car race with General Motors. *Tech Crunch*. Retrieved March 21, 2018, from https://techcrunch.com/2016/01/04/lyft-now-worth-5-5-billion-plans-to-get-into-the-autonomous-car-race-with-general-motors/

Buxton, M. (2017, February 2). Uber's CEO will leave Trump's economic advisory council after boycott. *Refinery 29*. Retrieved March 21, 2018, from www.refinery29.com/2017/01/138711/uber-response-delete-uber-backlash

Carson, B. (2017, February 2). Over 200,000 people deleted Uber after the company operated its service at JFK airport during the Trump strike. *Business Insider*. Retrieved March 21, 2018, from www.businessinsider.com/over-200000-people-deleted-uber-after-deleteuber-2017-2

Chapin, A. (2015, July 29). Introducing Xchange leasing: lease options built for Uber driver-partners. *Uber Newsroom*. Retrieved March 21, 2018, from https://newsroom.uber.com/a-flexible-vehicle-leasing-pilot-in-california-georgia-maryland/

Dogtiev, A. (2016, September 5). Uber revenue analysis. *Business of Apps*. Retrieved March 21, 2018, from www.businessofapps.com/uber-revenue-analysis/

DougH. (2016a, June 8). What's the difference between Lyft, Lyft Plus, Lyft Line, and Premier? *Ridesharing Driver*. Retrieved March 21, 2018, from www.ridesharingdriver.com/whats-the-difference-between-lyft-lyftplus-and-line/

DougH. (2016b, August 30). What's the difference between UberX, XL, UberSelect, and Black Car? *Ridesharing Driver*. Retrieved March 21, 2018, from www.ridesharingdriver.com/whats-the-difference-between-uberx-xl-uberplus-and-black-car/

Dua, T. (2017, January 31). What brands can learn from the three-day #DeleteUber outrage cycle. *Digiday*. Retrieved March 21, 2018, from http://digiday.com/marketing/brands-can-learn-three-day-deleteuber-outrage-life-cycle/

Hartmans, A. (2016, August 25). Uber says it has over 80% of the ride-hailing market in the U.S. *Business Insider*. Retrieved March 21, 2018, from www.businessinsider.com/uber-majority-ride-hailing-market-share-lyft-us-2016–8

Hartmans, A. and McAlone, N. (2016, August 1). The story of how Travis Kalanick built Uber into the most feared and valuable startup in the world. *Business Insider*. Retrieved March 21, 2018, from www.businessinsider.com/ubers-history/#june-1998-scour-a-peer-to-peer-search-engine startup-that-kalanick-had-dropped-out-of-ucla-to-join-snags-its-first-investment-from-former-disney-president-michael-ovitz-and-ron-burkle-of-yucaipa-companies-1

Helling, B. and Ajma, S. I. (2017, January 9). 2017: the year the rideshare industry crushed the taxi [infographic]. *Rideshareapps.com*. Retrieved March 21, 2018, from https://rideshareapps.com/2015-rideshare-infographic/

IRR Labs. (n.d.). Uber: what it can teach investors about market analysis and unit economics. Retrieved March 21, 2018, from www.irrlabs.com/what-uber-business-model-can-teach-investors-about-market-analysis/

Isaac, M. (2017, February 19). Uber investigating sexual harassment claims by ex-employee. *New York Times*. Retrieved March 21, 2018, from www.nytimes.com/2017/02/19/business/uber-sexual-harassment-investigation.html?_r=0**

Jain, S. (2015, December 8). How did Uber get its first batch of users? *Quora*. Retrieved March 21, 2018, from www.quora.com/How-did-Uber-get-its-first-batch-of-users

Kraemer, H. (2017, March 1). Don't let Travis Kalanick off the hook for Uber's sexual harassment culture. *Fortune*. Retrieved March 21, 2018, from http://fortune.com/2017/03/01/travis-kalanick-uber-ceo-amit-singhal-sexual-harassment/

Lashinsky, A. (2015, June 3). Uber: an oral history. *Fortune*. Retrieved March 21, 2018, from http://fortune.com/2015/06/03/uber-an-oral-history/

Lekach, S. and Flynn, K. (2017, January 30). Uber fights against #DeleteUber hashtag with targeted ads. *Mashable*. Retrieved March 21, 2018, from http://mashable.com/2017/01/30/delete-uber-trump-immigration-ads/#be_drzr8YOqn

Marks, G. (2017, January 5). Yes, you're reading this right: Uber is projected to lose $3 billion in 2016. *Washington Post*. Retrieved March 21, 2018, from www.washingtonpost.com/news/on-small-business/wp/2017/01/05/yes-youre-reading-this-right-uber-is-projected-to-lose-3-billion-in-2016/?utm_term=.e2f85abdac99

Medium. (2015, November 10). Uber business model canvas: know what led Uber to success. *Medium*. Retrieved March 21, 2018, from https://medium.com/uber-for-x/uber-business-model-canvas-know-what-led-uber-to-success-7bca35472546

Newcomer, E. (2017, February 28). In video, Uber CEO argues with driver over falling fares. *Bloomberg*. Retrieved March 21, 2018, from www.bloomberg.com/news/articles/2017-02-28/in-video-uber-ceo-argues-with-driver-over-falling-fares

Nickel, B. (2016). How Uber and Lyft run their paid traffic campaigns. *Adbeat*. Retrieved March 21, 2018, from www.adbeat.com/blog/uber-lyft/

Sekar, A. (n.d.). Uber competitors: top companies in the on-demand ridesharing industry. *DataFox*. Retrieved March 21, 2018, from http://blog.datafox.com/6-uber-competitors-demand-ridesharing-space/

Smith, A. (2016, May 19). On-demand: ride-hailing apps. *Pew*. Retrieved March 21, 2018, from www.pewinternet.org/2016/05/19/on-demand-ride-hailing-apps/

Smith, J. (2017, February 28). "I'm ashamed": Uber CEO Travis Kalanick issues groveling memo to staff admitting he needs to "grow up" after video surfaces of him yelling at one of his own drivers. *Daily Mail*. Retrieved March 21, 2018, from www.dailymail.co.uk/news/article-4269350/Uber-CEO-Travis-Kalanick-lashes-driver-video.html

Swisher, K. (2014, December). Man and Uber Man. *Vanity Fair*. Retrieved March 21, 2018, from www.vanityfair.com/news/2014/12/uber-travis-kalanick-controversy

TMZ. (2017, January 30). Uber drivers pissed re: Muslim ban response ... bailing for Lyft gigs. *TMZ*. Retrieved March 21, 2018, from www.tmz.com/2017/01/30/uber-drivers-quit-muslim-ban-donald-trump/

Trading Economics. (n.d.). United States GDP per capita forecast 2016–2020. *Trading Economics*. Retrieved March 21, 2018, from www.tradingeconomics.com/united-states/gdp-per-capita/forecast

Zhang, S. (2014, October 3). Uber. *Prezi*.

World Fuel Services: leading internal marketing

When we think about what separates a good company from a great one we need to look no further than the employees. Employees set the tone for the business. They are the ones who provide the service needed to service customers and to keep revenue flowing. World Fuel has grown to be one of the largest companies in the world, but the company still has not focused more of its attention to keeping and retaining employees. This revolving door can have a negative effect on company morale and the cost of continually training and losing employees is a wasted expense.

The internal marketing team must develop a plan that will first, reduce company turnover, second increase employee morale, and third make its employees believe in the company's vision and goals. In order to gain a better understanding of what life is really like as an employee of World Fuel, a former employee of the firm, Ms. Basile, was interviewed. She worked for World Fuel in 2012 for two years, leaving the company in 2014. Ms. Basile stated that during her tenure with the company she felt like just a number among many other employees, "I think because the company has so many employees the departments are a little segregated. Some people don't really even know what the other person in their own department does at least on a detailed level."

Although this is a common issue in many large companies, management must come up with a strategy to deal with the situation and bring their employees together. Many larger companies are trying to bring back the "small company feel," so their employees don't feel like just a number. The company has made some efforts in its Miami office to at least bring their employees together for functions according to Ms. Basile; it does have Christmas functions, team building meetings, and celebrations after goals are met. If everyone stays late during busy times the company buys dinner, and there is a huge corporate run group. "So, they do try to add in events to help us all connect." Now the efforts by the Miami office are steps in the right direction, but why aren't employees staying with the company? As stated by an anonymous ex-employee: "The atmosphere is very toxic, and they do not listen to a word you say. Plus, they continue to hire inexperienced people. The turnover rate is very high, and that says a lot about the structure." Based on employer reviews on websites like Glassdoor there are a few common issues that are driving factors in retention issues for the company. For example, lack of employee training, no room for growth, no work-life balance, and no transparent communication from senior management, are some of the issues mentioned.

History of World Fuel Services

World Fuel Services began operations as a used oil recycler located in the South/ East United States in 1984. The company entered the aviation fuel services business in 1986 through an acquisition. In 1995, World Fuel acquired Trans-Tec Services to further solidify its fuel services operations. During the next 15 years, World Fuel acquired numerous oil and petroleum companies such as TGS Petroleum, Inc., Tramp Oil Group and Oil Shipping Group of Companies (ICD Research, 2013).

Currently World Fuel Services describes itself as the "global leader in fuel supply, specializing in fuel distribution and sale of land, aviation, and marine fuel products and services including trade credit, price risk management, fuel control and fuel procurement" (NetWise, 2017). Its segments are not just limited to aerospace, it also conducts business within agriculture, manufacturing, and the automation industries. In addition to fuel, World Fuel sells credit cards, machinery, and electronic components.

Michael Kasbar and partner Paul Stebbins formed Trans-Tec services in 1985 which was their own marine fuel brokerage company. In 1995, aviation fuel supply company International Recovery Corporation acquired Trans-Tec and the combined companies are now World Fuel Services. Realizing that its products and services could be extended to more than the aviation industry, World Fuel determined that it would be able to assist the logistics industry and the millions of trucks that operate yearly, especially the small fleet companies.

Headquartered in Miami, Florida, with over 60 offices worldwide and operating in more than 200 countries, World Fuel has increased its annual revenues at a rate higher than Apple – 39.8 percent compared to 39.2 percent (Fortune, 2013). Its organizational structure is made up of about 20 executives, ranging from CEO to regional managing director and general counsel, and almost all of them being a part of the corporation for over ten years. With over 4,000 employees worldwide, World Fuel's current CEO, Michael Kasbar, has positioned this organization to produce over $30 billion in revenue.

However, many are not aware of the company's name or what it does. Simply put, for anything associated with fuel and logistics services, World Fuel is involved. By the end of 2015, World Fuel had supplied 20 billion gallons of fuel to its clients (World Fuel Services, 2016a). World Fuel has positioned itself to become one of the leading names in regards to aircraft fueling. In early 2016, it acquired fuel operations at over 83 airports in Canada, the United Kingdom, Germany, and Australia, which were previously being handled by petroleum giant ExxonMobil (World Fuel Services, 2016b).

Financial overview

World Fuel's largest revenue producer in 2015 was its aviation sector at 39 percent followed by marine at 31 percent and land at 30 percent. Leading revenue geographically is Europe ($6.3 billion) and the Middle East ($5.8 billion), followed by Asia ($2.6 billion). The revenue growth the organization has experienced over the past 15 years, with its largest growth period from 2010 to 2014, resulted in 126 percent revenue increases during this time period.

Company strengths and weaknesses

One of World Fuel's strengths is its solid international presence; with operating offices in the U.S., U.K., Germany, Russia, Japan, and Latin America the ability to provide services to thousands of clients is due to good name recognition and ability to deliver no matter where the client is located. For example, 49 percent of its revenue in 2015 was generated in countries outside of the United States (World Fuel Services, 2016a).

With the inclusion of its own credit facility, World Fuel's weakness is its outstanding borrowings within its internal credit facility. Holding loan borrowings over $400 million by the end of 2015 "impacts the financial soundness of the company and thereby limiting World Fuel's ability to face adverse market developments" (World Fuel Services, 2016a). In addition, World Fuel's outstanding debt interest payments within 2016–2018 would result in interest payments of over $7 million, adding to its financial instability.

Although World Fuel has experienced significant growth during the past decade, there are opportunities within petroleum consumption which can bring continued growth for years to come; especially with the acquisition of ExxonMobil fueling operations. The United States Energy Information Administration (EIA) expects the global petroleum consumption, which was 93.7 million barrels per day in 2015, will grow by more than 1 million barrels per day in the future. "World Fuel, through these service offerings, is well positioned to capitalize on the rising demand for liquid fuels, diesel, and gasoline and increase its sales and market share in the US and internationally" (World Fuel Services, 2016b).

The largest threat is the increase in competition. Other companies are recognizing the demand for and opportunities for aviation fuel services. Although World Fuel has established itself within the industry, there are other corporations that have larger capital resources. There are some major oil companies which have positioned themselves to compete with World Fuel. Their ability to direct market, provide more competitive pricing and credit terms, could pose a threat.

Competitors

World Fuel describes its competitors as those that "range in size and complexity from large multinational corporations, principally major oil producers, which have significantly greater capital resources, to relatively small and specialized firms" (World Fuel Services, 2016a). In the oil refining industry, its top three competitors are Adams Resources & Energy, Inc., Global Partners LP, and Suburban Propane Partners, LP whose combined total revenues in 2015 were not even half of World Fuel's total revenue for the same year (World Fuel Services Corporation INT, 2016).

Market outlook

Fuel and oil prices greatly affect the future success of the major segments of World Fuel's operations (aviation, marine, and land). The aviation segment provides fuel to the major commercial airlines, the marine segment provides fuel and other products to tanker fleets and commercial cruise lines, while the land segment supplies fuel and natural gas petroleum operations to commercial and residential customers (World Fuel Services, n.d.a). Its future outlook is heavily impacted by the price and production of oil and jet fuel.

The International Air Transport Association (IATA) expects that passenger traffic demand will increase in the future; that coupled with the decline of oil and jet fuel prices should allow World Fuel to experience the revenue growth it did prior to 2015 (KPMG Transport, 2016).

World Fuel is known by many as a Fortune 500 company based in Florida and that it provides marketing and financing of aviation, marine, and ground transportation fuel products and related services to commercial and corporate aircraft, petroleum distributors, and ships at more than 8,000 locations around the world. It also is known as a giant company that employs over 4,700 people globally.

What is not so well known is that currently the company has been dealing with a high employee turnover rate and that it is a costly situation it is looking to solve. The management team has come to realize that a lot of its employees are eager to be employed by the company because it represents a great resume builder, but they never become fond of the company. Happy employees are good employees that are actively involved with the company they work for and take pride in it. Building employee retention by lowering employee turnover and creating a positive corporate culture can be achieved partly through an internal marketing program, and this will be reflected in the company's customer service.

Internal marketing and branding is needed in order to have happy employees and, therefore, better retention. Having employees that know, trust, and like the company and believe in the company vision, mission, and objectives will translate into a better customer service and customer interaction. Strategies to achieve this are part of the strategies that World Fuel Services is looking to implement.

The leadership

Michael Kasbar has been the CEO of World Fuel since 2012, and under his leadership the company has experienced tremendous success in generating revenue. In 2013, World Fuel was ranked #74 out of the Fortune 500 list, with $38.9 billion in revenue (Fortune, 2013). World Fuel has been able to continuously grow its revenue for the past decade. It also ranked #1 in ten-year revenue growth in the Fortune 500 (Fortune, 2013). After graduating and earning an environmental science degree from the State University of New York in 1978, Brooklyn native Kasbar began working in the fuel industry selling marine fuel to shipping companies. After a short period of time working for a marine fuel brokerage company called KPI, he quit his job and ventured out on his own. In 1985, he decided to set up his own business using the knowledge he had gained from his fuel industry experience. Kasbar and his partner Paul Stebbins formed their own marine fuel brokerage company named Trans-Tec Services. Backed by a few Greek ship owners and outside investors, the two worked their way to the top and turned that business into the largest marine fueling company in the world.

In 1995, a Miami-based company in the aviation fuel business, International Recovery Corp., acquired Trans-Tec for $14.5 million. After the acquisition, International Recovery Corp. was renamed World Fuel Services. Kasbar and Stebbin begin working for World Fuel, running Trans-Tec as a subsidiary. With the two companies combined, World Fuel expanded its reach to the marine fuel business, in addition to its aviation, oil recycling, and other fuel segments. In the same year, both Kasbar and Stebbins became executives and directors of World Fuel with Kasbar serving as the CEO of the company's marine fuel service segment and Stebbins as the president.

In their evolving roles in the company over the years, Kasbar and Stebbins have directed the company to being a leader in revenue generation. It continues to grow by acquiring many different companies and expanding into different businesses. One such business is servicing small fleets of trucks. This market presents great opportunity for growth, with around 3.5 million trucks on the road, operated by more than 500,000 companies. An acquisition for $137 million for select assets of Multi Service, a transaction management company with a card system for fleets, is the latest effort in capturing the small fleet fuel market.

Internal marketing and branding

An organization's core values are driven by its employees who represent the company and build customer relationships to create true value for them. A strong brand is associated with employees who are aligned with the core corporate values (Chong, 2007). The values set by World Fuel are critical in how it develops committed employees, drive internal and external behaviors, and service its customers.

World Fuel Services' core values, as stated on its website, include its mission, vision, culture, ethics and compliance, and QHSSE (quality, health, safety, security, and environment) (World Fuel Services, n.d.b):

Mission: Create value for our business partners by delivering innovative solutions and logistics through a global team of local professionals.

Vision: Become the world's leading provider of credit, finance, services, and logistics to our business partners in the energy market.

Culture: Embrace sustainable, responsible growth while expanding in capabilities and footprint. Maintain our entrepreneurial vision. Be committed to delivering value with integrity and ethics to our customers, suppliers, and shareholders.

Ethics & Compliance: We are committed to doing the right thing. We communicate this commitment to our customers, business partners, investors, and communities by acting with honesty in all that we do.

QHSSE: We believe in the protection of our natural environment. Our ISO- and OHSAS-based integrated management system guides our operations to: safeguard worker health; ensure stringent safety controls; secure operations; steward the environment; and maintain product quality.

If Word Fuel employees adopt the organization's core values and are motivated to represent the brand, the overall customer experience will improve and bring growth and brand awareness. Leaders of the organization should aim to develop and inspire employees by creating relevant internal marketing efforts to improve their experience at work and care for their personal growth and work-life balance. This is a key strategic resource to drive the business. These efforts should include continued education and training, employee recognition, cross-functional collaboration, consistent and transparent communication from upper management, and flexible schedules to name a few possible initiatives. Happy and knowledgeable employees will drive superior value when servicing World Fuel customers through their interactions and will build strong customer relationships.

Continued monitoring of employees' performance is key in developing customer-conscious employees at every level. Bringing all employees' ideas and actions to the table will drive employee engagement and build strong internal collaboration. Employees' attitudes and opinions shape the work environment and make the difference from them doing a good job to delivering excellent customer service. There is a true link between employee satisfaction and the performance of the organization.

A strategic approach to World Fuel's internal marketing and branding efforts will create external marketing and customer service success. Addressing the issues of internal marketing will allow the organization to set itself apart from the competitors by delivering high-quality service, maintaining market share, and driving more sales.

Implementing an internal marketing and branding program

The synergy between corporate values, employees' effective enactment of these values, and customers' appreciation of them is critical to the success of a corporate brand. When looking at World Fuel, the management team must bridge the gap between meeting company needs and making employees feel valued and appreciated. A happy employee provides the best service, a happy employee will go the extra mile, and a happy employee will stay and grow with the company. World Fuel needs to invest in the growth and wellbeing of its employees. How to do so is a major decision facing management.

References

Chong, M. (2007). The role of internal communication and training in infusing corporate values and delivering brand promise: Singapore Airlines' experience. *Corporate Reputation Review*, 10(3), 201–212. doi:10.1057/palgrave.crr.1550051. Retrieved April 30, 2017, from https://link.springer.com/article/10.1057/palgrave.crr.1550051

Forbes. (2016, May). The world's biggest public companies. *Forbes*. Retrieved April 30, 2017, from www.forbes.com/companies/world-fuel-services/

Fortune. (2013, May 20). The only Fortune 500 company that's grown faster than Apple. *Fortune*. Retrieved April 30, 2017, from http://fortune.com/2013/05/20/the-only-fortune-500-company-thats-grown-faster-than-apple/

ICD Research. (2013, June 20). ICD Research – history. Retrieved April 30, 2017, from www.lexisnexis.com/hottopics/lnacademic

KPMG Transport. (2016). KPMG Transport Tracker. Retrieved April 30, 2017, from https://assets.kpmg.com/content/dam/kpmg/pdf/2016/03/kpmg-transport-tracker.pdf

NetWise. (2017, February 24). NetWise company profiles. Retrieved April 30, 2017, from www.lexisnexis.com/hottopics/lnacademic

World Fuel Services. (n.d.a). *Annual Report*. Retrieved April 30, 2017, from http://ir.wfscorp.com/phoenix.zhtml?c=101792&p=irol-reportsAnnual

World Fuel Services. (n.d.b). Our values include our mission, vision, culture, ethics & compliance, and QHSSE. *World Fuel Services*. Retrieved April 30, 2017, from www.wfscorp.com/About-Us/Our-Values

World Fuel Services. (2016a, February). Business – competitors. *World Fuel Services*.

World Fuel Services (2016b). World Fuel Services. *MarketLine*.

World Fuel Services Corporation INT. (2016) *World Fuel Services Corporation (INT) – Oil & Gas – Deals and Alliances Profile*. London: Global Data Ltd.

Weatherby Healthcare: increasing turnover and declining engagement

Weatherby Healthcare (Weatherby), established in 1995, is a subsidiary of Salt Lake City-based CHG Healthcare, the originator of *locum tenens* staffing. Locum tenens, a Latin term meaning to hold one's place, refers to a type of physician staffing for short-term or part-time assignments. Weatherby is located in Fort Lauderdale and has swiftly grown to be a formidable force in the locum tenens staffing space, its largest competitor being its sister company CompHealth. Together, Weatherby and CompHealth hold the lion's share of the market at 31 percent, making CHG, by far, the largest locum tenens firm in the United States.

CHG Healthcare has set itself apart from many other staffing organizations because of its rapid growth and impressive metrics, namely its industry-low turnover. With growth ambitions exceeding prior years' performance and that of competitors, CHG had several obstacles to overcome. Specifically, Weatherby was seeing spikes in employee turnover, up to 34 percent in 2014 from 11.5 percent in 2011. Weatherby was also experiencing decreased employee engagement, and an inability to train employees in a way that would foster internal growth and attractiveness to new-hire candidates.

After hiring a new president, Bill Heller, in the first quarter of 2015, Weatherby's leadership team set out to improve morale, reduce turnover, and more thoughtfully and methodically train its current and new employees.

Staffing industry analysis/micro-environment

Industry analysis

According to the American Staffing Association, more than three million individuals work for an American staffing organization in a given week (Poole, 2015). The staffing industry is a fiercely competitive sales environment with staffing employees working in nearly all business sectors. While other sectors of the economy seem to languish with a slow 8.9 percent projected growth rate from 2012 to 2022, healthcare is booming by comparison with a projected 26.5 percent growth rate (Weiner, 2016). This growth will presumably lead to mirrored growth in the healthcare staffing industry.

Due to several shifts and new legislation in the healthcare market in recent years, the locum tenens staffing model is expected to pick up increasing momentum and become a strategic staffing solution for many healthcare systems across the country. A combination of an aging population, including physicians reaching retirement age, and a decreased number of medical school graduates each year means more physicians are retiring than are entering the medical field. This will lead to a shortage of approximately 90,000 physicians by 2025 (Bernstein, 2015).

Additionally, the implementation of the Affordable Care Act in 2015 means more Americans have access to and coverage for healthcare today. This shortage only increases the demand for temporary physicians, who can fill gaps in staffing ratios for short periods of time. For instance, if a facility has a physician go out on medical leave or sabbatical, or if a hospital wishes to bulk up staffing ratios during busy seasons, locum tenens physicians provide the necessary coverage in order to maintain a continuum of care for patients. In addition, locum tenens physicians also help to keep the practice up to speed.

Staffing, like many sales organizations, tends to be a fast-paced, metrics-driven industry. A cut-throat sales environment often leads to discouraging turnover rates, and in staffing alone, the rate exceeded 45 percent in 2015. Weatherby's Learning and Development (L&D) supervisor Shannon Miele expressed, "The training in competitor organizations is often limited to a day or two, and sales personnel are then thrown to the wolves." "This sink or swim approach," Miele added, "lends itself to very low employee engagement scores" (Miele, 2016).

Organizational analysis/macro-environment

Organizational structure

Weatherby's parent company, CHG Healthcare Services, is based in Salt Lake City, Utah, and has under it three other brands: CompHealth, RN Network, and Foundation Medical Staffing. Each sister brand has its own president and leadership teams, as well as dedicated brand-marketing teams within the corporate marketing department. The brand teams serve as marketers and strategists for each brand, planning, implementing, and maintaining channel marketing, advertising campaigns, conferences, social media, websites, thought leadership, etc. The size of each brand team depends on the size and scope of the brand. CompHealth, CHG's largest brand, has a brand team made up of ten people, where Weatherby's is made up of seven. These brand teams work with various business units within their designated brands to strategize both internal and external marketing initiatives.

It is worth mentioning that Weatherby has two office locations, its headquarters in Fort Lauderdale, Florida, which has approximately 430 employees, and a satellite location in Durham, North Carolina with approximately 120 employees. This split-campus structure will be important to remember when analyzing the importance for internal communications and marketing.

Business model

Weatherby's employee base is made up of sales consultants, business partners (nonsales), and leaders. The more than 250 sales consultants are broken into teams that specialize in staffing specific medical specialties and subspecialties. Consultants within each specialty team are further divided into two categories, those who call on physicians looking for locum tenens work and those who call on medical facilities and practices that may need physician coverage. The industry growth and demand within certain medical specialties dictates the size of each of Weatherby's sales teams and the growth rate they maintain. For instance, a growing need for more primary care physicians throughout the U.S. has spurred Weatherby to grow its Family Practice, Urgent Care, Hospitalist, and Emergency Medicine specialty teams. Additionally, the deficit in physicians has encouraged states to increase medical credentials for nurse practitioners and physician assistants, who are able to provide a similar level of patient care to physicians. The growing number and effective integration of nurse practitioners in our healthcare system could help alleviate pressures on primary care capacity. It takes much less time to produce new nurse practitioners than new physicians – an average of 6 years of education and training, compared to 11 or 12 years for physicians, including education and residency (Vleet and Paradise, 2015).

Weatherby's sales teams are supported by a myriad of business partner teams, nonsales personnel. These teams include finance, IT, administrative staff, payroll, sales coordinators, travel and housing (for physicians who travel on assignment), facilities management, talent acquisition, human resources, marketing, learning and development, and events, to name a few. The growth of sales teams largely dictates the growth of support teams.

The rapid growth of the locum tenens industry has spurred equally rapid growth for Weatherby. Since 2011, the company approximately doubled its employee base to more than 550. CHG Healthcare as a whole hired 680 people across all divisions in 2015. In 2016, Weatherby planned to add at least 80 new sales positions, including sales leaders, sales consultants, and nonsales.

Business goals

Weatherby, and its parent company CHG Healthcare, are privately held, making financial data closely guarded company information. The company was willing to share, however, that in 2015, CHG grew revenue by 20 percent, and Weatherby's by 13.5 percent. In 2016, CHG aimed to grow revenue by an additional 17 percent (2016 CHG Road Show, 2016).

Another primary corporate goal for 2016 was to drive more community involvement and volunteerism. CHG launched the Making a Difference campaign, which included its own brand and messaging. Each employee was given a black, Making a Difference shirt and encouraged to wear it on designated "blackout days" aimed at building awareness and comradery around volunteering and charitable involvement. Since 2014, CHG has granted each employee eight hours of volunteer time off (VTO) per month, to be used in the same way paid time off is used. Employees are encouraged to donate time to the cause of their choice, and they are paid to do so. In 2016, CHG is encouraging more employees to use their VTO.

The Weatherby division, under the tutelage of new president Heller, has also set three areas of focus for 2016 which include: Engagement & Culture, People Development, and Hiring & Retaining. In a great company culture, employees trust leaders, have a sense of pride in their work, and enjoy their colleagues – and the culture serves the strategy (Becker, 2016). Heller knows these goals are only achievable through increased internal collaboration, communication, and marketing.

Company culture and leadership structure

With CHG as a parent company, Weatherby adopts the culture and core values of CHG, as do its sister brands. This culture is a major focus of CHG's, as it is worked into all marketing and communications efforts. The core message of CHG's culture is "Putting People First," and all other cultural elements or values build upon that. Putting People First permeates all areas of business and serves as a baseline for many company decisions.

CHG and its brands are proud of the company culture that has been cultivated through the years. To show both employees and new-hire candidates just how special the "Putting People First" employee-engagement platform is, CHG and its brands pursue industry and workplace awards each year. CHG, for instance, has made *Fortune* magazine's 100 Best Companies to Work for in America seven years in a row. This award is perhaps the most prestigious, as it is shared with the likes of Google, SAS Institute, and REI. Another key award earned by CHG is *Training* magazine's Top 125, which recognizes the top 125 organizations with exceptional employee training programs. In 2016, CHG ranked #3 (Friefeld, 2016).

Weatherby accolades include *South Florida Business Journal* and *Triangle Business Journal* Best Places to Work and Healthiest Employer awards, United Way of the Triangle partnership award, *Florida Trend* magazine's Best Companies to Work for in Florida, and Modern Healthcare's Best Places to Work in Healthcare award. Each has been won multiple times over the years (Weatherby Healthcare, 2016).

Lastly, Weatherby has been recognized for its superior client and provider (physicians, nurse practitioners, and physician assistants) service levels by Inavero, a satisfaction survey company. The annual Best of Staffing survey recognizes the top staffing organizations based solely on customer satisfaction. Only 2 percent of staffing companies make the list, and Weatherby has been named for more than five years in a row. For comparison, in 2016 more than 61 percent of Weatherby's clients rated the company a nine or ten out of ten for service. As for providers, more than 62 percent rated Weatherby a nine or ten. The industry standard for clients and providers is −3 percent and 24 percent, respectively. It is clear Weatherby's commitment to service was being felt externally, but could the same be said for internal customers?

Internal customers and external stakeholders

Leadership and business unite

Along with Heller, Weatherby is guided by four vice presidents and a chief strategy officer. Together these individuals make up the 6-Pack, an internal name for this team of six heavyweights with extensive business, finance, and staffing knowledge and experience. Leadership then filters down to senior directors, directors, managers, and supervisors, making up a leadership team of more than 100.

Sales teams of more than 250 consultants cover approximately 50 medical specialties. These consultants are supported by business partner teams (nonsales employees) made up of more than 200 employees.

External stakeholders

The sole purpose of CHG–Weatherby sales and business partner teams is to place physicians, nurse practitioners, and physician assistants in open locum tenens jobs across the country. The openings these medical providers are filling occur in healthcare facilities, private practices, hospitals, and clinics. Both the medical providers and healthcare facilities are customers of Weatherby.

Thanks to the efforts of CHG sales and business partner teams, approximately 730,000 days of coverage were provided in 2015 (measured by counting all providers working each day throughout the year) by more than 12,000 providers. This healthcare coverage from CHG's providers impacted more than 21 million patient lives.

Delivering on company promise

Previously, CHG's corporate marketing team had little insight or input into the marketing efforts of the Weatherby brand team. This led to disjointed, inconsistent messaging for both internal and external audiences. Weatherby has a workforce of varying ages and tenures. Some employees have been with Weatherby for nearly 20 years, seeing the company grow from a handful of sales consultants to a formidable workforce of more than 250 sales consultants, more than 200 nonsales employees, and more than 100 leaders. To keep such a rapidly growing workforce engaged, more effort was needed to connect them to the brand.

From 2011 to 2015, Weatherby's business and market share grew rapidly, making the company a serious competitor to its sister brand, CompHealth, for the first time. To match the company's growth, many employees were hired very quickly, and sales goals were accelerated. With CompHealth in leaders' sites, slowing down was simply not an option.

Unfortunately, this rapid growth and fierce-competition approach left many employees feeling left in the dust. Weatherby's L&D director Robert Jones shared, "Back then, many people left because they didn't feel prepared or supported in their roles, it took too long for consultants, especially new ones, to learn and understand their jobs" (Jones, 2016). He expressed there was no marketing presence with regard to employee training initiatives, so few of the brand messages that were being communicated to external customers were heard or understood by internal ones. Internal communications was relegated to announcing fun office activities, fundraisers, new hires, and promotions, with little mention of key marketing initiatives (successes and impact) in the field.

The detriment of Weatherby's lack of focus on employee connectedness to the brand was felt through decreasing employee engagement scores and increasing turnover rates. It became clear something had to give, and leadership decided it was important to reconnect employees to the brand. This first began with a decision to give employees of all levels and in all departments more visibility into current, ongoing, and upcoming marketing initiatives, as well as how those initiatives impact the business. It was also identified that marketing should have more insight into what those employees are seeing, hearing, and experiencing in interactions with customers.

Luckily for the Weatherby brand, its new president, Heller, sought to improve many of the company's woes by simply inviting the marketing team to the table. With marketing playing a fundamental, foundational role for the Weatherby brand, it was believed many of the inconsistencies, miscommunications, and mistrust in the brand could be corrected. Not everything could be corrected overnight, though. Heller chose two ways in which to kick off a new marketing focus.

First, Heller approved for a new, Fort Lauderdale-based marketing team, fully dedicated and fully present in Weatherby's day-to-day operations. The goal behind this new team was for its members to see and hear what was and was not working in each of the division's teams. This insight could then drive marketing conversations and collaboration about best practices and business pain points not previously shared with marketing. The second initiative was to drive an overhaul and restructuring of Weatherby's employee-training program. This program, called CORE, would be the first opportunity for the Weatherby brand team to flex its marketing muscle through an internal campaign, thereby exhibiting the importance of collaboration with marketing. Since people development was one of his 2016 goals, Heller chose to first infuse marketing into employee learning and development.

Learning and development team

Weatherby's brand team kicked off 2016 with one of its most impactful internal-branding efforts, the launch of the new employee training program called CORE. CORE, which stands for Creating Optimal Results Education, was an initiative originally launched in Weatherby's sister brand, CompHealth. CompHealth saw many early successes in the program, thanks largely to intensive planning and marketing input from the start.

CompHealth assistant brand manager Chad Stone stated,

> Marketing's role in the development and implementation of CORE was to bring legitimacy to the program. How things are packaged helps consumers [internal customers] gain brand awareness and acceptance. The well-defined CORE brand was carried throughout the build-out, from look and feel of signage and brand assets to messaging in internal communications. Marketing ultimately helped employees gain trust in the abilities of the Learning and Development team.
>
> (Stone, 2016)

What is the importance of launching new marketing efforts with new hire training? Weatherby's L&D team is the first face of the company seen by every new hire. These new employees base many of their opinions of brand, company structure, leadership teams, and job processes on their interaction with the members of the L&D team during the first few weeks of training. At the rate Weatherby is hiring, the L&D team is able to ingrain new employees with brand messaging from day one.

Marketing outfitted the training area with CORE-branded signage, the team members with CORE-branding shirts and hats, and new-hires with CORE-branded training manuals and office supplies. An internal communications plan was launched in the weeks leading up to CORE's launch. CORE-branded internal email communications served several purposes: increased awareness of the program; explained the purpose CORE serves and problems it overcomes; highlighted L&D team members responsible for implementation of CORE; and got leaders involved in upcoming new-hire events. Monthly best practices and success stories from CORE are shared at leadership meetings.

Prior to CORE, new-hire training lasted only two weeks, which had a very limited impact on engagement levels of new hires. As previously expressed by Jones, this short amount of time left many new consultants feeling unprepared for the fast-paced, high-stress sales job. Two weeks also made it difficult, Jones shared, for his team members to feel as though they were training employees correctly. "Trainers, by nature, want to do something worthwhile. They want to make a positive difference. The stress of the previous training model left my team members disengaged with their jobs and the company. We were stretched too thin" (Jones, 2016).

Under the CORE model, training is stretched to seven weeks; one week of Foundational Training at CHG's headquarters in Salt Lake City and six more weeks of Weatherby CORE training in Fort Lauderdale. CORE graduates then receive refresher courses and participate in events with their CORE comrades throughout their first two years of employment with Weatherby.

Through the implementation of CORE, Weatherby's leaders ultimately aimed to improve employee engagement scores by 70–80 percent and turnover by 25–30 percent. Jones said,

> These goals are already being realized, and it has a lot to do with sales consultants being better prepared, which leads to reduced stress levels on sales teams. Once a new hire finishes CORE, they go to sales team fully prepared, and tenured consultants don't have to continue to train new employees. Sales leaders are also impacted, because they can give ample time to all team members, not just new hires.
>
> (Jones, 2016)

Importance of internal marketing

All too often marketing must prove its worth to a company's leadership. People designated as marketers are sometimes assigned to sales support (lead generation and trade shows, for example) or communications (advertising and promotional materials).

Weatherby's decision to invite a branch of its dedicated brand team to join its ranks in the Fort Lauderdale office shows how important leadership, led by Heller, now felt marketing's input was. CHG's marketing department then added four new members to the Weatherby brand team, increasing the team member count from three to seven. These four new members would work out of Weatherby's Fort Lauderdale headquarters, allowing for a boots-on-the-ground level of interaction with the brand. This new branch could now see, hear, and experience, in real time, the regular, day-to-day challenges and successes of sales teams, drive new marketing initiatives to grow business, and eliminate marketing initiatives that have lost impact. One of the brand team's first objectives was to work on branding Weatherby's new CORE training program.

Marketing's role in CORE's development and rollout was to give the training program legitimacy through a consistent look and feel. Since the Weatherby brand is thought of so highly by external customers, it was believed internal customers should be marketed to just as strongly. By doing so, the marketing team aimed to build more trust in the company and the brand, starting with employees' first impression in new-hire training. The branding imagery was coupled with an internal communication plan for CORE's rollout, as well as for ongoing CORE communications. These included updates to leaders on best practices and successes.

Ultimately, the success of this marketing goal to build better brand trust would be measured against how much the company realized improved employee engagement scores and a reduced turnover rate. While internal marketing played a backstage, behind-the-camera role, it served as a platform, communication outlet, and the glue that created and maintained better brand and messaging cohesion. It made the brand feel real to Weatherby employees again.

References

2016 CHG Road Show. (2016, February). Internal CHG presentation.

Becker, J. (2016). The best way to build company culture. *Fortune*. Retrieved April 30, 2017, from http://fortune.com/2016/01/04/best-way-to-build-company-culture/

Bernstein, L. (2015, March 3). U.S. faces 90,000 doctor shortage by 2025, medical school association warns. *Washington Post*. Retrieved April 30, 2017, from www.washingtonpost.com/news/to-your-health/wp/2015/03/03/u-s-faces-90000-doctor-shortage-by-2025-medical-school-association-warns/

Friefeld, L. (2016, February 11). *Training Magazine* ranks training top 125 organizations. *Training Magazine*. Retrieved April 30, 2017, from https://trainingmag.com/training-magazine-ranks-2016-training-top-125-organizations

Jones, R. (2016, March 31). Personal communication.

McDuffie, G. (2015, May 4). Why internal marketing could be the most important marketing. *CMO Exclusives*. Retrieved April 30, 2017, from www.cmo.com/articles/2015/4/27/why-internal-marketing-could-be-the-most-important-marketing.html

Miele, S. (2016, March 30). Personal communication.

Poole, C. (2015). Staffing industry statistics. *American Staffing Association*. Retrieved April 30, 2017, from https://americanstaffing.net/staffing-research-data/fact-sheets-analysis-staffing-industry-trends/staffing-industry-statistics/

Stone, C. (2016, March 30). Personal communication.

Vleet, A. and Paradise, J. (2015, January 20). Tapping nurse practitioners to meet rising demand for primary care. *The Henry J. Kaiser Family Foundation*. Retrieved April 30, 2017, from http://kff.org/medicaid/issue-brief/tapping-nurse-practitioners-to-meet-rising-demand-for-primary-care/

Weatherby Healthcare. (2016, April 13). Weatherby Healthcare provides award-winning red ribbon service. *Weatherby Healthcare*. Retrieved April 30, 2017, from www.weatherbyhealthcare.com/about-weatherby/recent-awards.aspx

Weiner, L. (2016, January 4). 2016 healthcare staffing trends. *Health Leaders Media*. Retrieved April 30, 2017, from www.healthleadersmedia.com/hr/2016-healthcare-staffing-trends

Chapter 6

Corporate reputation management

Corporate reputation is increasingly being regarded as a valuable asset to an organization as it gives it a sustainable competitive advantage. In fact its sustainability is largely reliant on its reputation. Abratt and Kleyn (2012, p. 1057) defined corporate reputation as "a stakeholder's overall evaluation of an organization over time." *Fortune Magazine* publishes a list of the World's Most Admired Companies (http://fortune.com/worlds-most-admired-companies/). It is not surprising to see the top five on the list in 2017 being Apple, Amazon, Starbucks, Berkshire Hathaway, and Disney.

When the reputation of a company has been harmed, it is costly for them and sometimes difficult to recover. Recent reputational lapses have hit the motor industry with the Volkswagen emissions scandal in September 2015 (www.bbc.com/news/business-34324772) and Toyota's defect cover-up in 2014 (www.abc.net.au/news/2014-03-20/toyota-pays-1-3-billion-for-defect-cover-up-statements/5332894). In 2016 alone, Wells Fargo opened up thousands of fraudulent accounts. This was due to pressure from bank executives for employees to meet growth targets. Samsung had to recall its Galaxy Note 7 because the batteries in the phones were exploding. A formal recall process was then initiated, but not before phones began harming consumers in various ways, leading to lawsuits for the electronics giant (http://fortune.com/2016/12/28/biggest-corporate-scandals-2016/).

According to Gaines-Ross (2010) organizations may be caught unawares by small-scale adversaries in command of a social network arsenal. Facebook protest sites, blogs, tweets, text messages, and online petitions can damage reputations of large organizations. Critics do not need large resources to attack an organization. Management needs to review the reputational risks facing the organization and build and manage its corporate reputation. Noncompliance by organizations with socially responsible standards constitutes a risk to their reputations across all significant stakeholders. Gaines-Ross (2010) suggests that the battle over reputation does not always favor the organizations with the deepest resources.

Reputational risk

Loss of reputation affects competitiveness, positioning, loyalty of stakeholders, media relations, and the legitimacy of operations. Reputational risk can be divided into business and socio-political. Business risks for an organization include: product failure/recall, poor advice and service, fraudulent activities, poor governance and decision making, intervention by governmental authorities, litigation by stakeholders, unethical behavior towards competitors, infighting of the board of directors and senior managers, security-related issues like data breaches, and poor policy or strategic decision making. Fombrun, Gardberg, and Barnett (2000, p. 88) defined reputational risks as "the range of possible gains and losses in reputational capital." Stakeholders are a source of risk to be managed as they are a threat to an organization's reputation.

Dimensions of corporate reputation

There are many dimensions to corporate reputation and many are specific to each stakeholder and organization. These include:

Vision and leadership quality

CEOs can be important in generating admiration and trust with customers and other stakeholders. Some leaders have media appeal and often attract investments to their company. One only has to think of Bill Gates of Microsoft, Richard Branson of Virgin, Steve Jobs of Apple, and Howard Schultz of Starbucks as leaders who have aided their organization's reputation in mainly positive ways.

Corporate governance

Corporate governance is the system of rules, practices, and processes by which a company is directed and controlled. It essentially involves balancing the interests of a company's many stakeholders, such as shareholders, management, customers, suppliers, investors, government, and the community. Having adequate and ethical governance practices enhances an organization's reputation.

Financial performance

Profitability is an important signal to investors about an organization's success and indicates that it will likely grow in the future. Different stakeholder groups interpret financial success differently and it is how an organization uses its financial strength that influences stakeholder perceptions of the organization.

Investment in product development and innovation and product quality

Products, whether they are goods or services, are at the core of what organizations do. Therefore most stakeholders know an organization by its products or service offerings. Perceptions of these organizations are formed by stakeholders largely by the price, quality, communication, and distribution strategies of the organization. Innovation is an important asset in reputation development. Apple's reputation is built largely on its ability to launch new innovation products.

Investments in human capital workplace (good employer)

Stakeholders respect companies who are regarded as good employers and maintain a good workplace. Satisfied employees are more likely to perform brand citizenship behavior and therefore contribute to customer satisfaction. This dimension of reputation has become important as there are regular publications of rankings. *Forbes* magazine publishes "The Best Places to Work" and *Fortune* magazine publishes "The 100 Best Companies to Work For."

Corporate citizenship

The corporate social performance of an organization has a major impact on its reputation. Corporate citizenship includes sustainability practices, environmentally sound behavior, corporate social responsibility practices, and working in an ethical way. Many stakeholders form perceptions of an organization based on these dimensions and it is becoming an important part of corporate identity and strategy. "Everyday all around the globe, McDonald's is putting people, processes and practices into place to make sustainability the new normal – for our business, society and the world at large" (http://corporate.mcdonalds.com/mcd/sustainability.html).

The portfolio of corporate reputation dimensions is varied. They each contribute to the overall reputation of the organization. In order to build and management its reputation, an organization must manage all the dimensions that are applicable to them.

Value of corporate reputation

Fombrun and van Riel (2004, p. 32) defined reputational capital as "an organisation's stock of perceptual and social assets – the quality of the relationship it has established with stakeholders and the regard in which the company and brand is held." A loss of reputational capital was detrimental to stakeholder relationships and impacted on the firm's long-term vision and the firm's creation of shareholder wealth (Fombrun and van Riel, 2004). An organization needs to build reputational capital so that it has an abundance of it in case of need. The Deepwater Horizon accident and BP's actions in its aftermath led to numerous fines and a multi-billion dollar clean-up and business recovery costs. BP survived this major incident because it had reputational capital and it can be argued that it redeemed itself in the eyes of many stakeholders.

According to Floreddu, Cabiddu, and Evaristo (2014), superlative handling of a crisis can mitigate long-lasting reputational damage. They suggest a well-crafted online strategy, combining the right mix of social media, should contribute to a positive reputation. As a manager, they suggest organizations need to assess their current level of reputation; then consider the cost-benefit of expanding their communication presence especially online; and then engage with customers regularly. Successful corporate reputation management requires successful communication, including on social media.

Corporate reputation is a summary view of the perceptions held by all relevant stakeholders of an organization and what they believe the organization stands for, and the associations they make with it. It is therefore likely that organizations have reputations, rather than a single reputation, as the different stakeholder groups may have different perceptions.

Conclusion

This chapter highlights the importance of organizations having a good reputation among stakeholders and the risks of losing a good reputation. The dimensions of reputation are discussed in detail and then the value of corporate reputation is highlighted. The importance for an organization to build its reputational capital is also discussed as it would serve it well if it is faced with a crisis.

References

Abratt, R. and Kleyn, N. (2012). Corporate identity, corporate branding and corporate reputations. *European Journal of Marketing*, 46(7/8), 1048–1063.

Floreddu, P.B., Cabiddu, F., and Evaristo, R. (2014). Inside your social media ring: how to optimize online corporate reputation. *Business Horizons*, 57(6), 737–745.

Fombrun, C.J. and van Riel, C.B.M. (2004) *Fame and Fortune: How Successful Companies Build Winning Reputation*. New Jersey: Pearson Education.

Fombrun, C.J., Gardberg, N., and Barnett, M.L. (2000). Opportunity platforms and safety nets: corporate citizenship and reputational risk. *Business and Society Review*, 105(1), 85–106.

Gaines-Ross, L. (2010). Reputation warfare. *Harvard Business Review*, December, 2–7.

Lennar Corporation

Lennar began as a successful construction company that did very well by building quality homes and establishing a reputable name in the housing industry. In the midst of high-level returns, Lennar made the pivotal move to get away from construction and change its business structure to a full service model. The company ventured into real estate and the complete home buying and selling sector. This timely move beat the downturn in the housing market, before the economy fell, and as a result put Lennar in great position to skyrocket. By making another wise commitment to target affordable homes, Lennar became a power in the game. Within its new model, the company would completely end its construction business and use subcontractors to build its homes. This would initially prove to be cost effective and a positive step, but would eventually lead to trouble for the brand. The company gained loyalty through great quality and detailed construction, yet subcontractors eventually ruined the fiber of that trust. The gap began to close and competitors gained ground. As the market began to improve, demand increased and more people began to purchase homes. Buyers looked for both affordable and low-cost homes. At this point, price was just one strong determining factor. Quality became paramount, along with location and trust. Business shifted as consumers' interest became more about location, reputation, and quality, not only price. As Lennar still struggled to overcome its poor quality stain, rental and resale business gradually fell into the mix and became game changers. Therefore, Lennar marketed an "Everything Included" format that proposed a dream home concept with a high-quality guarantee.

Company overview

Florida's largest homebuilder and one of the largest residential builders in the country, Lennar Corporation began as a Miami-based residential homebuilding company, then later diversified into real estate investments and financial services to mitigate its dependence on a cyclical housing construction market. By the 1990s, Lennar was a full-service real estate company principally involved in designing, building, and selling all types of residential housing, but primarily focused on the market for first-time homebuyers, or those homes selling for under $100,000 (Funding Universe, n.d.). Lennar primarily sells single-family attached and detached homes in communities targeted to first-time, move-up, and active adult homebuyers. Although the company operates primarily under the Lennar brand name, other brands of the company include Cambridge, Greystone, NuHome, Patriot, U.S. Home, and Village Builders (Barnes, 2015a).

Its original founders were Gene Fisher and Arnold Rosen, and the company operated as F & R Builders. Two years after its inception, Leonard Miller replaced Gene Fisher. Miller would eventually become the company's CEO, and the company's name changed to Lennar. Together, Rosen and Miller were able to grow their business and to expand by establishing strong core values, and by staying ahead of the curve with changing their business approach. Their most pivotal movement occurred in the early 1980s when they decided to stop constructing homes and became a full service provider, focusing more on real estate and the homebuying and selling process. Conservative behavior during boom times maximized the profit of existing holdings at the expense of rapid expansion, which placed Lennar in a position of great strength as the economy faltered. While most of its competitors were struggling to meet costs and stay in business, Lennar was able to take on debt and purchase land and projects at a significant discount (Hamilton, Church, and Dornbach-Bender, 2009). In the mid-1990s, Lennar entered into its first out-of-state markets, expanding to Texas, California, and Nevada, and the Pacific Northwest, establishing its self as a power-house in its industry.

Through its financial services subsidiary, Lennar originated or serviced mortgage loans in 48 states, provided title services, and operated a mortgage loan brokerage business, while the company's asset management business purchased and managed commercial real estate, including shopping centers, office buildings, warehouses, apartment properties, and mobile home parks (Funding Universe, n.d.). The struggling economy of the late 1980s and early 1990s brought about a booming need for lower-priced more affordable homes. Homebuilders struggled during the early 1990s, as construction costs rose, the economy struggled, and demographics shifted. Coinciding with the failing savings and loan industry, a new market niche was developing: the market for low- and medium-priced homes made available to the newly spendthrifty homebuyers; a niche that Lennar had already mastered in its business model (Hamilton, Church, and Dornbach-Bender, 2009). Its business model through full service lined up perfect with a "New Movement" on lower-priced more affordable homes. Lennar was ahead of the curve and primed for this movement, while its competitors faltered. Lennar was in a prime position, increasing its revenues while the rest of the American economy was only beginning to recover in 1993, earning $666.9 million, a 55 percent improvement over its revenues of 1992. Earnings increased by 80 percent during this period, amounting to $52.5 million in 1993 (Hamilton, Church, and Dornbach-Bender, 2009). In 1997, Stuart Miller replaced his father and became the new CEO of the Lennar Corporation. It was at this time that the company started to aggres-sively expand its commercial real estate operations under the name LNR Property, which would be entirely dedicated to providing homebuilding and mortgage services. The purchase of U.S. Home Corporation in 2000 for $1.1 billion made Lennar a national heavyweight, doubling its size. In 2001, Lennar became one of Forbes' 500 largest companies, and in 2003 and 2004, Lennar earned Fortune's most admired homebuilding company title (Hamilton, Church, and Dornbach-Bender, 2009). Lennar's Homebuilding segment primarily includes the construction and sale of single-family attached and detached homes as well as the purchase, development, and sale of resi-dential land. Homebuilding is the most significant part of the company's business, earning revenue of $7 billion, or 90 percent of the total in fiscal 2014, and having employee strength of 3,578 (Barnes, 2015b).

In 2012, Lennar introduced its NextGen Home-Within-a-Home. Lennar was the first national homebuilder to provide a solution for the growing needs of long-term guests and family members in terms of additional space, privacy, and functionality (Steele, 2012). An estimated 51.5 million people live in multi-generational housing, which typically means three generations under one roof. That number is expected to increase as baby boomers get older. At least 10,000 Americans will turn 65 each day for the next 19 years, according to the Pew Research Center (Glink, 2013). Lennar saw an opportunity to serve the aging demographic by providing homes that served a need across the board. Today, through organic and inorganic growth, Lennar has expanded to become the nation's fourth largest homebuilder (measured by revenues), operating in 17 states across the United States. (Hamilton, Church, and Dornbach-Bender, 2009).

Industry overview

Lennar Corporation is part of the homebuilding industry. It is currently a very tough industry as the economic downturn, mortgage market crisis, and bursting of the housing bubble has adversely affected homebuilders, and Lennar is no exception even though there are some improvement trends that have been generating positive expectations for the future (Hamilton, Church, and Dornbach-Bender, 2009). Lennar operates primarily under the voice "General Contractors: Single-family housing construction" (Hamilton, Church, and Dornbach-Bender, 2009). The industry is defined by residential construction of single-family attached and detached homes. Additionally, the industry in general has about 170,000 companies in the United States and as a unit generates generally revenues of $140.65 billion total single-family construction homebuilding per year.

The homebuilding industry is relatively big compared to Lennar's total revenue; this indicates an opportunity for Lennar to expand its market. In this industry, Lennar's major competitors are DR Horton, Inc. and Pulte Homes, Inc. as well as other national, regional, and local homebuilders (Hamilton, Church, and Dornbach-Bender, 2009). As reported by Fortune, the industry has been going through several tough years, but now it is definitely coming back at good levels (Matthews, 2015). The bursting of the housing bubble sent many homebuilders into bankruptcy for different reasons. The industry not only built too much over the bubble years from 2002 to 2006, but also the financial crisis meant that credit was nowhere to be found for many builders in need.

The positive trend, for the homebuilders, turned to be attractive again in 2012 when home prices began to recover and have continued to surge ever since (Matthews, 2015). At the same time Americans' balance sheets were recovering, leading to an increase in the personal average incomes. Therefore, the year 2012 represented the year where Americans were able again to purchase a new home. The post-bubble slump, in which new housing construction fell to all-time lows, helped create a shortage of housing and primed the sector for a strong comeback (Matthews, 2015).

Currently the situation is further changed into a positive. An article from Forbes underlined how the homebuilders' housing market index has been the highest since 2005 (Schiffman, 2015). This is even though personal income growth is still slow and consumer debt recently hit an all-time high of $3.2 trillion (Schiffman, 2015). The improvement of the job market over the last few years has been considered as a stimulator for the homebuilder industry's growth. Wages have not gone up rapidly, but still faster than inflation.

The National Association of Home Builders has released some very detailed updates about the industry in general. With its November 2015 press release, it stated that markets in 79 of the approximately 360 metro areas nationwide exceeded their last normal levels of economic or housing activities in the third quarter of 2015 (National Association of Home Builders, 2015). This analysis confirms the idea that the market has been having a modest but positive recovery trend during the last few years. Furthermore, to confirm this information, 69 percent of these markets have shown an improvement year over year (National Association of Home Builders, 2015).

These positive trends make it possible for the industry to become more affordable for the general population. Lower interest rates and home prices are boosting housing affordability across the country (Home Builders, 2015). Relying on numbers, the national median home price declined from $215,000 in the fourth quarter of 2014 to $210,000 in the first quarter of 2015 and the average mortgage interest fell from 4.29 percent to 4.03 percent in the same period (Home Builders, 2015).

Competitor overview

According to Occupational Safety & Health Administration (OSHA), the homebuilding industry is defined as "general contractors primarily engaged in construction, including new work, additions, alterations, remodeling, and repair of single-family houses" (OSHA, n.d.). The residential homebuilding industry is very competitive and Lennar faces a high degree of rivalry and price competition. One of the main issues it faces is the domino effect within the industry regarding valuation. For example, a decline in the value of one home leads to falling valuations of surrounding homes, and so on. To respond to these market pressures, homebuilders must be sensitive to price reductions by providing sales incentives as well as incentive brokerage fees; however, an increase in competition and pressures has ultimately led to industry-wide price reductions and housing deflation. Due to a decline in the housing market, Lennar and its competitors are forced to compete for homebuyers on the basis of a variety of factors, including location, price, reputation, quality, and financing (U.S. Securities and Exchange Commission, 2011).

Lennar competes with numerous national and regional homebuilders for homebuyers in each of the market regions in which it operates, encompassing over 170,000 companies that build homes within the United States. Several top companies rival Lennar, including the following major competitors in the homebuilding space: PulteGroup (Atlanta), D.R. Horton (Texas), Toll Brothers (Pennsylvania), and NVR, Inc. (Virginia) (Oasis Consulting, 2009).

In addition to homebuilding, Lennar is also competing for resales of existing homes as well as within the rental housing market (U.S. Securities and Exchange Commission, 2011). Resale market competition with others in the homebuilding space can ultimately reduce the number of homes Lennar is able to deliver, or can lead to it accepting reduced margins in order to maintain its sales volume. Furthermore, efforts to sell foreclosed homes have resulted in an increasingly more competitive homebuilding industry. Finally, it is important to note that Lennar isn't just competing with others for homebuyers, it is also competing for desirable properties, raw materials, and access to skilled employees, as well as with third parties for land buyers in an effort to sell great properties to homebuilders and others.

Product differentiation could set these competitors apart from one another; however, the physical homes, which Lennar sells, have very little differentiation from its competitors. As a result of reduced variable costs associated with homebuilding, homebuilders have shifted away from custom homes and have focused on developing model homes. This decision has increased the homebuilders' efficiency and ability to presell more homes; however, it has decreased the product differentiability among competitors in the industry. In an effort to separate itself from its competitors as well as differentiate itself, Lennar currently operates under additional brand names, including Greystone, Village Builders, Patriot, and Cambridge (Oasis Consulting, 2009). Special attention has been paid to brand reputation, quality, and home features as Lennar focused on an advertising campaign that coined the slogan "Everything's Included." This approach was a unique way to determine what homebuyers wanted in their dream homes and then commit to providing the high-quality features and upgrades as default elements of a home. Again, these efforts didn't provide much in the way of differentiability for Lennar since both the brand and its competitors seem one and the same for consumers. Although the homes themselves provide little product differentiation, location plays a major role for competitors within the industry. As multiple homebuilders operate within the same location and as land becomes more constrained, Lennar holds a competitive advantage due to its extensive investments and land acquisitions, giving it developable land that is greater than its competitors (Oasis Consulting, 2009).

Lennar also operates in the financial service segment with competitors that include CTX Mortgage, D.R. Horton, Pulte Homes, and other mortgage lenders, including national, regional, and local mortgage bankers, brokers, banks, savings and loans associations, and other financial institutions. In this regard, Lennar competes in the origination and sale of mortgage loans, which includes interest rates and mortgage plan products. In the financial service space, Lennar is facing stronger competition with regard to mortgage origination and the potential loss of incentive-based programs as well as repurchased securities. Additionally, Lennar offers ancillary services and competes with other title insurance agencies and underwriters for title insurance and closing services, with competitive factors including service and price. Finally, the homebuilder operates as a communication service provider in the sale of cable television and high-speed internet services. Major factors that contribute to the competition in this space include price, quality, service, and availability.

Consumer overview

Market segmentation is essential to a company's success and is a driving characteristic of a company's market strategy. Lennar's market segmentation is primarily made up of first-time, move-up, and active adult homebuyers (Barnes, 2015a). Due to the rise of multigenerational households, Lennar has also added them to its target market segments. Within these target segments, married couples and single females have the highest homebuying rate in all age groups except those of 34 and younger. Within the age range of 34 and younger, homebuyers primarily consist of couples.

First-time buyers

First-time buyers used to make up 50 percent of existing home sales; however, as of 2013 they only made up approximately 35 percent. Generation Y, which has an age range of individuals that are 34 and younger, are 68 percent of first-time homebuyers, with the average first-time buyer age at 33. Thus, the share of first-time buyers declines as age increases (National Association of Realtors [NARS], 2015).

The average first-time buyer has an average income of $64,074, with a median home purchase value of $150,000. Thirty-nine percent of first-time homebuyers state that their primary reason for buying a home is due to a desire to own a home of their own. This could be in relation to the fact that 77 percent of first-time buyers were previously renters.

First-time homebuyers are more likely to buy older and previously owned homes due to a better price and better overall value. They are also most likely to purchase a home based on convenience to the location of their job and overall neighborhood affordability. In addition, younger homebuyers are more likely to buy homes that are within 10 miles of their previous residence.

Move-up homebuyers

Move-up homebuyers are buyers that buy a home that is generally larger and more expensive than the home they already own. This segment usually consists of homebuyers that have acquired a substantial increase in their income. The average age of a move-up homebuyer is 45, with an average income of $84,170 and an average household size of 2.7 persons. Furthermore, approximately 17 percent of move-up homebuyers bought a house that cost more than $500,000.

Adult homebuyers

Adult homebuyers consist of Generation X (ages 35–49), Younger Boomers (ages 50–59), Older Boomers (ages 60–68), and the Silent Generation (ages 69–89). Among these groups, Generation X had the highest income levels, with an average household income of $104,600; the Silent Generation had the lowest income levels, with an average household income of $63,600. Similar to Generation Y, 23 percent of Generation X homebuyers placed a high importance on owning a home of their own, yet many purchased homes due to a change in family situation or a job-related relocation. Younger Boomers are more likely to purchase a home to downsize, while Older Boomers and the Silent Generation are more likely to move for retirement and to be closer to friends and family.

Among the adult homebuyer segment, there is a difference in the homebuying preferences and deal-breakers based on generations. Generation X homebuyers consider the quality of school districts and the convenience of school locations when purchasing a home. Yet Older Boomers and the Silent Generation are more concerned with convenience to friends, family, and health facilities. Older Boomers and the Silent Generation are also more likely than other generations to purchase a brand new home due to the amenities and in order to avoid renovations or structural/utility problems. Like younger first-time homebuyers, Generation X homebuyers are more likely to move within 10 miles of their previous residence. However, the Silent Generation is more likely to move within 20 miles and the Older Boomers are more likely to move the farthest with a distance of up to 30 miles. Moreover, the older the homebuyer, the fewer compromises the buyer tended to make with their home purchase; 48 percent of the Silent Generation made no compromises on their home purchase (NARS, 2015).

The type of homes purchased also varies within the adult homebuyer segment. At least 80 percent of buyers who are aged 59 and younger bought a detached single-family home, yet buyers over the age of 59 purchased townhomes and condos. Additionally, 13 percent of buyers over the age of 49 and one-quarter of buyers over the age of 69 purchased a home in a senior-related housing for themselves or others.

Multigenerational households

One of the newer trends of the homebuying market involves the increase of purchasing multigenerational homes. Multigenerational households consist of three generations with usually adult children over the age of 18, and/or grandparents residing in the home. Thirteen percent of all homebuyers purchased a multigenerational home, with 21 percent of them being Younger Boomers. The three most common reasons for the formation of multigenerational households were cost savings, children over 18 moving back into the house, and caretaking of aging parents.

Brand reputation and customer complaints

Lennar Corporation prides itself on being a professional organization that is committed to its founding principles of quality, value, and integrity. It builds upon its industry-leading reputation of experience, expertise, and financial strength. However, as a result of competition within the industry as well as reduced variable costs associated with homebuilding, Lennar, as well as its competitors, had to shift away from custom homes. Although this approach allowed the brand to presell more homes and increased the homebuilders' efficiency, it also resulted in more model-style homes with little to no product differentiability among competitors throughout the industry. The brand also shifted its attention and advertising to brand reputation, quality, and home features and coined the slogan "Everything's Included." This shift focused on the consumer and what they, as homebuyers, sought in their dream homes. Lennar then committed to providing the high-quality features and upgrades its homebuyers' sought as a default element of the home.

Although the brand took a strong approach to forging a strong brand reputation, consumers' perceptions of the brand were not as strong. Looking at a review of complaints and resolutions on the Better Business Bureaus (n.d.), top complaints by consumers included cheap quality materials, poor craftsmanship, unreliable appliances and equipment, providing high-risk mortgages, and useless warranties. However, in 2010, the *J.D. Power and Associates Overall Customer Satisfaction with Home Builders and New-Home Quality Report* noted a consecutive improvement in customer satisfaction with new-home builders, new-home quality, and overall customer satisfaction. Additionally, new-home quality increased, reaching a record high, and the top problems focused on were issues with landscaping, kitchen cabinet finish and quality, and heating and air conditioning. The study also noted that satisfaction improved in a variety of categories, most notably in workmanship and material and home readiness. Also, the only factor not improved was the recreational facilities provided by the builder. Additionally, in 2015, Lennar Corporation ranked second in the Homebuilders Industry of Forbes' Most Admired Companies, with the brand being ranked first in innovation and social responsibility. It is important to note, however, that despite these industry-wide improvements, Lennar Corporation is still witnessing complaints in regard to its poor construction, bad design, and cheap materials. One of the most common complaints also notes that consumers felt that the brand was deceptive, showing a "cutaway" model which suggested the brand would provide the highest quality design and material, but that that is not what the brand is delivering. To continue to grow, corner the homebuilders' market, and build brand loyalty, Lennar Corporation will need to make changes to its construction processes.

How consumer trust affects brand reputation

For a company to be successful in its industry it has to win consumer trust and build a strong relationship. The type of investment the customer has to make towards these types of acquisitions is very significant. Very often customers have the chance to acquire only one house throughout their lifetime. This makes it even more important to have a brand reputation that is not only positive but also solid enough to attract the customers that are ready for this expensive investment. Studies have demonstrated that companies may not have the biggest sales or market share in their categories, but the trustworthiest brands have created relationships with consumers through experiences that trigger a visceral response (Andruss, 2012). Lennar is well known in the homebuilding industry, being the leader, and in time has been working a lot on its brand reputation.

One of the key aspects that Lennar has worked on to enforce its brand has been the diverse customer segmentation of the market. Lennar is conscious that diversifying its customer segments helps in the growth of trustworthiness. Lennar has divided this market into active seniors, empty nesters, young professionals, singles, young families with children, and first-time homebuyers (Barnes, 2015a). Giving each segment a great variety of products is the key to fulfilling their different needs. It is logic that having a great variety of products means that the brand will have to be considered very flexible to succeed. Customers expect always the best from the product offered, in this case a new house. They feel the trust growing only when the first transaction has been completed with positive outcomes and the customer feels really satisfied by the purchase, considering how he/she has been treated by the company too.

In the business world as in life they say that it takes years to build trust with the customers and only seconds to destroy it all. An article from Forbes underlines the importance of being able to build trust with consistency during time. Trust is not enough at times, what counts a lot too is the integrity of the company. Integrity means doing the right thing at all times and in all circumstances (Anderson, 2012). Lennar Corporation has been an example of integrity for the whole industry. The integrity of Lennar's operation is reported under its core principles where Lennar states a strong commitment to quality, value, and integrity as its underlying foundation upon which it was built (Lennar Corporation, 2015). This integrity is directly connected to the reason why Lennar has built a very strong trust with its customers during its many years of activities.

Lennar's primary goal has to be to encourage its customers to have trust in the corporation. The client, who will purchase the house, will have to be already confident in Lennar's brand and will have to have trust in its operations throughout the purchase and afterwards. After the purchase, many times, is where the company can establish the deepest trust with the customer. When the company follows in detail the customer after the purchase it will have a positive outcome and the customer will very likely share this experience with the community and expand Lennar's popularity. Lennar has been demonstrating throughout its growth how it has been able to establish good and in-depth trust.

Building a reputation

The goal of the brand should be to establish a culture that is conducive to the vision of the brand. In order for the Lennar Corporation to improve its brand reputation, it must promise its customers that it will actually live up to the image it projects. This includes listening to the feedback from the previous homebuyers in order to improve the experiences of its future customers. From that point, it is vital that the company follows through and delivers to the standards that are promised. In order to achieve true change and overcoming such a negative brand reputation all employees must be committed to the overall change. That includes all positions from entry level to upper management. In the case of Lennar, the subcontractors that are used to supply the materials and build the homes must also understand the standards being set by the Lennar Corporation. There must be an overall understanding of the organizational goal to improve its brand reputation and revive the brand trust that was lost among the buyers who had previously purchased from Lennar Corporation.

References

Anderson, A. (2012, November 28). Success will come and go, but integrity is forever. *Forbes*. Retrieved November 19, 2015, from www.forbes.com/sites/amyanderson/2012/11/28/success-will-come-and-go-but-integrity-is-forever/

Andruss, P. (2012, March 20). Secrets of the 10 most-trusted brands. *Entrepreneur*. Retrieved November 19, 2015, from www.entrepreneur.com/article/223125

Barnes, P. (2015a). Market segmentation in Lennar Corporation. *Market Realist*. Retrieved November 19, 2015, from http://marketrealist.com/2015/03/market-segmentation-lennar-corporation/

Barnes, P. (2015b). Lennar Corporation – one of the largest US homebuilders. *Market Realist*. Retrieved November 19, 2015, from http://marketrealist.com/2015/03/lennars-deliveries-average-selling-price/

Better Business Bureaus. (n.d.). Consumer complaints for Lennar Homes, Inc. – *South East Florida BBB*. Retrieved November 19, 2015, from www.bbb.org/south-east-florida/business-reviews/home-builders/lennar-homes-in-miami-fl-6718/complaints

Forbes. (n.d.). *World's Most Admired Companies 2015*. Retrieved November 19, 2015, from http://fortune.com/worlds-most-admired-companies/lennar-100000/

Funding Universe (n.d.). Lennar Corporation history. *Funding Universe*. Retrieved November 19, 2015, from www.fundinguniverse.com/company-histories/lennar-corporation-history/

Glink, I. (2013). Housing trend: builders offer "home-within-a-home." *CBS Money Watch*. Retrieved November 19, 2015, from www.cbsnews.com/news/housing-trend-builders-offer-home-within-a-home/

Hamilton, C., Church, T., and Dornbach-Bender, R. (2009). *Strategic Report for Lennar Corporation*. Oasis Consulting. Retrieved November 19, 2015, from http://economicsfiles.pomona.edu/jlikens/SeniorSeminars/oasis/reports/LEN.pdf

Home Builders. (2015, June 1). Increasing housing affordability opens doors to homeownership for more Americans. *NAHB*. Retrieved November 8, 2015, from www.nahb.org/en/news-and-publications/Press-Releases/2015/june/increasing-housing-affordability-opens-doors-to-homeownership-for-more-americans.aspx

J.D. Power and Associates. (2010, September 15). *J.D. Power and Associates Reports: Satisfaction with New-Home Builders and New-Home Quality*. Retrieved November 19, 2015, from http://businesscenter.jdpower.com/news/pressrelease.aspx?ID=2010177

Lennar Corporation. (2015). *Lennar*. Retrieved November 19, 2015, from www.lennar.com/about/core-values

Matthews, C. (2015, August 25). It's good to be a homebuilder in 2015. *Fortune*. Retrieved November 19, 2015, from http://fortune.com/2015/08/25/homebuilders-fastest-growing/

National Association of Home Builders. (2015, November 15). Housing markets continue to recover at modest pace. Retrieved November 8, 2015, from www.nahb.org/en/news-and-publications/Press-Releases/2015/november/housing-markets-continue-to-recover-at-modest-pace.aspx

National Association of Realtors (NARS). (2015). *Home Buyer and Seller Generational Trends Report 2015*. Retrieved November 19, 2015, from www.nar.realtor/sites/default/files/reports/2015/2015-home-buyer-and-seller-generational-trends-2015-03-11.pdf

Oasis Consulting. (2009, April 22). *Strategic Report for Lennar Corporation*. Retrieved November 19, 2015, from http://economics-files.pomona.edu/jlikens/SeniorSeminars/oasis/reports/LEN.pdffiles.pomona.edu/jlikens/SeniorSeminars/oasis/reports/LEN.pdf

Occupational Safety & Health Administration. (n.d.). Description for 1521: General Contractors-Single-Family Houses. Retrieved November 19, 2015, from www.osha.gov/pls/imis/sic_manual.display?id=405&tab=description

Schiffman, B. (2015, October 19). Homebuilders: everything is awesome. *Forbes*. Retrieved November 6, 2015, from www.forbes.com/sites/betsyschiffman/2015/10/19/homebuilders-everything-is-awesome/

Steele, A. (2012). Lennar's NextGen Home-within-a-Home provides multigenerational living. *New Home Source*. Retrieved November 19, 2015, from www.newhomesource.com/resourcecenter/articles/lennars-nextgen-home-within-a-home-provides-solutions-for-multigenerational-living

U.S. Securities and Exchange Commission. (2011, November 30). Lennar Corporation Annual Report Form 10-K. Retrieved November 19, 2015, from www.sec.gov/Archives/edgar/data/920760/000119312512029792/d257946d10k.htm

Chipotle: the cost of fresh fast food

Chipotle is a fast casual dining restaurant headquartered in Denver, Colorado. During middle to late 2015, Chipotle was connected to a number of health concerns related to E. coli, salmonella, and norovirus incidents at several of its restaurants in as many as 12 states. As a result of these incidents, related restaurant closures, and the negative publicity that comes with the health concerns, Chipotle's sales were significantly impacted during the last months of the year 2015. Comparable restaurant sales (the change in period-over-period sales) fell 14.6 percent for the fourth quarter of 2015. The negative impact carried over to 2016, with comparable restaurant sales declining more than 36 percent in January 2016 (Chipotle Mexican Grill, Inc., 2016). As a result of the slumping sales, Co-CEO and founder Steve Ells, along with Chipotle's board of directors devised a number of marketing and promotional strategies beginning the first quarter of 2016 to invite customers back to the stores and work on getting their trust back. Just two months before the decision by the Centers of Disease Control (CDC) to declare the E. coli outbreak connected to Chipotle restaurants over, Ells penned a letter posted on the company's website where he apologized to consumers and pledged to turn Chipotle into a leader in food safety in the food industry. Ells added, "To achieve our goal of establishing leadership in food safety, we collaborated with preeminent food safety experts to design a comprehensive food safety program that dramatically reduces risk on our farms, throughout the supply chain, and in our restaurants" (Ells, 2015).

Ells wanted to address consumers' concerns that the food being served at all Chipotle restaurants is as safe as it can be. To do this, he designed a collaboration with food safety experts to determine a comprehensive food safety program that would reduce the risk of illnesses at its farms, throughout the supply chain, and ultimately at the restaurants. Some of the changes being implemented at the supply chain level include high-resolution sampling and testing of all ingredients to prevent contamination, working with food suppliers to enhance their food safety programs, introduction of additional steps to eliminate the risk of bacterial contamination, rolling out of enhanced sanitation procedures and incentives at Chipotle restaurants, as well as additional food safety training for all employees (Chipotle Mexican Grill, Inc., 2016). In an effort to invite customers back to the restaurants, a number of promotional activities have been implemented involving promotional offers for free or discounted food. In February 2016 Chipotle rolled out its "Burrito raincheck" promotion aimed at luring back customers by giving away free burritos. Last month, the company announced an extension to its free food promotion by sending out 21 million coupons by mail for free menu items, good until May 15 (Feeney, 2016). Ells is now counting on the new food safety protocol and promotional activities to bring customers back to the restaurants and stop the declining sales, but the question remained, will these efforts be enough for Chipotle to earn customers' trust back and stop the decline in sales?

Chipotle history

Founded in 1993, in a former ice cream store in Denver, Colorado, founder Steve Ells opened the very first fast casual restaurant called Chipotle Mexican Grill. Using an $85,000 loan from his father, Ells committed to selling high-quality and fresh burritos daily, near the campus of the University of Denver (Brand, 2006). After only one month in business the restaurant saw great success and led to Ells opening a second location less than two years later and soon after a third. With great success and a determination to keep growing Ells worked with his father, who became an investor, created a board of directors, and began searching for investors, eventually raising enough to grow the business.

As business grew, so did the attention of its success. In 1998, McDonald's made an investment in the business (Brand, 2006). Making it the largest investor of the company, McDonald's fueled the momentum taking the small company to more than 500 locations just seven years later (Brand, 2006). As the company grew, the focus of serving high-quality fast food remained a driving force for Ells and his team. As a result, in 2009, Ells announced a new focus for the company and released a new mission statement defining it as "Food with Integrity" (Barnes, 2009). To demonstrate a commitment to serving fresh ingredients to its customers, it began focusing on where its ingredients came from. First beginning this change by eliminating dairy products that included the bovine growth hormone, this would include its sour cream and cheeses (Barnes, 2009). Ells then worked with suppliers who were committed to producing and maintaining sustainable, safe, and healthy practices to raise animals and produce. As such, paired with its mission for "Food with Integrity," Chipotle moved to a "naturally raised" criteria for its chicken, beef, and pork used in its products (Biondich, 2008). To continue this change the company began working with certified organic growers to produce almost 60 percent of the company's black beans used in their products (Czaplewski, Olson, and McNulty, 2014).

Now with over 22 years of building a successful business, these same standards ring true for the company. It is still devoted to finding and serving only the very best ingredients while maintaining its commitment to giving respect to the animals, the farmers who provide the produce for its restaurants, while limiting its negative impact on the environment, what some now label as having a "green marketing strategy" (Czaplewski, Olson, and McNulty, 2014).

This focus of a green marketing strategy has driven sales and profits and it has also impacted the company's culture. In 2005, the company did a major overhaul and transformed the way management teams were recognized, promoted, and motivated (Nisen, 2014). During this time it implemented a new system that would promote managers from within the company, rather than hiring from outside the company. The motivation for doing this was to encourage, motivate, and prove to its employees that it was investing in them and essentially the company. To supplement and support the program it also implemented the "restaurateur program" (Nisen, 2014). The program is designed to allow hourly crew members the ability to transition and be promoted to managers. These individuals are chosen from the current pool of general managers, are then promoted based on skill, ability to manage their store successfully, but also through their ability to train new employees including their peers. When promoted they are presented with a one-time bonus, stock options, and the ability to earn an extra $10,000 bonus for each additional crew member they train and support to become a general manager (Nisen, 2014).

The refocus of reinvesting in its employees and focusing on fresh, healthy ingredients has paid off for Chipotle. Since its formative days in the late 1990s, Chipotle has grown from a three-store business to having approximately 1,500 locations, in 43 states, Canada, and with international expansion in the works. Its employee count has grown to more than 37,300 and counting as expansion continues and new stores open. Its success skyrocketed until a massive health concern plagued the company beginning in mid to late 2015, resulting in loss of profits by 14.6 percent in the final quarter of 2015 (Giammona, 2016). This was the first decline for the company since it opened in 1993. Still at the helm, it is now up to Co-CEO and Founder Steve Ells, Co-CEO Montgomery Moran, their top management and decision-making officials Chief Financial Officer John Hartung, Chief Creative and Development Officer Mark Crumpacker and the remaining seven other board of directors to make decisions to benefit the company and turn sales around.

Background information

As is the case with most consumer-related industries, fast food restaurants have realized the need to adapt in efforts to stay aligned with trends and changing consumer tastes if they are to remain relevant and competitive. With the obesity epidemic plaguing the United States, many quick service restaurant chains have come under increasing scrutiny for low food quality and poor preparation, shown to have negative health consequences and opposing a general change in consumer attitudes towards healthy diet and lifestyles (Amidor, 2013). Many fast food offerings are high in calories, artery-clogging saturated fat, and sodium (Amidor, 2013). In 2010, the U.S. Food and Drug Administration unveiled guidelines for a mandatory menu calorie count to be implemented in March 2011 for all chain restaurants with 20 or more locations (Amidor, 2013). Once these numbers were reported, there was no doubt that most choices at fast food joints were unhealthy ones, causing an increase in consumer demand for healthy fast food and changes throughout the fast food industry (Amidor, 2013).

A survey was conducted of the nation's 100 largest quick service chains, as defined by the number of locations, and found that many quick service and fast casual restaurants are creating menus that look more and more like what consumers would cook at home in efforts to meet customer expectations (Minkin and Renaud, 2016). The survey scored the chains on such factors as the use of healthy fats and preparations, healthy sodium counts in entrees, availability of nutritional information, and the use of organic produce to determine the ten highest-ranking restaurants, with Chipotle ranked as sixth (Minkin and Renaud, 2016). But as the traditional definitions of "healthy" continue to change, consumers are not only looking for low-calorie meals but transparency in regards to how the food is sourced and ingredients used (Taylor, 2015). Overall, 87 percent of fast food operators say their customers are paying more attention to nutrition than they were two years ago (National Restaurant Association, 2012).

Over the last decade, fast food restaurants or, more technically, quick service restaurants (QSRs), have grown at a much faster pace than any other segment in the restaurant industry (Trefis Team, 2014). Best described by concepts such as McDonald's, KFC, and Burger King, they are characterized by fast food cuisines with average quality of food, minimal to no table service, limited menus, and price of meals ranging from $3 to $6 per person (Trefis Team, 2014). In typical QSRs, fast food is highly processed and prepared in bulk using standardized cooking procedures. Moreover, QSRs are typically part of a restaurant chain or franchise operations, with drive-thru outlets for most of these chains (Trefis Team, 2014).

The biggest shift that the QSR industry has seen in recent years is the push for healthier food. As more Americans become obese and face resulting health problems, many people are trying to take control of their eating and want their favorite restaurants to follow suit. QSRs like McDonald's and Wendy's are not typically known for their diet-friendly meals, but are making significant changes to their menus in order to cater to the health-conscious crowd. This can be seen with new menu items including oatmeal breakfasts, fresh salad options, and grilled alternatives to fried chicken. McDonald's has been leading the fast food restaurant category in terms of system-wide sales and total number of restaurants worldwide followed by Subway and Starbucks (Trefis Team, 2014). In the fiscal year 2013, system-wide sales for the fast food giant rose 2 percent to reach nearly $28 billion and its total store count reached nearly 35,000 with 7,000 company-operated restaurants (Trefis Team, 2014).

However, fast casual restaurants such as Chipotle Mexican Grill have started eating into the market share of these leading QSR chains. According to Technomic's 2014 Top 500 chain restaurant report, sales for fast casual chains grew by 11 percent and store count by 8 percent in 2013 (Trefis Team, 2014). This is due to the fact that fast casual restaurants are zeroing in on consumers' desire to eat healthy, affordable food on the run (Trefis Team, 2014). It is at this intersection of higher-quality food and the need to be quick that fast casual has found its niche.

Fast casual restaurants are a relatively fresh and rapidly growing concept, positioned somewhere between fast food restaurants and casual dining restaurants (Trefis Team, 2014). They provide counter service and offer more customized, freshly prepared, and higher quality food than traditional QSRs, all in an upscale and inviting ambiance (Trefis Team, 2014). They also have minimum table service but the typical cost per meal ranges from $8 to $15 (Trefis Team, 2014). This higher range is due to the additional costs of high-quality organic ingredients and flavors in the dishes and other conveniences such as nonplastic proper dining utensils and plates (Trefis Team, 2014). Sales at fast casual franchises tend to be strongest at lunch and have nearly the same share of lunch customers as casual dining restaurants (Sena, 2016). Brands such as Chipotle Mexican Grill, Panera Bread, Qdoba Mexican Grill, and Baja Fresh are considered the top restaurants in this category (Trefis Team, 2014). Although the menu offerings are slightly more expensive than QSRs such as McDonald's and Burger King, customers perceive them as having better quality ingredients and food.

Sixty percent of frequent fast food diners cite healthy menu options among their top reasons for choosing a fast casual restaurant (Sloan, 2014). This consumer shift is primarily due to the fact that people with higher disposable income are more inclined towards quality and hygienic food, unlike less nutritional "junk food" in most of the quick service outlets (Trefis Team, 2014). However, recent statistics over the last four years have shown that Millennials have also been increasing their consumption of fast casual by 5 percent annually, whereas their consumption of fast food has remained largely flat (O'Sullivan, 2015).

Current company status

Chipotle over the years has been a fast-growing company that found its niche in the market between a fast food company and sit-down restaurant that is able to deliver high-quality food. The company has opened over 2,000 restaurants in the U.S. and has now made itself one of the most desirable Mexican grill restaurant chains. In order to continue with its rapid growth, it needed to pick up investors along the way and

Chipotle was able to have McDonald's invest heavily in the company in 1998. Now that Chipotle had the backing of a major company it wanted to continue to grow the company as it felt it had established itself as one of the safest restaurants you can eat at. Due to the major success in the U.S. Chipotle went international with its Mexican grill restaurant with locations in the United Kingdom, Canada, Germany, and France.

Chipotle experienced two separate E. coli outbreaks that included 58 people in October 2015. Once word got out about the outbreak Chipotle's stock began a steady decline and hasn't recovered since. Chipotle's stock at the high point was $750.42 and as it sits on March 21, 2018 it was at $334.52. As Chipotle struggled on the financial market it did not stop trying to find a way to become cleared of the E. coli virus from the CDC. On February 1, 2016 Chipotle was finally declared free of the E. coli virus (Whitten, 2016). Between the initial outbreak in October 2015 and the end of the outbreak in February 2016 Chipotle put together new processes and procedures to limit the risks of this outbreak or any other outbreak from happening again. This not only helps it live up to its mission of "Food with Integrity," but helps the brand of Chipotle move forward into a positive direction.

As Chipotle moves into the future it now must think of ways to grow the company internationally and how to diversify itself and it has done just that. "We have two non-Chipotle brands open now – ShopHouse and Pizzeria Locale – and have noted before that the Chipotle model could be applied to a wide variety of foods," said Chris Arnold, a Chipotle spokesman (Yu, 2016). Chipotle has also just applied for a trademark of Better Burger to get into the U.S. burger industry. ShopHouse is a restaurant in Asia and the Pizzeria Locale is in Italy. These two restaurant hopefuls delivered on a promise made by Chris Arnold that Chipotle would branch out into a wide variety of foods.

Value proposition/target market

As the brand continues to grow and prosper the company has put together a value proposition that has built a foundation for it going forward that it can rely on. "Food with Integrity" (Chipotle, n.d.). This value proposition has a major impact on the company as it continues to invest in the research and development stages of being able to produce its food at the highest quality. It has been able to fund its own farms and testing facilities so the company knows it is offering the highest quality of food money can buy. Chipotle has also taken this a step further by putting together a layout of its restaurants that lets the customers into the kitchen. The food is prepped, cooked, and put together right in front of the customers' eyes. This not only speaks to the quality of food it is offering, but translates to the customers that the company has nothing to hide and wants the customer to feel at ease.

As Chipotle was introduced into the market it did not know who would walk through its doors – the young, the old, or the in between. Chipotle did target the University of Denver as it opened its first location near there. As the company grew it began to define who its target market was. "Chipotle has recently found a primary customer segment in millennials" (Naguilar, 2015). This has helped Chipotle focus its marketing strategies to this segment of the market. The millennials are a younger group that is tech savvy and they like to get in and out of restaurants as quickly as possible, but still want high-quality food, even if that means paying a higher price than the likes of McDonald's and such.

Integrated marketing strategies

As Chipotle looks to move the company forward and past the food safety concerns such as E. coli, it will steer its marketing strategies to hit the issue head on. It has and will continue to improve on the food handling processes. Part of the marketing strategies will be not to hide what it is doing to improve the food handling process, but it wants its customers to know what it is doing. "Founder and co-CEO Steve Ells said steps such as high-resolution testing of fresh produce and chopping tomatoes in central commissaries rather than in restaurants will reduce the risk of another outbreak 'to near zero' " (Beaubien, 2016).

One of the first strategies Chipotle will do is send a letter to all its loyal customers (those who have signed up to receive special offers and to create accounts online) explaining what took place with the E. coli virus and what the company did to take action to make sure its customers knew Chipotle had their best interests. The company then would work on bringing customers back through its doors offering promotions such as buy-one get-one free (this would only be offered for a limited time to protect the brand). Any other communication that goes out with the marketing strategies would have a positive spin on the message being delivered and with these new strategies Chipotle vows to keep the customers' health and safety its number one priority.

Food safety concerns

Ells founded Chipotle under the brand promise of "Food with Integrity" (Whipp, 2016). It was this core concept that came into question in 2015 when restaurants across 12 states were linked to E. coli, norovirus, and salmonella (Table 6.1). Centers for Disease Control (CDC) investigations were initiated along with court-ordered subpoenas for food-safety documents dating back to 2013. In the end, the source of the outbreaks was unknown, as it is often in multi-ingredient cases, but the CDC pointed to produce as the likely culprit while Chipotle blamed its Australian free-range beef (Whipp, 2016). Chipotle posits this was a cross-contamination issue while the CDC blames source ingredients. Furthering the confusion is Chipotle's lack of traceability of ingredients from source farm to restaurant (Jargon and Newman, 2016).

Table 6.1 Timeline of outbreaks

When	Where	Cases reported	Culprit	Source
July	Seattle	5	E. coli	Unknown
August	Simi Valley, CA	234	Norovirus	Unknown
August and September	Minnesota	64	Salmonella	Tomatoes
Began Oct. 19	CA, IL, MD, MN, NY, OH, OR, PA, WA	52	E. coli	Unknown
December	Boston	136	Norovirus	Unknown

Source: www.foodsafetynews.com/2015/12/a-timeline-of-chipotles-five-outbreaks/.

QSRs have battled similar food-related illness in the past and successfully recovered. For example, in 2006 Taco Bello (Yum! Brands Inc.) suffered an E. coli outbreak that sickened 71 people across four states (Duggan, 2015). As a publicly traded company, Yum! Brands stock fell 3.5 percent in December 2006 but has since fully recovered.

The road to recovery

Duggan (2015) posits that happy customers have "short memories" and providing Chipotle handles the outbreaks appropriately, the brand should fully recover; however, according to Jeffery Bernstein of Barclays, Chipotle may have a harder time recovering given its "Food with Integrity" brand promise "thereby making the E. coli outbreak more damaging" and given its "more educated customer base and greater social media awareness" (Derrick, 2015). Attempting to leverage these obstacles, in 2016 Chipotle pushed two large digital media campaigns:

1. Burrito raincheck, an SMS/web promotion for a free burrito.
2. Guac Hunter, an online digital game where customers could win free guacamole and chips.

The free burrito campaign was meant to lure back Chipotle customers and for the most part, customer traffic increased with the free vs. paid entrees declining from 30 percent in early January to 20 percent in early March (Jargon, 2016). Still, Chipotle has a lot of work to do to win back its customers. Surveys show between 5 and 7 percent of customers state they "will never come back" and the majority will be waiting some time before returning (Jargon, 2016). It may be a long road for Chipotle whose recovery will also be affected by "incremental costs of labor to better insulate the supply chain and a lack of pricing power" (Derrick, 2015). Chipotle's decision to focus on food safety policy and supply-chain management are forcing the 23-year-old company to redefine its position and value proposition.

Food safety policy

Since extensive CDC investigations failed to identify the source of the outbreak, Ells decided to mitigate risk factors by instilling tougher food safety protocols along with supply-chain adjustments. On February 8, 2016 all Chipotle restaurants closed for a few hours to hold a company-wide meeting with its more than 60,000 employees (Jennings, 2016). New food safety measures include, but are not limited to:

- increasing standards for suppliers;
- high-resolution DNA testing of ingredients for various pathogens;
- prepping higher-risk ingredients like tomatoes and romaine lettuce in a central kitchen where kill-step methods can be used;
- making sure restaurant-level staff are observing the most up-to-date food safety practices (Jennings, 2016).

Moreover, Chipotle's contamination risk from meat is much higher than any other chain since beef was brought fresh into its kitchens (Jargon and Newman, 2016). New procedures now call for the handling of all beef after-hours. Also, the beef is now precooked at a central kitchen and restaurants are simply responsible for adding spices and warming up the meat. Each restaurant has an appointed food-safety leader and managers' bonuses are tied directly to food safety (Jargon and Newman, 2016). Chipotle has always been dedicated to obtaining the best ingredients, eliminating GMOs when possible, and being transparent on the source ingredients. Chipotle will continue this promise with an added emphasis on food safety.

Supply-chain management

Supply-chain management "encompasses organizing the optimal flow of high-quality, value-for-money materials from a suitable set of innovative suppliers" (Eltantawy, 2008). Chipotle asserts that its Australian supplier of beef is the best option and although the outbreak may have been tied to this supplier, Chipotle will not be dropping its Australian source of grass-fed beef; however, it is testing meat for pathogens before it arrives on restaurants (Jargon and Newman, 2016). Chipotle was unable to trace back certain ingredients to its source farm. It has since required suppliers to label shipments to get scanned at distribution centers. Additionally, restaurants will soon be able to scan incoming items to aid in traceability within the supply chain. This type of supplier integration is a "valuable source of competitive advantage because it enhances responsiveness, flexibility, and timesaving" (Eltantawy, 2008). More importantly, this process will make source farms accountable for the ingredients. By making these changes, Chipotle can use its supply-chain process as a strategic tool for competitive success.

The future of Chipotle brand

This food safety crisis fueled Ells to reenergize its "Food with Integrity" mantra. Ells told investors that Chipotle "prided itself on being a safe place to eat but that the [outbreaks shows they] need to do better" (Jargon and Newman, 2016). The February 8th meeting was both a rally and a public sign of "additional comfort" for Chipotle customers (Jennings, 2016). According to Ells, the policy changes "will make Chipotle the safest restaurant to eat at and bring outbreak risks to near zero" (Jargon and Newman, 2016). A bold and risky statement. Although Ells will try to mitigate all risk factors, he may never be able to positively guarantee zero outbreak, and this could be a problematic position for the brand. Still, as Ells states, in the future, the broader marketing push will not focus on food safety but rather what has made Chipotle successful thus far – its food.

Does fresh fast food come at a price?

In February 2016 Chipotle announced its full-year 2015 results and the end of the CDC investigation into the E. coli incidents. The fourth quarter of 2015 was one of the most challenging in Chipotle's history, but as the CDC investigation concluded, Chipotle hoped to leave that in the past and start a new chapter. Ells stated, "We are pleased to leave this behind us and can place our full energies to implementing our enhanced food safety plan that will establish Chipotle as an industry leader in food safety." He further stated, "We are extremely focused on executing this program, which designs layers of redundancy and enhanced safety measures to reduce the food safety risk to a level as near to zero as is possible" (Business Wire, 2016). Commenting on Chipotle's battle to ensure food safety, Melinda Wilkins, Director of the Master of Science in food safety at Michigan State University, wrote, "The more complicated your supply chain is, the more opportunity you have to introduce problems" (Alba, 2016). Wilkins added that by trying to meet customers' demands of serving fresh and fast food, Chipotle is walking a fine line between "offering fresh, local ingredients and decentralized food preparation and the risk of introducing foodborne pathogens" (Alba, 2016). Now that Chipotle has switched to a centralized food preparation system, these risks will be minimized. But there are still challenges ahead.

In February 2016, comparable sales were down by 26.1 percent, 21.5 percent the first week of March and 27.3 percent the second week of March. Although this is an improvement from the 36 percent in January, it's still a far cry from the improvement investors expected. Wedbush Securities analyst Nick Setyan estimated that the company would not bounce back to the $2.5 million sales per restaurant that Chipotle once generated until at least 2018 (Levine-Weinberg, 2016). Moreover, even if sales continue to improve, Setyan commented that due to Chipotle's enhanced food-safety procedures, the company's profits would continue to suffer.

Market analysts pointed out that Chipotle is capable of growing sales fairly quickly, as it did during the year 2014, where sales per restaurant increased from $2.17 million to $2.47 million (Levine-Weinberg, 2016). According to analyst Mark Kalinowski at Nomura Securities, what Chipotle needs the most at this moment is avoid any food safety scares and to stay out of the news for a while.

The food tastes good. The speediness of the customer service is good. So, if they're out of the news for a while, and people aren't being reminded that over and over again about their food safety issues, then the customers will eventually gravitate back.

(Berr, 2016)

References

Alba, D. (2016, January 15). Chipotle's health crisis shows fresh food comes at a price. *Wired*. Retrieved April 8, 2016, from www.wired.com/2016/01/chipotles-health-crisis-shows-fresh-food-comes-at-a-price/

Amidor, T. (2013, October 21). Has fast food become healthier? *US News*. Retrieved from http://health.usnews.com/health-news/blogs/eat-run/2013/10/21/has-fast-food-become-healthier

Barnes, S. (2009, November 5). Integrity is key to Chipotle brand. *Times Union*. Retrieved March 20, 2018, from www.timesunion.com/living/article/Integrity-is-key-to-Chipotle-brand-547662.php

Beaubien, G. (2016, January 14). With new marketing plan, Chipotle looks to move forward. *PRSA*. Retrieved April 10, 2016, from www.prsa.org/SearchResults/view/11374/105/With_New_Marketing_Plan_Chipotle_Looks_to_Move_For#.VwpaLhMrKRs

Berr, J. (2016, April 3). Wall Street has a mixed appetite for Chipotle. *CBS News*. Retrieved April 8, 2016, from www.cbsnews.com/news/wall-street-has-a-mixed-appetite-for-chipotle/

Biondich, S. (2008, February 6). Food with integrity: Chipotle's fresh Mex. *Shepherd Express*. Retrieved April 8, 2016, from http://shepherdexpress.com/article-763-food-with-integrity.html

Brand, R. (2006). Chipotle founder had big dreams. *Rocky Mountain News*. Retrieved April 8, 2016, from http://rockymountainnews.com/news/2006/dec/23/chipotle-founder-had-big-dreams/

Business Wire. (2016, February 2). Chipotle Mexican Grill, Inc. announces fourth quarter and full year 2015 results; CDC investigation over; Chipotle welcomes customers back to restaurants. *Business Wire*. Retrieved April 8, 2016, from www.businesswire.com/news/home/20160202006613/en/

Chipotle. (n.d.). Food with Integrity. *Chipotle.com*. Retrieved March 21, 2018, from www.chipotle.com/food-with-integrity

Chipotle Mexican Grill Inc. (2016, February 5). 10K SEC filings.

Czaplewski, A. Olson, E., and McNulty, P. (2014). Going green puts Chipotle in the black. *American Marketing Association*. Retrieved April 8, 2016, from www.ama.org/publications/MarketingNews/Pages/Going-Green--Puts-Chipotle-in-the-Black.aspx

Derrick, J. (2015, December 7). Wall Street mixed on Chipotle: more educated customer base and food with integrity branding complicates. *Benzinga*.

Duggan, W. (2015, December 7). Taco Bell proves Chipotle can overcome E. coli outbreak. *Benzinga*.

Ells, S. (2015, December). Comprehensive food safety plan. Retrieved April 7, 2016, from www.chipotle.com/founderletter

Eltantawy, R. (2008). Supply management contribution to channel performance: a top management perspective. *Management Research News*, 31(3), 152–168.

Feeney, N. (2016, March 16). Chipotle is giving away more free burritos. *Time*. Retrieved April 8, 2016, from http://time.com/4261720/chipotle-burritos-free/

Giammona, C. (2016, January 6). Chipotle sales plunge as troubled chain gets federal subpoena. *Bloomberg News*. Retrieved April 8, 2016, from www.bloomberg.com/news/articles/2016-01-06/chipotle-says-sales-dropped-even-more-than-expected-last-quarter

Jargon, J. (2016, March 16). Chipotle to offer more free burritos: free-burrito campaign has worked to woo back wary customers, restaurant chain says. *Wall Street Journal*. Retrieved April 8, 2016, from www.wsj.com/articles/chipotle-to-offer-more-free-burritos-1458155867

Jargon, J. and Newman, J. (2016, February 3). Fresh ingredients came back to haunt Chipotle: after E. coli outbreak, CEO Steve Ells revamps food-safety practices; source remains a mystery. *Wall Street Journal*. Retrieved April 8, 2016, from www.wsj.com/articles/fresh-ingredients-came-back-to-haunt-chipotle-1454463065

Jennings, L. (2016, January 13). Chipotle CEO "extremely confident" food-safety crisis is over. *Nation's Restaurant News*. Retrieved April 8, 2016, from www.nrn.com/food-safety/chipotle-ceo-extremely-confident-food-safety-crisis-over

Levine-Weinberg, A. (2016, April 3). A slow comeback for Chipotle is fine for investors. *The Motley Fool*. Retrieved April 8, 2016, from www.fool.com/investing/general/2016/04/03/a-slow-comeback-for-chipotle-is-fine-for-investors.aspx

Minkin, T. and Renaud, B. (2016). America's top 10 healthiest fast food restaurants. *Health*. Retrieved April 10, 2016, from www.health.com/health/article/0,,20411588,00.html

Naguilar, D. (2015, March 19). Chipotle's segmentation and target marketing: millennials. *Medium*. Retrieved April 10, 2016, from https://medium.com/@d_stellanorth/chipotle-s-segmentation-and-target-marketing-millennials-ed510781fe16#.n4qrf9b70

National Restaurant Association. (2012, February 14). Diners seem more healthful meals at restaurants. *National Restaurant Association*. Retrieved March 20, 2018, from www.restaurant.org/News-Research/News/Diners-seek-more-healthful-meals-at-restaurants

Nisen, M. (2014, March 20). How Chipotle transformed itself by upending its approach to management. *Quartz*. Retrieved April 8, 2016, from http://qz.com/183224/how-chipotle-transformed-itself-by-upending-its-approach-to-management/

O'Sullivan, M. (2015, June 9). Shifting consumer tastes change fast-food industry. *VOA*. Retrieved April 10, 2016, from www.voanews.com/content/shifting-consumer-tastes-change-fast-food-industry/2814926.html

Sena, M. (2016). Fast casual industry analysis 2016 – cost & trends. *Franchise Help*. Retrieved April 10, 2016, from www.franchisehelp.com/industry-reports/fast-casual-industry-report/

Sloan, E. (2014). Fast foods slim down. *IFT*. Retrieved April 10, 2016, from www.ift.org/food-technology/past-issues/2014/march/columns/consumer-trends.aspx

Taylor, K. (2015). These 5 trends will dominate fast food in 2016. *Business Insider*. Retrieved April 10, 2016, from www.businessinsider.com/5-fast-food-trends-to-watch-out-for-2015-12

Trefis Team. (2014). How the fast casual segment is gaining market share in the restaurant industry. *Forbes*. Retrieved April 10, 2016, from www.forbes.com/sites/greatspeculations/2014/06/23/how-the-fast-casual-segment-is-gaining-market-share-in-the-restaurant-industry/#25a1d4131d48

Whipp, L. (2016, February 5). Chipotle founder Steve Ells forced to rework recipe for success. *FT*. Retrieved April 8, 2016, from www.ft.com/content/c08d85cc-cb8e-11e5-a8ef-ea66e967dd44

Whitten, S. (2016, January 1). CDC declares Chipotle-linked E. coli outbreak over. *CNBC*. Retrieved April 10, 2016, from www.cnbc.com/2016/02/01/cdc-declares-chipotle-linked-e-coli-outbreak-over.html

Yu, R. (2016, March 30). Chipotle plans to open burger chain. *USA Today*. Retrieved April 10, 2016, from www.usatoday.com/story/money/2016/03/30/chipotle-open-better-burger-chain/82440378/

Index

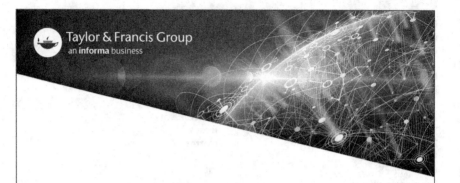

Printed in the United States
by Baker & Taylor Publisher Services